CLIMBING ROSES

Stephen Scanniello
and
Tania Bayard

A **Horticulture** Book

Prentice Hall
New York   London   Toronto   Sydney   Tokyo   Singapore

PRENTICE HALL GENERAL REFERENCE
15 Columbus Circle
New York, New York, 10023

A **Horticulture** Book
An affiliate of *Horticulture*, The Magazine of American Gardening

Library of Congress Cataloging-in-Publication data
Scanniello, Stephen.
Climbing roses / Stephen Scanniello and Tania Bayard.
p.   cm.
Includes bibliographical references (p.   ) and index.
ISBN 0-671-85046-6
1. Climbing roses. I. Bayard, Tania. II. Title.
SB411.65.C55S23   1994
635.9′33372—dc20   92-32101   CIP

Manufactured in the United States of America

10 9 8 7 6 5 4 3 2 1

First Edition

Page iv: *A tunnel of arches enveloped with the bright pink blossoms of 'American Pillar' spans a walkway at La Roseraie de l'Haÿ-les-Roses near Paris. This beautiful and versatile climber was created by one of America's preeminent rose hybridizers, Dr. Walter Van Fleet.*

For Dana and Robert

Acknowledgments

The authors would like to thank the following for their time and expertise with the research for this book:

Brenda Weisman and **Alan Kramer** at the Brooklyn Botanic Garden library
Walter Punch and staff of the Massachusetts Horticultural Society library
Bernadette Callery and staff of the New York Botanical Garden library
Katherine Powis, New York Horticultural Society library
Sheila Connor, Arnold Arborctum library
Paul Cyr, New Bedford Free Public Library
Alain Renouf and staff of the library of the Société Nationale d'Horticulture de France, Paris
Bernard Vouillot and **Michel Traversat** at the Bibliotheque Nationale Department des Livres
    Imprimés, Paris
The library staff of the Bibliotheque Centrale du Museum National d'Histoire Naturelle, Paris
The New York Public Library Annex
Royal National Rose Society library, Chiswell Green, England
Charles Walker, Heritage Rose Foundation
Dr. Steve Clemants and **Dr. Kerry Barringer**, Brooklyn Botanic Garden
Dick Hutton, Conard-Pyle Roses
Leonie Bell, The Heritage Rose Group
Virginia Hopper, Heritage Rose Gardens
Ben Williams, J. B. Williams Associates
Dr. Felicitas Svejda, Central Experimental Farm at Ottawa

Special thanks to the Cranford Rose Garden volunteers, Jeffrey C. Keil, Ellen Minet, Dave Lajoie, Alain Meilland, Peter and Joan Beales, Peter Harkness, Leon R. Gerberich of Hershey Gardens, the associates of the Atlanta Botanical Gardens, the staff of La Roseraie de l'Haÿ les Roses, the staff of La Roseraie de Bagatelle, Robert Cammarota, Dana Twining, Susan Newman, Black Lamb Studios, Tom Cooper, Rebecca W. Atwater, Rachel Simon, and Janet Manus.

CONTENTS

INTRODUCTION

Climbing roses are the acrobats and aerialists of the rose garden, the carefree plants that tumble over fences, scale walls and trellises, fling themselves across arches, and swing aloft on ropes and chains. The most versatile and ornamental of all the roses, they add movement, texture, and color at various heights; soften straight lines; accentuate curves; create depth; and provide a feeling of abundance that is afforded by no other type of rose. Their flowers have glorious color, and the foliage of some varieties turns red, yellow, or orange in the fall. A few have red- or plum-colored canes and scarlet hips to brighten the winter landscape. Many are so rugged and disease resistant that they can thrive and produce spectacular blooms even when they receive no care at all.

Climbing roses have a natural charm that lends itself to picturesque effects. They are the perfect cottage garden plants, but they also work wonderfully in formal settings. They can be used in innumerable ways: wrapped around pillars, columns, poles, and arches; trained on lattices, trellises, and pergolas; shaped as weeping standards; formed into tunnels and bowers; coiled around ropes and chains; pegged to the ground; or induced to scramble up into the branches of trees. In the early part of this century, some varieties were grown in containers and fashioned into globes, pyramids, fans, baskets, windmills, ships, and umbrellas.

The climbing rose family is so enormous that it would be impossible to include all its members in one book. Rather than treat a large number of these roses superficially, we decided to discuss sixty-five of our favorites in detail. Many other, equally worthwhile climbers are listed at the ends of various sections. In addition to varieties that are officially classified as climbers, we have included roses from other classes that can be used as climbers: bush roses and old garden roses such as hybrid Chinas, hybrid Bourbons, and hybrid Noisettes. Some of the wild climbing roses that have played an important role in the development of modern climbers are also here, for these too have a place in the garden or the landscape.

In order to follow the evolution of climbers in modern times, we have arranged the sixty-five roses chronologically. This is intended as an overview of the development of climbing roses, not as a complete history. We tracked

'White Cockade' and 'Seagull' climb a rustic cedar arch in a private garden in Amagansett, New York.

down much of the background on these roses in old books, periodicals, and garden catalogs here and in Europe. This information is included in an historical sketch at the beginning of each rose portrait. Many of the hybridizers have written about their work, and wherever possible, we tell the stories of the roses in their words. For roses developed since 1930, we have consulted the hybridizers' patent applications; much information gleaned from these documents is provided here.

Many climbers can survive for years on their own, often outlasting the gardeners who planted them. Some of the early varieties are no longer in commerce but still can be found, thriving, in old dooryards, along highways and railroad embankments, in abandoned gardens, in cemeteries, and in the refuse of vacant city lots. Sometimes the names of these old friends have been forgotten. For each rose discussed here, we include botanical details to help in identifying unknown specimens. (Botanical details also provide clues to the cultural requirements of the roses.) We hope this information will stimulate interest in the rediscovery of old varieties, and we would like to hear from readers who know the whereabouts of "mystery" climbers.

Since its foundation in 1899,[1] the American Rose Society has played an important role in the promotion of roses and dissemination of knowledge about them. In the pages of its yearbook, *The American Rose Annual*, first published in 1916, one can follow the progress of the rose in America during the twentieth century. Beginning in 1926 the editors included in each volume of the *Annual* a section entitled "Proof of the Pudding," which is a compilation of pithy comments from gardeners around the country who are trying out newly introduced roses. The gardeners evaluate each rose for five years, and their observations tell a great deal about how well certain varieties can be expected to perform in various regions of the United States. We refer often to the "Proof of the Pudding" when discussing roses introduced after 1926.

The search for the perfect climbing rose is never ending. Many of today's climbers are everblooming, disease resistant, carefree, and large flowered. Complete hardiness in all climates, however, has yet to be achieved. Many climbers will not live through cold northern winters; some of those that do survive are reduced to a nonclimbing form because their canes die back in freezing weather. On the other hand, a rose that requires a period of winter dormancy may gradually weaken in a southern garden unless extraordinary measures are taken to stop it from producing flowers and leaves for a few months every year. The growth habits of roses vary according to climate, as well; a variety that is a rampant climber in Louisiana may remain a shrub in upper New York state. We cannot be specific about how hardy each climber we discuss will be in every region of the United States.

The information in this book is based on Stephen Scanniello's many years of experience as rosarian of the Cranford Rose Garden at the Brooklyn Botanic Garden. All the climbers discussed here grow in the Cranford Rose Garden, and we present them as Stephen knows them, not merely as beautiful flowers, but as complete plants—each with its own growth habit, type of foliage, pruning requirements, degree of hardiness, and special use in the garden or landscape. (Hardiness zones are very general, and within each there are many microclimates. The best way to determine how well a rose will fare in your region is to talk to other gardeners, your local extension agent, and members of the nearest rose society.) We hope to provide sound information on how to choose, plant, and care for these roses. Several of the varieties we discuss are now rare or out of commerce; this book will perhaps reintroduce gardeners to some long-lost acquaintances.

1

THE EVOLUTION OF MODERN CLIMBING ROSES

NO ROSES are true climbers in the sense that they have tendrils or other means of scaling tall structures. Climbing roses are simply vigorous shrubs with long canes that will, if not trained, grow up and arch over under their own weight. They can only be induced to "climb" if they are tied to a support.

Throughout history, gardeners have recognized the decorative appeal of rose-covered arbors, trellises, arches, and tall fences. Before the nineteenth century, however, there were only a limited number of rose varieties in the West with canes long enough to be trained on such supports: two European wild roses—the eglantine (*Rosa eglanteria*) and the dog rose (*Rosa canina*); and two naturally occurring varieties—the alba (*Rosa alba*) and the musk (*Rosa moschata*), both of which are capable of sending out ten- or twelve-foot canes. It is also possible that lower-growing shrub roses, such as gallicas or damasks, were grafted onto *R. eglanteria* or *R. canina;* this would have made the shorter varieties appear to be climbing roses, an illusion captured in medieval paintings.

The evolution of roses that can be trained on tall supports, especially pillars, is inseparable from the history of other hybrid roses created during the nineteenth century when hundreds of new cultivars and varieties of roses came into being, many with canes long enough to be used for ornamental purposes. All the new varieties resulted from efforts to combine the best qualities of several types of roses: wild roses (those indigenous to the West as well as those that were being discovered in the East); old European garden roses; and China roses, the remarkable hybrids that were then being introduced into Europe from China.

Most species roses (roses that occur naturally in the wild and are commonly called "wild roses") and almost all the old European garden roses flower only once a year, in the spring and early summer. It was therefore an extraordinary moment in the history of the rose in the West when, in the late eighteenth century, everblooming roses were introduced from the Orient into Europe. These new hybrids were not as hardy as species roses or the old European garden roses, but they possessed the ability to bloom all season long. They also had flowers with vibrant colors that were unknown in Western roses at that time, and glossy, long-lasting foliage. These roses were called China roses. When they were crossed with species roses and the old garden roses of Europe, many new classes of roses came into being: Bourbons, Noisettes, hybrid Chinas, hybrid Bourbons, hybrid Noisettes, damask perpetuals, and hybrid perpetuals. Within each of these classes were roses with canes just the right length for wrapping around pillars. Rose-covered pillars were very much in fashion in the 1840s, especially in the United States. At the same time, certain roses with longer canes, the Ayrshire roses and hybrids of *Rosa sempervirens*, became the preferred choices for covering taller structures, such as arches and pergolas. These roses lost their popularity after the introduction of the hardier multifloras and wichuraianas, whose long, flexible canes, rampant growth habits, and profuse blooms made them ideal for covering large surfaces and training on high supports.

Page x: 'Tausendschön' (Thousand Beauties) is the perfect name for this climber, which produces masses of large, multicolored flowers. (Photograph by Saxon Holt.)

Another type of rose, called the tea rose or the tea-scented China, came to Europe from China in the nineteenth century and became the progenitor of more new roses with climbing habits. The original tea rose is thought to have been a cross between *Rosa chinensis* (the original China rose) and *Rosa gigantea*, an extremely vigorous and tender wild rose native to China and Burma. During the mid-1850s, crosses with *R. gigantea*—which sometimes has canes as long as fifty feet and flowers as large as six inches in diameter—resulted indirectly in a number of varieties known as climbing tea roses; these include the famous 'Gloire de Dijon' and the hardy, exquisite 'Sombreuil'. The tea roses were very influential in the development of other classes, including the Noisettes.

Some of the new roses introduced during the nineteenth century resulted from accidental fertilization (natural pollination) when roses of different classes were planted close together. But in many cases they were created by deliberate hybridization, a process whereby the hybridizer transfers pollen from one variety to the stigmas of another. Four roses from China actually became known as "stud roses" because they were grown in the West expressly for purposes of hybridization. These stud roses were two Chinas—'Slater's Crimson China' and 'Old Blush'—and two tea-scented Chinas—'Parks' Yellow Tea-scented China' and 'Hume's Blush'.

Many of the earliest deliberate hybrids, including some of the first cultivated climbing roses, came from France, where interest in roses was stimulated by Empress Joséphine. From 1804 to the time of her death in 1814, Joséphine collected at Malmaison, her estate near Paris, all the varieties of roses then known throughout the world. She also encouraged the work of the foremost hybridizers of the day,

many of whom produced new roses that were ideal for training on supports.

One of the most influential early hybrids with a climbing habit came from the United States. Around 1811 John Champneys, the owner of a rice plantation in Charleston, South Carolina, raised a seedling produced by the accidental crossing of one of the "stud" Chinas, 'Old

In June, a lattice fence in a partially shaded area of the Cranford Rose Garden is covered with a colorful display of the hybrid Bourbon 'Great Western', the wichuraiana hybrid 'Christine Wright', and the ever-blooming Noisette 'Fellenberg'.

Blush', and *R. moschata*. This rose, originally called 'Champneys' Pink Cluster', yielded a number of offspring that were later called Noisettes when they were marketed in France by the nurseryman Louis Noisette. The Noisettes are everblooming, and because of their musk rose parent, many of them are vigorous enough to use as climbers. Throughout the nineteenth century hybridizers created beautiful climbing roses by crossing the Noisettes with roses of other classes. Eventually the infusion of blood from the more tender tea roses diminished the hardiness of the Noisettes.

Other significant varieties of climbing roses were developed in nineteenth-century America. During the 1830s and 1840s Samuel Feast in Baltimore and Joshua Pierce in Washington D.C., used *Rosa setigera* (the prairie rose), a native North American rose with long canes, to produce several successful climbers. But although *R. setigera* seemed a promising parent for a hardy new race of climbers because it flourishes just about everywhere in this country, it proved to be very difficult to cross with other roses. It was not until the work of Dr. Walter Van Fleet in the early twentieth century that it gave rise to other notable climbing offspring. In the 1930s and 1940s Michael Horvath also successfully used *R. setigera* in hybridizing.

Many species roses played a role in the development of climbers, but the two most influential were *R. multiflora* and *R. wichuraiana*, both from the Far East. *R. multiflora* is a hardy, rampant rose with large pyramidal clusters of small flowers. Many varieties of this rose were known in the West throughout the nineteenth century, but it was not until the species itself was introduced into Europe in the 1860s that its decorative potential was fully appreciated. The first

multiflora hybrid produced in the United States was 'Dawson', created in 1888 by Jackson Dawson at the Arnold Arboretum in Massachusetts. Many other hybridizers in the West worked with *R. multiflora,* but its most remarkable offspring was a hybrid from Japan, 'Crimson Rambler', which took the world by storm in 1893. 'Crimson Rambler' opened up new possibilities in the world of climbing roses. Not only was it the first climber with massive clusters of brilliant red flowers, it was also hardy and had long, pliable canes that could easily be used to achieve decorative effects not possible with earlier, stiffer climbers. 'Crimson Rambler' was the first of a group of roses that eventually came to be classed as ramblers: climbing roses with very supple canes that grow from the base of the plant each year and produce laterals that bear large clusters of small flowers during one bloom period the following summer.

In England during the early part of this century, the Reverend Joseph Pemberton developed a race of small-flowered shrub roses that are everblooming and can be used as climbers. These roses, which he called hybrid musks even though they are only distantly related to *R. moschata,* were important early pillar roses. They derive their everblooming ability from an early multiflora rambler, 'Trier' (created in 1904 by the German hybridizer Peter Lambert), one of the first perpetually blooming rambling roses.

R. wichuraiana holds an equally important place in the evolution of modern climbing roses. This vigorous trailing wild rose from Japan was introduced into America through the Arnold Arboretum in 1888. Gardeners immediately recognized its decorative possibilities, for it is a vigorous and hardy rose with dark, glistening foliage, fragrant flowers, and long, flex-

'Dr. W. Van Fleet' (in the foreground) and 'Silver Moon' cover more than twenty-four feet of a lattice fence. After the blooms have faded, the dark glossy foliage creates a dense, long-lasting and disease-free screen.

ible canes that are easy to train. In addition, it crosses readily with other varieties of roses. The first successful wichuraiana hybrids were produced in the late 1890s in Rhode Island by Michael H. Horvath. Horvath's work led to further experiments with this rose, and soon a multitude of wichuraiana hybrids appeared on the market. These were considered superior to the multiflora hybrids because they have shiny, long-lasting leaves that are more attractive than the coarse foliage of the multifloras; canes that are even more pliable than those of the multifloras; and a longer flowering period. In addition, while the multiflora hybrids are notoriously susceptible to mildew and blackspot, the wichuraiana hybrids are more disease resistant. The most notable wichuraiana hybrid at the turn of the century was 'Dorothy Perkins', introduced by the Jackson and Perkins Company in 1901. This rambler with huge clusters of pink flowers quickly eclipsed 'Crimson Rambler' in popularity.

In the early years of the twentieth century, Michael H. Walsh in Massachusetts used both *R. multiflora* and *R. wichuraiana* to produce many distinguished climbers with large clusters

of small flowers. In 1909 Walsh introduced 'Excelsa', a rambler with crimson blossoms. 'Excelsa' set a new standard for wichuraiana hybrids, and it was soon grown everywhere, for it was healthier and easier to train than 'Crimson Rambler'—the other popular red rambler of the day.

Hybridizers in the United States have been at the forefront of the development of climbing roses, striving for varieties that will succeed in harsh climates and less-than-ideal soils. Dr. Walter Van Fleet, one of the leading hybridizers of the early twentieth century, frequently wrote about his desire to provide Americans with roses that would flourish without the pampering required by the hybrid teas and the other tender varieties that were being imported from England and the Continent. Using *R. setigera*, *R. wichuraiana*, and other wild roses, he created hardy climbers that he called "dooryard roses"—varieties that he hoped would combine beautiful flowers, luxuriant foliage, disease resistance, and the ability to thrive anywhere in the United States. One of them, 'Dr. W. Van Fleet', introduced into commerce in 1910, was particularly significant because of the large size of its flowers. Gardeners at that time considered 'Dr. W. Van Fleet' a great improvement over the ubiquitous multiflora and wichuraiana hybrids with their clusters of small flowers. 'Dr. W. Van Fleet' and other Van Fleet hybrids also differ from ramblers because they have heavier, stiffer canes. They exemplify the type of roses now classed as "climbers."

Although the large-flowered climber 'Dr. W.

Magnificent weeping standards in the Bagatelle rose garden in Paris. From left to right: 'New Dawn', 'American Pillar', and 'Paul Noël'. The tall tripods in the background are covered with the scarlet climber 'Décor'.

Van Fleet' did not fulfill the hybridizer's dream of a hardy, large-flowered climber that would bloom all season long, it later produced a sport (mutation) that did. This sport, 'New Dawn', introduced in 1930, marks a turning point in the history of climbers, for it is everblooming, producing clusters of large flowers from the middle of May right up until the first frost. ('New Dawn' also holds the distinction of being the first plant ever patented.)

The introduction of 'New Dawn' and the subsequent development of other large-flowered, everblooming climbers achieved many of the hybridizers' goals. Since then hundreds of other new and beautiful climbing roses have been introduced. Among these are varieties that are sports of bush roses. These sports, which are simply climbing versions of the bush forms, are called climbing hybrid teas, climbing grandifloras, climbing floribundas, and climbing polyanthas. Climbing sports, which usually bloom on the previous year's growth, are very popular in the South, but because their canes often die back in freezing weather, they have limited use for decorative purposes in regions with cold winters. There are, however, a few varieties that are hardy in the North. These include: 'Climbing Queen Elizabeth' (a climbing grandiflora), 'Climbing Iceberg' (a climbing floribunda), 'Climbing Yesterday' (a climbing polyantha), and 'Climbing Peace' (a climbing hybrid tea). The climbing miniature, developed largely through the efforts of Ralph Moore in California, is another new addition to the family of climbing roses. Most climbing miniatures are cultivars, not sports.

One objective has so far eluded hybridizers: to develop a climbing rose that is completely hardy in even the coldest climate. There are modern climbers that come close to this goal,

Trained on a barn wall in the private garden of rosarian Peter Beales in Attleborough, England, 'Goldbusch' puts on an outstanding display of large, semidouble, golden yellow flowers early in the rose season. This particular specimen sometimes reblooms in the fall.

however. Notable examples are some of the introductions of Dr. and Mrs. Walter Brownell in Rhode Island; the setigera hybrids created in the 1930s and 1940s by Michael Horvath in Ohio; varieties produced by Captain George C. Thomas in Pennsylvania and California; and the roses developed by Griffith Buck at the University of Iowa. One especially noteworthy step in the direction of a perfectly hardy climber was made in the 1940s and 1950s by the German hybridizer Wilhelm Kordes, the originator of the Kordesii hybrids. These hardy roses go back to 'Max Graf', a procumbent rose that was a spontaneous cross between *R. wichuraiana* and *R. rugosa*, an extremely hardy wild shrub from the Far East. Kordes, who had the patience to wait many years for the usually infertile 'Max Graf' to produce hips, raised a seedling that proved suitable for breeding with modern garden hybrids. From this he developed a completely new race of hardy, disease-resistant, everblooming shrub and climbing roses that combine all the best qualities of *R. rugosa* and *R. wichuraiana*.

Important work with the Kordesii hybrids is currently going on in Canada, where the Department of Agriculture is involved in a program of breeding hardy shrub roses. Many of these lovely shrubs, part of the so-called Explorer series, can be used as climbers, and they have proved to be remarkably hardy in harsh northern climates.

Some of the most notable new climbers are everblooming groundcover roses that are the offspring of *R. wichuraiana* and its hybrids. In addition, there are a number of hardy new shrub roses with 'New Dawn' in their ancestry that can be used as climbers. Peter Beales in England has also introduced a recent sport of 'New Dawn' called 'Awakening'. And in France at the 1991 *Concours International de Roses Nouvelles de Bagatelle*, Alain Meilland showed 'Climbing Rimosa', a sport of the floribunda 'Rimosa'. This large-flowered yellow climber will soon appear on the market. Many other new climbers are being developed, as well, for there is a resurgence of interest in these wonderful roses.

2
THE ROSES

ROSA MOSCHATA

Introduced into England during the sixteenth century

ROSA MOSCHATA, the musk rose, is a late summer-flowering rose that was brought to England from the Mediterranean region sometime during the sixteenth century.[2] Although some authorities claim that there is a China rose in its heritage, its exact origins are not known, and no species of rose that can be called its ancestor has ever been found. Of the many references to the musk rose in literature, the most famous is probably the passage in Shakespeare's *A Midsummer Night's Dream* in which Oberon describes Titania's bower as being over-canopied with woodbine, sweet musk roses, and eglantine. Shakespeare overlooked the fact that the musk rose starts to bloom only in late summer. Other, more accurate, descriptions appear in herbals of the sixteenth, seventeenth, and eighteenth centuries. In his *Herball* of 1597, John Gerard discussed the single musk rose, whose "flowers growe on the tops of the branches of a white colour, and pleasant sweete smell, like that of Muske, whereof it took his name."[3] Gerard is explicit about the bloom period: "The Muske Rose flowreth in Autume, or the fall of the leafe."[4] John Parkinson, in his *Paradisi in Sole Paradisus Terrestris* of 1629, said that single and double musk roses "flower not untill the end of summer, and in Autumne. . . ."[5]

Parkinson recognized the climbing ability of this rose, for he wrote: "The Muske Rose, both single and double, rise up oftentimes to a very great height, that it overgroweth any arbour in a garden, or being set by an house side, to bee ten or twelve foote high, or more, . . ."[6]

In the late nineteenth century the musk rose became confused with a summer-blooming wild rose from the Himalayas, *Rosa brunonii*, which closely resembles it. *R. brunonii* was often sold as the musk rose, and the true musk rose virtually disappeared from commerce until Graham Stewart Thomas pointed out that this "musk rose" that bloomed in early summer had to be an imposter. Thomas subsequently discovered a magnificent specimen of the true musk rose in an old garden in England.[7]

Inspired by Thomas's work, American "rose rustlers" (collectors of old garden roses who search out neglected and forgotten varieties) found other specimens in Virginia and North Carolina. Interestingly, many of the specimens in the United States have been traced to one family, the Burwells, who came to this country in the early seventeenth century. In 1837 a member of this family, a Presbyterian minister named Robert Burwell, founded a women's academy, the Burwell School, in Hillsborough, North Carolina; it is thought that many of the musk roses that have been discovered in this region came either from the grounds of that school or from the graves of members of the Burwell family. Descendants raised from the cut-

Page 10: 'Climbing Cécile Brünner', a climbing sport of the polyantha 'Cécile Brünner', scales a lattice fence and scrambles into a Japanese tree lilac at the Cranford Rose Garden.

Left: A double flower of the true musk rose in Hollywood Cemetery, Richmond, Virginia. There is another fine specimen of this elusive species, which starts to bloom in late summer, on the grounds of the Burwell School in Hillsborough, North Carolina.

tings of these musk roses still exist today. In her garden at Chatwood, in Hillsborough, North Carolina, the late Helen Watkins grew a musk rose that came directly from the grounds of the Burwell School. Another specimen in the Hollywood Cemetery in Richmond, Virginia, has also been traced back to the Burwell family; this bush produces both single and double flowers, just like the musk roses Parkinson described more than three hundred fifty years ago.

The musk rose holds an important place in the history of climbing roses. Before the nineteenth century it was one of the few roses that could be used as a climber; although it is not commonly cultivated today, its blood lives on in the Noisettes, a class of rose that originated from the accidental crossing of a China rose and a musk rose.

A few specialty nurseries in the United States, England, New Zealand, and Italy now sell the true *R. moschata*.

UNLIKE MOST modern climbers and ramblers, which produce flowering laterals all along their canes, the musk rose bears the majority of its flowers at the ends of its canes, a characteristic noted by both Gerard and Parkinson. Each inflorescence is on a continuation, or growth, of the last blooming lateral; new blooms originate from the second or third bud eyes behind the previous bloom. There are also some flowers on the ends of the long canes that spring from the base of the plant. The small white flowers, which are borne in large clusters, open from very long, tapered buds, and they may be both single and double on the same plant; when double, they can have as many as thirty-five petals. Numerous clusters of flowers make up an entire inflorescence. The sweet, spicy fragrance, especially noticeable in the evening, is strong and unforgettable.

The musk rose is a vigorous shrub whose canes can reach ten to twelve feet in length. It is capable of surviving for centuries without pruning or other care, as evidenced by the specimens found at old grave sites. Left on its own, it becomes a huge mound, often seven feet high and four feet wide, with blooms at the tips of a few long canes. Dead wood builds up in the center, probably due to lack of sun. To prevent this, periodically cut out some of the older canes and central clutter (old and new tangled laterals that grow inward and compete with new growth coming up from the center). No other pruning is required to induce blooming.

The musk rose will thrive without winter protection as far north as Richmond, Virginia, where its climbing habit is limited. In colder climates it will not be a successful climber; even in Virginia it is more of a tall shrub than a climber. At the Burwell School in North Carolina, it starts to bloom in July and continues right through the fall.

The dark green leaves are susceptible to blackspot, mildew, and a host of insects and other diseases. Nevertheless, *R. moschata* is a survivor, as we know from the durable old specimens of the true musk rose that have recently been found in England and the United States.

ROSA EGLANTERIA (FORMERLY ROSA RUBIGINOSA)

Cultivated before 1551

ROSA EGLANTERIA, the eglantine or sweet-brier rose that is much praised for the delicious apple scent of its foliage, is a wild rose native to England and the Continent. It was probably the fragrance of its leaves rather than the beauty of its flowers that inspired Shakespeare to combine it with the musk rose on Titania's bower in *A Midsummer Night's Dream*.

The eglantine was one of the plants the colonists brought to the New World, and it became naturalized in the eastern United States. Because it is a tall-growing bush with fierce prickles, it was then, as now, used as a hedge. In the past it was also popular as a decorative rose, and it is sometimes still grown that way, particularly in France and England. At Mannington Hall, near Norwich, England, for example, there are several magnificent specimens on arbors and rustic fences. Arbors covered with *R. eglanteria* are showpieces at La Roseraie de l'Haÿ-les-Roses, the famous rose garden south of Paris.

Like the flowers of most wild roses, those of *R. eglanteria* are single. However, varieties with more than five petals, naturally occurring or otherwise, have long been known. A semi-double eglantine is pictured in the 1633 edition of John Gerard's *Herball*. During the nineteenth century, nurserymen Thomas Rivers and William Paul in England and William and Robert Prince in the United States sold several double varieties.

In the 1890s an English judge, Lord Penzance, created a number of eglantine hybrids, which became known as the Penzance hybrids.

He used eglantine specimens as the seed parents, fertilizing them with pollen from hybrid perpetuals, Bourbons, hybrid Chinas, 'Austrian Copper', 'Persian Yellow', and certain species roses. In 1894 and 1895 the Keynes, Williams and Company of Salisbury put them on the market, while Lord Penzance first exhibited them at Kew Gardens in 1895. The sixteen hybrids, thirteen of which he named after characters in the novels of Sir Walter Scott, had a wider range of colors and more vigor than the wild eglantines; some retained more of the wonderful scented foliage than others.

THE EGLANTINE is one of the later-flowering wild roses, reaching its peak bloom at the same time as the hybrid teas. The five-petaled blossoms, borne singly or in clusters, are pale pink with whitish centers. The flowers are fragrant, but their scent is insignificant; it is the perfumed foliage that makes this such an enchanting rose. The leaf buds start to break in early spring (at the beginning of April in the Cranford Rose Garden), and all through the season, whenever the bush is brushed against or touched with rain or dew, the foliage gives off the wonderfully spicy, apple scent that earned this prickly rose the name "sweet-brier."

The eglantine is a large shrub that can reach a height of ten or twelve feet with the support of neighboring trees or shrubs. On its own it makes a forbidding, intruder-proof barrier, for it has very prominent prickles. Many gardeners would think it an unusual candidate for training as a climber, but it has a naturally graceful, arching growth habit, and anyone with the courage to battle its armed canes can take advantage of this. Trained on an arch, an eglantine makes an inviting entrance to a garden, especially in a shaded area, for its leaves dispense their perfume every time a visitor brushes against them. To create such an eglantine-covered portal, plant two bushes, one on each side of a six- to eight-foot-wide arch. The bush will send up from the base six-foot canes that can be either wrapped around the arch and tied to it, or simply pulled up onto the support following their own natural curve. There will also be many long continuing laterals (secondary canes that spring from the main canes on the upper parts of the plant) that can be trained. To utilize some of the excess growth, construct a low fence next to the arch and attach the canes to that as well. Another way to show off the eglantine is on a fence surrounding a garden or bordering a piece of property. When planting the bushes against such a fence, set them at least eight feet apart. Do not try to train the eglantine on a single pillar, however; it is much too prickly and rampant.

A mature eglantine on an arch or on any support that is near a foot path requires constant pruning, for this shrub is large, dense, and spreading, and it can be extremely invasive. Its rampant canes could easily take over the garden or fill in the opening of the arch, creating a dangerous barrier rather than an inviting entrance. After the eglantine blooms, trim back any unwanted growth throughout the rest of the season. Your reward for this hazardous work will be lush and abundant new foliage that will constantly provide fresh fragrance. Start pruning as soon as the flowers have faded and continue almost until the first frost. If enough of the flowering laterals are left behind, the bush will be covered with a multitude of red, one-inch hips in the fall. After a few seasons continue the pruning regimen during the winter by removing all unnecessary old wood and thinning out from the center any crowded and crossing branches.

The eglantine is a very hardy rose that will flourish in full sun or partial shade. It should not be grown against a wall or in any area that lacks good air circulation, for it is susceptible to blackspot. In hot, dry weather it tends to drop its leaves, not because of disease but because the foliage is short lived. When this happens, simply prune the canes back a bit, and there will be an explosion of healthy new growth.

The Penzance hybrids are more suitable and interesting for a garden than the species eglantine. The hybrids have a wider range of color and are more easily adapted to archways and fences because they have a more vigorous and graceful growth habit. Like all the eglantines, they produce blooms on very short laterals at every node along the canes. Therefore, the more the canes are arched over a support, the greater the flower production.

The leaves of the eglantine hybrids are not always as fragrant as those of the species rose, and sometimes they are a brighter green. One Penzance hybrid that has especially aromatic foliage is 'Brenda', which was introduced by Keynes, Williams and Company in 1894. This vigorous eglantine, whose parentage is unknown, has delicately colored peach-pink blossoms that occasionally repeat their bloom in the fall, especially after an Indian summer. This variety is rarely seen today.

'Greenmantle', introduced in 1895, is per-

The delicate flowers of Rosa eglanteria *bloom in June, later than most other species roses. The delicious apple scent of its leaves earned this rose the name "sweetbrier."*

haps the most fragrant of all the Penzance hybrids, producing sweet-smelling flowers as well as strongly scented leaves. Its blooms are bright pinkish red with prominent white eyes and yellow stamens.

R. eglanteria and its hybrids are delightful additions to informal gardens, appealing for their nostalgic associations as well as for their beauty and fragrance.

Lord Penzance Hybrids

'Amy Robsart'	'Flora McIvor'	'Lord Penzance'
'Anne of Geierstein'	'Greenmantle'	'Lucy Ashton'
'Brenda'	'Jeannie Deans'	'Lucy Bertram'
'Catherine Seyton'	'Julia Mannering'	'Meg Merrilies'
'Edith Bellenden'	'Lady Penzance'	'Rose Bradwardine'

ROSA CANINA

Cultivated before 1737

ROSA CANINA, known as the dog rose or brier rose, is a wild rose native to Europe and western Asia that was brought by colonists to the New World, where it has become naturalized in many areas. The name dog rose is sometimes attributed to the fact that it has large, curved prickles that resemble dogs' teeth. It is also possible that "dog" is a corruption of "dag," an old word meaning to pierce or stab, also a reference to its prickles. Another hypothesis is that it got this name because a substance made from its roots and hips was thought to be a cure for the bite of a mad dog. Although their value in treating rabies is questionable, the delicious hips, which were once much used in desserts, are a rich source of vitamin C. Gerard wrote in his *Herball:* "The Brier Bush or Hep tree, is also called *Rosa canina*, which is a plant so common and well knowne, that it were to small purpose to use many words in the description thereof: for even children with great delight eate the berries thereof when they be ripe, make chaines and other pretie gewgawes of the fruite: cookes and gentlewomen make Tarts and such like dishes for pleasure thereof. . . ."[8]

Many old garden roses, such as albas, damasks, and centifolias, have *R. canina* in their ancestry. The dog rose is often used as an understock for modern roses, but it has been very little used in hybridizing.

ROSA CANINA is so common a wild rose in Europe and the United States that its potential as a garden climber is usually overlooked. This is a shame, for in June a dog rose enveloping a pillar with its dainty pink blossoms is a delightful sight. This rose is also spectacular in the fall when it is decorated with hundreds of large, hanging, elongated orange-red hips. The lightly scented flowers, borne singly or in small clusters, are composed of five petals, each with a band of pink and a band of white, and they have a festive air, for the two colors encircle a sunburst of golden anthers. The shades of pink vary greatly from flower to flower.

The natural growth habit of *R. canina* is dense and rampant, and its twelve-foot canes are armed with fierce, hooked prickles. In its wild state this rose creates a forbidding, impenetrable barrier. If you are courageous and well covered with protective clothing, you can curb its ferocious nature and train it as a climber. Stephen discovered the decorative potential of *R. canina* by accident. A specimen in the Cranford Rose Garden threatened to take over one of the beds. To make room for the other roses growing near it, he removed nearly all of its growth except for two or three canes, which he wrapped around an eight-foot pillar. Because the canes were mature and extremely stiff, this was a difficult task, but the result was surprisingly beautiful. If you decide to train this rose, start while the canes are young and still pliable. Spiral two or three of them around a pillar, tripod, or other support, and attach them tightly to it. From these canes will come others, four to six feet long, that will arch gracefully away from the support and produce on their short, four- to six-inch laterals masses of pink blooms, and later, wonderful hips. Even when trained in this fashion, *R. canina* requires a lot of room, so relegate it to the background in a garden, away from paths and walkways.

19

No deadheading is necessary, but invasive growth must be cut away to keep *R. canina* under control. After a few years, remove some of the oldest canes, especially those at the center of the bush, for overcrowding and lack of light will result in a build-up of unsightly dead wood and an ugly rose. If the rose is trained on a pillar, the older wood will always have to be removed, for it is hard to keep on the support.

R. canina is very hardy and disease resistant. It does well in shady areas; like all early-blooming wild roses, it produces its flowers before the overshadowing leaves of trees have developed.

Rosa canina *climbing a pillar. This European native with menacing hooked prickles is difficult to train. It is worth the effort, however, for in June it will envelop the support with flowers. In the fall it puts on a brilliant display of elongated orange-red hips that will last well into the winter.*

ROSA SETIGERA

Named by André Michaux; published 1803

ROSA SETIGERA is a wild rose native to North America that has the characteristics of a climber. It was named by the French botanist André Michaux (1746–1802), who described it in volume one of his *Flora Boreali-Americana*, published posthumously in 1803. In 1811 a British botanist, Robert Brown, found a form of this rose that he mistook for a new species; he called it *Rosa rubifolia* because of its black-berrylike leaves. As a result, there is much confusion in the old literature, where *R. setigera* is often listed as *R. rubifolia*.

Michaux, who collected plants from the New World for Louis XVI of France, recorded *R. setigera* along the coastal plain of the Carolinas; but this rose, which is known as the prairie rose or the Michigan rose, is widespread in most of the eastern, southern, and midwestern states. It is especially abundant in Missouri, Michigan, Ohio, and the Mississippi Valley. The Philadelphia nurseryman Robert Buist, who thought it the perfect rose for cultivation in all parts of the country, wrote in 1844: "This native is destined to convey to every hall, cottage, and wigwam of the Union, the Rose, the acknowledged queen of flowers."[9] He overestimated its climbing ability when he raved, "I have no doubt that in good soil it would reach one hundred feet in a very few years;" but he was certainly correct about the decorative possibilities of a rose that "is admirably adapted for covering rock work, old buildings, or any other object requiring to be hid; it also delights in a procumbent position, and can be used for covering naked spaces of rough ground. . . ."[10]

American hybridizers attempting to breed the hardiness of species roses into the Chinas, teas, Bourbons, hybrid perpetuals, and other large-flowered roses of the day were quick to recognize the potential of the rugged prairie rose. The Long Island nurseryman, William Prince, and his son, William Robert Prince, worked with it in the 1820s; unfortunately, the results of their efforts no longer exist. In the 1840s and 1850s, Samuel Feast in Baltimore and Joshua Pierce in Washington, D.C. had more success with it, introducing several setigera hybrids that are still grown today. At the end of the nineteenth century, Henry B. Ellwanger, of the firm of Ellwanger and Barry in Rochester, New York, tried to improve the Feast hybrids; however, since they were all sterile, his work was unfruitful.

In general, hybridizers had difficulty perfecting *R. setigera* and breeding its good characteristics into roses of other classes. None of its offspring repeated their bloom, and they were not reliably hardy. In addition, when they were crossed with hybrid teas, the resulting roses had flowers that were considered overly bright and foliage that was thin and unattractive. Hybridizers did succeed in breeding *R. setigera*'s vigorousness and adaptability into other roses, however. Dr. Walter Van Fleet, for one, felt that even though many seedlings resulting from experiments with *R. setigera* would be failures, there were still possibilities to be explored with this rose. One of the most successful setigera

Rosa setigera, the prairie rose, is a native American species that blooms as late as mid-July in Brooklyn, New York. The large scentless flowers are followed by clusters of vivid red hips that stay on the bush all winter.

hybrids was 'American Pillar', which he introduced in 1902. This beautiful and vigorous
climber is still popular today. Later, M. H.
Horvath used *R. setigera* in the creation of his
"Treasure Island" climbers. Two of the most
successful were 'Doubloons' and 'Long John
Silver', both of which were introduced in 1934.

As a decorative rose, *R. setigera* was extremely popular throughout the nineteenth century. Because it is late blooming, it extended
the rose season in an era when there were few
repeat-flowering roses. It was recommended as
a worthy plant for homesteads in the Midwest,
where it was planted as a natural fence and provided a bit of adornment around new houses.
Its long-lasting flowers, which open in succession in each cluster, were also used in bouquets.
Part of its popularity was due to the efforts of
Charles Sprague Sargent, the first director of
the Arnold Arboretum in Boston, who early in
the nineteenth century advocated it as a landscape plant for private as well as public gardens. It was planted extensively in Boston's
parks, which helped bring it to the attention of
the public. Before long it was in great demand
in urban areas and places where it did not grow
freely in the wild. People soon were complain-
ing that nurseries, which featured the more
spectacular double-flowered roses introduced
from England and the Continent, did not stock
sufficient quantities of one of our own native
roses.

R. SETIGERA is a hardy, vigorous rose that
is a familiar sight growing untended along the
edges of fields and woods throughout much of
the United States. The last of the wild roses to
come into bloom, it bears corymbs of scentless,
bright pink flowers in June, July, or August,
depending on the climate of the region in which
it is grown. In the Cranford Rose Garden it
starts blooming during the last week of June
and the first week of July, just as the hybrid
teas are passing their peak, and it continues its
display for about two weeks. The brightly colored flowers, two inches in diameter, have five
wavy petals that are a rich pink toward the
edge, fading to white at the center. Their festive
appearance is enhanced by sunny yellow "eyes"
of pollen-covered anthers. This is only the beginning of the show this rose puts on, however.
Following the flowers, which turn pale pink before they drop, there are myriad clusters of
long-lasting, vivid red hips that decorate the
bush throughout the fall and winter. In autumn, the leaves turn fiery red, and during the
coldest months, the canes also put on a show,
becoming a deep plum red that contrasts with
the pronounced white of their menacing
prickles.

The large, broad, rough leaves of *R. setigera*
resemble those of blackberry bushes, and the
canes, which can grow at least ten feet long in
one season, are also like those of the blackberry—arching, extremely prickly and quick to
root wherever they touch the ground. Because
it roots so easily, and also because birds, which
love the hips, distribute the seeds, *R. setigera*
spreads rapidly and can be invasive.

A coarse plant, far from dainty, this rose
lends itself to massed plantings in which it functions as a natural border or barrier. It was often
used this way in the last century, especially in
city parks, and its value as a boundary plant
should not be overlooked today. To create a
hedge of *R. setigera*, set the young bushes at
least twelve feet apart; their long canes will
quickly fill in the spaces. As the plants mature,
they can be cut back ruthlessly with hedge
shears to force them to fit the space you have

alotted to them. Otherwise, they require little care. Within two years the strong, erect laterals will produce colorful blooms. Do not deadhead the spent flowers, as that eliminates the wonderful hips.

R. setigera can be used as a covering for steep slopes, in clumps that add color to the edges of fields, in parks and other informal settings, or as a specimen plant standing on its own. In situations like these, it will thrive with no pruning at all. It does, however, mound up in the center, the new canes growing out of, and hiding, a mass of old, dead wood that may be as tall as six feet and about as wide. If you want to groom the bush, beginning in the late winter of its second year, after the hips have dropped, simply cut out the dead wood and the oldest canes.

Training *R. setigera* as a climber is a task. The old canes, which are stiff and hard to work with, must be assiduously removed to free the new, flexible growth that can be used for train-ing. The plant is also extremely vigorous and therefore difficult to keep under control on a single pillar or post. Nevertheless, with severe pruning it can be trained on a tripod or other wide support, such as a fence. To grow it on a tripod, simply reduce it each winter to two or three main young canes and wrap these as tightly as possible around the support, attaching them with strong twine. It can also be used to cover a lattice; in this case, leave a greater number of young canes to work with. Another impressive way to display it is against a white wall that sets off its colorful flowers, hips, leaves, and canes.

In addition to its other good qualities, *R. setigera* has coarse, tough, vigorous foliage that is not affected by insects and diseases. With its bright pink flowers in the summer, fiery leaves in the fall, and red hips and reddish-purple canes in the winter, this rose is a showpiece in the landscape year-round.

ROSA MULTIFLORA

Introduced into the United States before 1810

ROSA MULTIFLORA is a beautiful wild rose that bears large pyramidal clusters of small, single, white, blackberrylike flowers with golden anthers. Native to Japan and Korea, it was introduced into the United States before 1810, and in 1811 it was recorded as one of the plants growing in the Elgin Botanic Garden in New York City.[11] Because it readily crosses with other roses, *R. multiflora* has many hybrids that occur through natural pollination in the wild. A number of varieties of this rose had long been grown in the gardens of the Far East, and some of them reached the West even before the prototype, *R. multiflora,* itself. In 1804, Thomas Evans of the East India Company sent specimens of *R. multiflora carnea* from China to England. This multiflora, which has double, flesh pink flowers, was introduced into France in 1808, and Empress Joséphine grew it in her rose garden in Malmaison. P. J. Redouté included a superb painting of it in *Les Roses,* published between 1817 and 1824. In the early nineteenth century, another variety, *R. multiflora platyphylla,* was also sent to England from Japan. One name for this rose was 'Grevillia Rose', after Sir Charles Greville, who was supposed to have introduced it, although this is disputed. This rose was also called the 'Seven Sisters Rose' because its double flowers, borne in clusters of thirty to fifty blossoms, appear to go through at least seven color changes, from purple to white, as they age. These colors were described by one nurseryman in 1828 as "white, light blush, deeper blush, light red, darker red, scarlet, and purple—all on the same clusters."[12]

The species, *R. multiflora,* was first introduced into Europe in 1862 when seeds were sent from Japan to the mayor of Lyon, France, who gave them to the Guillot nursery near that city. In 1874 *R. multiflora* was raised at the Arnold Arboretum in Boston, Massachusetts, using seed sent from Europe. But it was not until 1875, when the owner of the Guillot nursery, Jean-Baptiste Guillot (who had earlier raised what is generally considered the first hybrid tea, 'La France'), sent seeds of *R. multiflora* to hybridizers and nurserymen in the United States and other European countries, that it became popular. With its profuse blooms, large growth habit, and hardiness, *R. multiflora* gained attention as an ornamental plant, especially in northern climates, as gardeners became aware that they could create lovely effects with this rampantly growing rose that spread and sprawled and quickly covered large areas.[13] This was the beginning of the craze for decorative roses that could be used in a variety of ways—as backdrops in gardens, following their wild, unrestrained growth habits; on fences; covering walls; even climbing up through the branches of trees. *R. multiflora* and its naturally occurring hybrids were also useful for masking unsightly structures such as old sheds and railway fences. It didn't take long, however, for gardeners to realize that a rampant

Rosa multiflora, *said to be "horse high, bull strong, and goat tight," was once promoted by the U.S. Soil Conservation Service as a "living fence." Unfortunately, this species rose is extremely invasive, often engulfing twenty-five-foot trees in a few years. In late spring the sweetly scented flowers provide a spectacular display in city parks and along country roads.*

rose quickly grows out of bounds. Hybridizers were soon at work refining the type.

Intrigued with its expansive growth habit and its massive and profuse clusters of small white flowers, each containing several dozen fertile blossoms, hybridizers used the multiflora to create many new cluster-flowered roses, including polyanthas and, to a lesser extent, ramblers. One of the first American hybridizers to work successfully with *R. multiflora* was Jackson Dawson, the plant propagator at the Arnold Arboretum. In 1888 he crossed *R. multiflora* and 'Général Jacqueminot', a red hybrid perpetual, to create 'Dawson', the first multiflora hybrid rambler produced in the United States. 'Dawson', which has double, bright rose-pink flowers, is no longer in commerce.

In 1902 two nurserymen in Rutherford, New Jersey, Lambertus C. Bobbink and F. L. Atkins, decided to experiment with *R. multiflora* as an understock for budded roses. Their idea paid off handsomely; the multiflora worked so well for this purpose that they soon had the first thriving business in budded field-grown roses in the United States.[14] A variety of multiflora that has no prickles is still used today as the understock of many budded roses.

While it is prized as a valuable understock, and has always been recognized as a beautiful landscape plant, a fast-growing hedge, and an expansive cover plant, *R. multiflora* now is reviled as a troublesome weed in many parts of the United States. Because its long canes grow quickly into a tangled mass, in the 1950s people seized upon the idea that it could be even more effective than *R. setigera* as an attractive, inexpensive, and impenetrable hedge. The multiflora was the famous "living fence" promoted by the U.S. Soil Conservation Service as an alternative to wire fencing. It was used widely to contain livestock, as a boundary barrier, as a windbreak, as a highway median barrier, and for erosion control along railway embankments. Said to be "horse high, bull strong, and goat tight," it formed such a dense mass that it was even planted as a crash barrier in the median strips of highways. After a few years, however, many people came to hate this rose, for birds devour its hips in great quantities and spread the seeds, causing *R. multiflora* to spring up in places where it is unwanted and almost impossible to eradicate. Today it is outlawed in several states. The variety without prickles is, however, still important as a rootstock.

DESPITE ITS reputation as a hateful weed, *R. multiflora* is a beautiful rose that has a place in the landscape, if not in the garden. For two or three weeks in late spring it is an elegant sight, its long, arching canes raining down massive pyramidal clusters of sweetly fragrant, single, creamy white flowers. The flowers of the species rose, like those of all its varieties, are unstable in color; it is not uncommon for individual clusters to contain blooms in subtle shades of pink as well as white. The blossoms are extremely fragrant and attract crowds of bees. After it blooms, the bush is a dense mass of green, festively laden with a multitude of the small, shiny, hard red hips that are so irresistible to birds. Extremely vigorous and adaptable, this rose flourishes in all types of soils, tolerates shade, is not seriously affected by diseases or pests, and thrives on neglect. It is much too large and invasive for most gardens, and it is not the ideal rose to plant near cultivated fields, where seedlings may spring up everywhere and be a permanent nuisance. However, it has many uses—scrambling up trees, spilling over embankments, defining property borders, masking unsightly buildings, providing windbreaks, breaking up the monotonous landscapes of industrial parks, or adding green to city parks. In addition, it provides food and an ideal nesting spot for birds and affords cover for small animals.

R. *multiflora,* which has an upright, arching growth habit, easily reaches a height of twelve to fifteen feet and a width of eight to ten feet in a single season. It can quickly make its way to the top of a twenty-five- to thirty-foot tree. It grows from a base of three or four heavy, very woody canes. It is the secondary canes, which may be ten feet long, that produce the elegant display of flowers in their second year. The variety without prickles, which has plum-colored canes, has more decorative appeal and appears to be hardier than the armed species.

R. *multiflora* needs little or no pruning, but you can improve its appearance by removing the thick undergrowth that will develop over the years. When it has finished blooming, prune away the heavy wood that has built up in the center and encourage the new canes, which will bear flowers when they are at least one year old. With careful pruning you can turn R. *multiflora* into a graceful bush with canopies of early-summer blooms and autumn hips.

R. *multiflora* roots easily from cuttings. Its foliage is somewhat susceptible to mildew, but it is basically *very* disease resistant. During periods of dry weather it may drop some leaves; pruning the affected canes back to any length will encourage healthy new growth.

In 1887 an English writer, newly familiar with R. *multiflora* (which was at that time also known as R. *polyantha*), enthusiastically described it as

one of the most decorative Roses in existence. It is true that the individual flowers are single, and not large, but the countless myriads in which they are produced, and the immense size of the trusses (each generally containing several dozens of blooms), render the display made by the plant in blossom, not only far more striking, but also of longer duration than that made by most double Roses. The flowers are pure white, with bright golden stamens, and owing to their being so abundantly produced it is almost incredible how dense a mass of snowy bloom the plant in flower appears literally to consist of, for practically all stems and foliage are obscured from view.[15]

Even more important than its beauty as a decorative plant, however, were the new possibilities for hybridizers. From R. *multiflora* sprang a whole new race of climbing roses, the multiflora ramblers.

'FÉLICITÉ PERPÉTUE'

Jacques, 1827
Probably R. sempervirens × *a Noisette*

'FÉLICITÉ PERPÉTUE' was one of the first successful cultivated climbing roses. It was raised by Antoine Jacques, the head gardener at the Château de Neuilly near Paris, one of the residences of Louis Philippe, duc d'Orléans and later king of France. Jacques, like many other French rosarians of his day, wanted to develop new roses by crossing varieties known at that time in Europe with China roses, or roses related to the Chinas. He was noted for hybridizing with *R. sempervirens* (the evergreen rose), a wild rose with a prostrate growth habit and native to the Mediterranean region. To create 'Félicité Perpétue' he almost certainly crossed *R. sempervirens* with one of the Noisettes, at that time a popular new class of roses with China blood.[16]

The Noisettes, which had been introduced into France in 1817, had been raised early in the nineteenth century from seeds of a rose that was a cross between a musk and a China. The original Noisettes, which had large clusters of small, double pink or white flowers, inherited a climbing habit from the musk rose, while from their China parent they derived the ability to repeat their bloom. 'Félicité Perpétue' retained some qualities indicating Noisette influence, for it has multiple clusters of small, double, blush pink flowers and a musk fragrance, another characteristic of the early Noisettes. Its red stipules and petioles, distinc-

tive traits in most roses with Chinas in their background, would also have come from the Noisettes. It did not, however, inherit the Noisette's repeat-blooming ability. From the evergreen rose, 'Félicité Perpétue' derived a prostrate growth habit and leaves that remain on the bush and are green nearly year-round.

Jacques named most of his hybrids for members of the royal family, but to this rose he gave the names of his twin daughters, who were called Felicitas and Perpetua, after two saints. The name, usually given as 'Félicité et Perpétue', has caused much confusion and sometimes heated debate. At least twelve variations can be found in rose literature. One of the most common forms in the nineteenth century was 'Félicité Perpétuelle', which has led to the false impression that this is a perpetually flowering rose. As Jacques himself wrote, its true name is 'Félicité Perpétue'.[17]

'FÉLICITÉ PERPÉTUE' has dark pink buds that open to very double, creamy blush white flowers, about one inch in diameter. These pompomlike blooms, borne in hanging clusters of fifteen to twenty, have tiny button eyes, and they are so full that they resemble double cherry blossoms. They do not set hips, but the spent flowers are not unsightly, so there is no need to deadhead. The short bloom period occurs at the peak of the hybrid tea season.

This is a very vigorous rose whose canes quickly grow to ten feet and develop long continuing laterals; the combined length of a cane and its lateral can easily reach twenty-five feet. Because of its prostrate habit, 'Félicité Perpétue'

The Noisette influenced rambler 'Félicité Perpétue' has dark pink buds and small, pompomlike blush white flowers. In mild climates the foliage sometimes remains on the plant throughout the winter.

left on its own makes a thick groundcover. In the walled garden of The Stephen-Coolidge Place in North Andover, Massachusetts, a specimen of 'Félicité Perpétue' is grown with its canes pegged to the ground; it makes a beautiful display of flowers in June and provides a profusion of healthy, glossy foliage until late autumn. Trained this way, the canes of 'Félicité Perpétue' must be shortened to keep them within bounds.

This rose is also easy to train as a climber. It is not suitable for a pillar because the severe pruning necessary to keep it under control will remove much of the blooming wood and encourage new growth that will not bloom until the following season. However, it can be trained in a way that takes advantage of its rampant yet beautiful growth habit—on a fence, tripod, high lattice, or wall of a house. It makes a graceful display festooned on a chain or a rope, and it is an excellent choice for a tall weeping standard. 'Félicité Perpétue' is especially effective set among hedges or growing up through the branches of an evergreen tree whose dark green foliage sets off the pale blush of its flowers. Wherever it is grown, this rose should have good air circulation, as it is somewhat susceptible to mildew.

The young canes are very pliable and easy to train, but they quickly become thick and inflexible. When the ends are tipped down, they die back, so try to keep them as nearly horizontal as possible. The flowers are generally borne on six- to eight-inch laterals, and the best bloom is on the oldest wood, which produces the greatest number of these laterals. This rose will not bear flowers if it is severely pruned. Therefore, if the canes become crowded over the years, just thin them lightly in early spring, removing from the center of the bush any that are dead or crowded. Thinning can also be done right after the plant has bloomed; this gives new growth time to harden off before the first frost. It is not necessary to shorten the laterals.

'Félicité Perpétue', which retains its leaves nearly year-round in warmer regions, is hardier than *R. sempervirens*. In cold climates, however, it suffers considerable dieback in the winter on new growth it sends out late in the season. In protected areas of the Cranford Rose Garden, the foliage of this wonderful rose stays green through mid-winter.

Jacques Hybrids of *R. sempervirens*
'Princesse Louise'
'Princesse Marie'
'Adelaide d'Orléans'

'MALTON'

Guérin, 1830
Parentage unknown but suspected to be a cross between a China and a gallica

ROSARIANS in the early nineteenth century were fascinated with the new roses being introduced into Europe from China. The China roses had qualities unknown in either the wild or the cultivated roses in the West at that time: they repeated their bloom throughout the summer, and they exhibited a wide range of vivid colors. 'Malton' is the result of an early attempt by a French hybridizer to breed these characteristics into one of the old garden rose groups of Europe.

It had been discovered that the first generation resulting from a cross between a China rose and an old European garden rose—such as a gallica, centifolia, damask, or alba—will create a vigorous but nonrepeating rose. These first generation crosses, all of which are ideal pillar roses, are called hybrid Chinas if one of the parents was a China rose, hybrid Bourbons if one was a Bourbon rose, and hybrid Noisettes if one was a Noisette. Some hybrid Bourbons and hybrid Noisettes may produce a rare repeat bloom, but the hybrid Chinas do not. It is likely that 'Malton' is a hybrid China, for it has flowers of a particularly rich crimson associated with the China roses and does not repeat its bloom. The other parent was probably a gallica, for it has a number of botanical characteristics typical of that class.

'Malton' was created by Modeste Guérin of Angers, France, who named it for M. Malton, his brother-in-law.[18] In the rose literature of the nineteenth and twentieth centuries it is often called 'Fulgens', from the Latin word meaning "bright" or "shining," probably because its flowers are such a radiant red. However, 'Malton' is the correct name.[19]

Although 'Malton' is not well known in the United States today, it was once very popular, especially for training on pillars or as a weeping standard. It was also frequently planted on grave sites, where specimens recently have been rediscovered by rose rustlers, primarily in the Northeast and in northern California. At first it was simply identified as a "mystery red hybrid perpetual," but after cuttings from this "mystery" rose were distributed to rose experts, its true identity was agreed on. 'Malton' has now been brought back into commerce, properly identified.[20]

Most of the hybrid Chinas were infertile. Several of them, including 'Malton', had the ability to reproduce, however. When they were crossed with each other and with roses of other classes, the resulting hybrids were everblooming; this was the beginning of the evolution of the hybrid perpetual class. Two early hybrid perpetuals were offspring of 'Malton': 'Gloire de Guérin', 1833, and 'Ernestine de Barante', 1842.[21]

'MALTON', which reaches its peak bloom at the same time as the modern roses and continues blooming for as long as a month, has fragrant flowers with luminous crimson petals. Borne singly or in clusters of three, these blossoms, which open from large, fat, ovoid buds, are at first cupped; as they age they become flat or reflexed. They are semidouble to double and noticeably quartered.

This is a very vigorous rose with many continuing laterals that are often over five feet long. Although 'Malton' has been described as graceful, the two specimens in the Cranford Rose

Garden, whose rigid canes grow straight out from all parts, are rather awkward and sprawling. The strong, thick canes, which are very prickly, like those of the gallicas, do not bend down under the weight of the abundant growth, and even without support 'Malton' can reach twelve feet in height. In the past it was often grown as a weeping standard, but it takes hard work to force the stiff, heavy canes into this shape. Perhaps grace comes with age. Like all the hybrid Chinas, it is an excellent pillar rose, but it can easily be spread out on a lattice or used to cover an arch. One of the specimens in the Cranford Rose Garden was not originally trained as a climber, but as it matured it became so laden with old wood that it fell over into a neighboring arch and took up residence with 'Zeus', a modern climber that was already there. 'Malton's' crimson flowers make wonderful companions for the large, yellow blooms of 'Zeus'.

Like several other roses of this class, 'Malton' blooms best on older growth and should be pruned only lightly, as heavy pruning removes valuable flowering wood. Cut out all the dead wood, and as the plant ages, rejuvenate it by working on some of the old canes; choose one third of these canes and either prune them back to their point of origin, or shorten them by two thirds, depending on how much wood there is. After this severe pruning the bush will send out luxuriant new growth that will flower the following year.

Today 'Malton', which appears to be very hardy, is often thought of as merely one of the ancestors of the hybrid perpetuals. In the nineteenth century, however, it was much admired. Thomas Rivers wrote: "Fulgens, or the Malton rose, is certainly one of the most brilliant and beautiful of roses; the entire plant is also worthy of admiration independent of its magnificent globular scarlet flowers, as its foliage is so abundant, and so finely tinted with red; its branches so vigorous, and yet spreading so gracefully, that it forms one of the finest of standard roses."[22]

'Malton' is one of the many neglected old-fashioned roses being rediscovered today. It was popular in the nineteenth century as a pillar rose, and this is always an effective way to use it; but it can also be adapted to a lattice, an arch, or any other broad structure that will support its strong canes and abundant growth. Its elegant, glowing red flowers make it a welcome addition to any contemporary garden.

The brilliant red flowers of 'Malton' envelop a pillar. This old-fashioned rose is becoming popular again today.

'MME. HARDY'

Hardy, 1832
A damask hybrid

IN HIS BOOK *The Rose Garden,* published in 1848, the English nurseryman William Paul painted a charming picture of Julien Alexandre Hardy, the curator of the Luxembourg Gardens in Paris, who devoted many years to the cultivation of roses and raised many thousands of seedlings, never selling them but exchanging them with his friends for other plants. "The Roses in the Gardens of the Luxembourg are seen from the public promenades," Paul wrote, "and M. Hardy is very courteous to foreigners. It is necessary to visit him early in the morning during the Rose season."[23] One rose among the thousands of seedlings Hardy raised in the Luxembourg Gardens made him famous, not only in his own time, but down to the present day. The exact origins of 'Mme. Hardy' are a mystery, but we know that it was raised from a seedling of a damask rose, that it first flowered in 1831, and that it was introduced to the world in 1832 bearing the name of the hybridizer's wife.[24] Beyond this we are ignorant of its history.

Hardy was one of a group of distinguished early nineteenth-century French rose growers who bred many new varieties. Unfortunately, these early hybridizers were not record keepers, so we have to speculate about the parentage of the roses they created. 'Mme. Hardy' is certainly not a pure damask, for it has clusters of large, globular buds and pure white flowers.

One of its parents could have been a China rose or a rose with China influence, such as a Bourbon or a Noisette. Hardy, like his contemporaries, was fascinated with the newly introduced roses from China. He grew Chinas, Bourbons, and Noisettes in the Luxembourg Gardens and often crossed them with the old European garden roses.

With its superb white blossoms and its luxuriant growth habit, 'Mme. Hardy' quickly became popular in France, where it was originally grown as a shrub, either on its own roots or grafted onto *R. eglanteria* rootstock. Throughout Europe and the United States it was also a favorite rose for growing in pots where it could be forced into bloom for festive occasions. In this country it was known as a rose vigorous enough to envelope low fences and short pillars; the many specimens of 'Mme. Hardy' found around old Victorian houses attest to its use for these purposes in a bygone era. With the advent of hybrid perpetuals and ramblers, the popularity of this nonrepeating rose waned, but it is still among the most prized of all the old garden roses. In 1991 at the meeting of the World Federation of roses, it was voted one of the top ten all-time favorites.

'MME. HARDY', which blooms from mid-May to mid-June, has large, fragrant flowers that are often described as the whitest of all the old garden roses, even though they are occasionally tinged with flesh pink in the center. Borne in clusters on short laterals, they are very full, cupped, and quartered, and have a green button eye. They set unattractive hips, so pinch

The flowers of 'Mme. Hardy', a fragrant white damask hybrid, have a distinctive green button eye. J. A. Hardy, the head gardener at the Luxembourg Gardens in Paris, introduced this rose, named for his wife, in 1832.

'Mme. Hardy' is not commonly used as a climber, but its rampant growth can be trained on a low support. In the Cranford Rose Garden the canes are attached to a pillar, where they create a fountain of white flowers.

off the spent flowers constantly throughout the flowering season of this rose.

'Mme. Hardy' does not produce many long canes from the base and so is not considered a climber. A creative gardener can take advantage of its extremely vigorous growth habit and make it the showpiece of a garden by training its long laterals on a pillar or spreading them out along a wall. It is especially attractive fanned out against a black wrought iron fence or highlighted against a shrub with dark green leaves, such as holly or boxwood. If you want to create a beautiful climbing effect with 'Mme. Hardy', the first rule is not to prune it until its

second or third season. By that time it will have developed canes with numerous, very long continuing laterals that, while they are still young and pliable, can be either pulled up onto an upright support or spread out on a horizontal structure. As it matures, 'Mme. Hardy' also produces a few new canes from the base; occasionally one of these will grow to ten feet and can also be attached to the support. No matter how you train it, keep 'Mme. Hardy' in an accessible spot where you will not miss any of the delicious fragrance of the flowers.

As 'Mme. Hardy' matures, its canes lose their flexibility, and this, combined with its insidious, almost invisible prickles, makes it difficult to work with. Therefore, after two or three seasons, thin out the stiff older wood yearly, keeping as many of the young, pliable canes as you need for training. A lot of dead wood will build up in the center of the plant; remove this as well. Prune with care, however, for the color of the canes is deceptive; they turn quickly from green to gray brown as they develop, and some desirable growth that is perfectly healthy may appear dead.

The leaves are dark green, coarse, and more susceptible to blackspot and mildew than those of other damask roses—this is one of the indications that 'Mme. Hardy' has some China heritage. The foliage recovers as the season progresses, but this rose tends to look messy in the heat of the summer. Plant it with tall summer-blooming perennials and annuals that will hide it when it is not at its best.

This is a very hardy rose that can withstand even cold New England winters. With its perfumed, magnificent large white flowers and vigorous growth habit, it is one of the most beautiful of the old garden roses, and one that is more versatile than most people realize.

'FELLENBERG'

Known before 1835
A Noisette × a red China

THE ORIGINS of this red Noisette have been the subject of much controversy. In recent literature it is usually dated 1857, but it was known long before that. The earliest reference we have found is 1836.[25] Many modern sources give 'Belle Marseillaise' as another name for 'Fellenberg', but they are two different roses.[26] 'Fellenberg' is often spelled 'Fellemberg'. We have chosen the former spelling because we believe this rose may have been named for either Philipp Emmanuel von Fellenberg (1771–1844), an influential Swiss philanthropist and educator, or M. de Fellenberg, professor at the Académie de Lausanne, whose name appears in a French horticultural journal of 1852.[27]

Soon after the Noisettes were introduced in France in 1817, hybridizers such as Antoine Jacques, who created 'Félicité Perpétue', began to work with them. The blush-colored flowers of 'Felicité Perpétue' are typical of the early Noisettes, whose colors were generally in the pink or white range. 'Fellenberg' on the other hand is one of the earliest red roses in this class. Some early nursery catalogs listed it as a China rose, possibly because red may not have been a color associated with the Noisettes at that time. Its multiclustered flowers, however, are strong evidence that it is a Noisette.[28] It appears to be the result of crossing a Noisette seedling and a crimson China such as 'Fabvier', 'Cramoisi Supérieur', or even 'Slater's Crimson China', one of the "stud" Chinas. The vertical white stripe on its red petals is characteristic of roses with crimson Chinas in their ancestry.

In *The Rose Manual*, Robert Buist discussed 'Fellenberg' under the heading of "Roses That Bloom the Whole Season." His characterization of it as a perfectly hardy Noisette is significant, for the early Noisettes had a ruggedness that was later lost when they were crossed with tea roses in the hybridizers' quest for a yellow variety.

'Fellenberg' was one of the parents of 'Gruss an Teplitz', an important Bourbon introduced in 1897. Because most modern red roses, including the famous climber 'Blaze', have 'Gruss an Teplitz' in their heritage, the blood of 'Fellenberg' has been carried down to the present day.

'FELLENBERG' was especially valued in the nineteenth century as one of the few roses that bloomed all season. It is traditionally grown as a colorful hedge that enlivens the landscape with its numerous clusters of raspberry red flowers from early May through late autumn. As each bush is liberally studded with blooms from top to bottom, a dense planting is extremely effective.

The double, medium-sized flowers have an unusual shape and a distinctive color. They are borne in clusters of twelve to thirty or more (a trait Noisettes inherited from the musk rose), and the central bud in each cluster, which is larger than the others, opens first, the others following in succession. The twenty-five to thirty-five crimson petals, which vary in size, are long and pointed and have dark red "veins." Each petal is brushed with white toward the center and may have a distinct vertical stripe of white, as well. As the flower unfolds, the petals curl back at the edges, so that its whitish center and exposed yellow stamens and pistils become prominent. The blooms have a strong tea scent and open quickly, and if the plant is protected

from the hot sun, they may last for several days. Unlike other short-lived roses, these do not become messy before the petals fall. Small, shiny, rust-colored hips follow.

Although 'Fellenberg' is often used as a hedge, with patience and care you can train the eight-foot-long canes on a pillar or along a low fence. Like many Noisettes, it does not produce much new growth from the base. A hard pruning at planting time, however, will force it to send up vigorous basal shoots. It also develops many four- to five-foot-long continuing laterals, and after two seasons it will have plenty of growth for training. To encourage the production of the continuing laterals, prune sparingly, simply removing faded flowers and any wood that is making the plant unshapely. Every spring, remove any wood that has succumbed to winter kill.

'Fellenberg' has a spreading growth habit, with canes that tend to grow away from the center. When training it, choose the most vigorous canes and spread them out in a horizontal position on the support. Horizontal training encourages plentiful blooms all along the length of the canes and keeps them from following their natural inclination to become top-heavy with flowers. They can even be pegged along the ground. Because its foliage is rather sparse, 'Fellenberg' is most effective when combined with other, more dense nonrepeating climbers such as wichuraiana hybrids, whose leaves can provide a backdrop for its continuous display of vibrant color.

In general, the growth habit of this rose is very much like that of a China, with new shoots from every possible node along the canes. This growth usually consists of twiggy laterals, but long continuing laterals also develop at random on some of the nodes throughout the season. Shortening some of the canes during the summer forces them to bloom and send out these continuing laterals near the base of the plant. Less vigorous shoots should be pruned down to a few inches.

'Fellenberg' blooms profusely all season long, even during the hottest part of the summer. Flowers appear everywhere from base to top—on old and new wood, on the terminal buds of the laterals, and on any basal shoots that develop. It is especially prolific in cooler weather, at which time the flowers become mauve-red and tend to ball up.

This is a vigorous rose that thrives in partial shade. The dark, glossy leaves have above-average disease resistance, though they are somewhat susceptible to blackspot. 'Fellenberg' is hardy for a Noisette, able to thrive as far north as New York City. In the Cranford Rose Garden, its reaches a height of eight feet and spreads out to six feet, suffering very little dieback in winter. In climates north of this, however, it needs winter protection in order to grow canes long enough for climbing.

'Fellenberg' seems to thrive on neglect, blooming profusely without pruning or other care. In the South, it is often found around old country homes, in cemeteries, and on abandoned farmlands. With its loose, brilliantly colored flowers and its lax growth habit, it is delightful in any informal setting, the perfect cottage garden rose.

'Fellenberg' produces enormous clusters of small red blooms throughout the summer and puts on an especially colorful flush in late autumn. This Noisette, which is often used as a hedge, should be pruned sparingly, for every bit of growth bears clusters of flowers.

'RUSSELL'S COTTAGE ROSE'

Before 1837
A hybrid of R. multiflora

'RUSSELL'S COTTAGE ROSE', a shrub of unknown origin, is often listed in old literature and catalogs under other names: 'Russelliana', 'Cottage Rose', 'Old Spanish Rose', 'Souvenir de la Bataille de Marango', and 'Scarlet Grevillei' (or 'Grevillea' or 'Grevillia'). It should not be confused with *R. multiflora platyphylla*—the 'Seven Sisters Rose' or 'Grevillia Rose'.

'Russell's Cottage Rose' is very vigorous and, in the past, was much used as a rootstock for other garden roses. When neglected, the rootstocks sometimes took over and grew on their own. This is one of the reasons why free-form specimens of this rose—enormous mounds of eight- to ten-foot canes covered with masses of magenta flowers in early summer—are often found in old cemeteries or around abandoned homesites. Equipped with a basic knowledge of botany, one can identify these old specimens and also join the ongoing debate about the classification of 'Russell's Cottage Rose'.

When first encountered, this rose may appear to be some sort of gallica, for it has quartered, mauve-red flowers with button eyes. The coarse foliage with resinous fragrance and the glandular bristles on the pedicels and other stem parts are also traits associated with the gallicas. The color of the flowers is extremely variable, ranging from mauve to pink and purple (some flowers are even streaked with white); this is reminiscent of the unstable colors of *R. multiflora*. The fringed stipules are a certain clue that this rose is related to the multifloras. To complicate matters, however, its very prickly canes, its stipules with a distinctive red rib down the center, and its plum-colored canes point to a possible connection with *R. setigera*.

Most nineteenth-century rosarians, including William Paul, Thomas Rivers, and Robert Buist, classified 'Russell's Cottage Rose' as a multiflora. Nevertheless, William Prince, of Prince's Nursery in Flushing, New York, wrote in 1846 that it was not a multiflora hybrid but, rather, 'Pallagi panaché', a French variety of hybrid China that he had imported from France many years earlier. Prince claimed that the British had deceived the public by changing the name from 'Pallagi panaché' to 'Russelliana Rose' and marketing it as a new variety.[29]

Most contemporary authorities place 'Russell's Cottage Rose' with the multifloras. Graham Stuart Thomas, however, thinks this very prickly rose may be derived from *R. setigera*.[30] On the other hand, Thomas notes that the name 'Scarlet Grevillea' could mean that it was brought from the Far East by Sir Charles Greville, one of the founders of the Royal Horticultural Society.[31]

Whatever its origin, 'Russell's Cottage Rose' was a very popular rose in the nineteenth century. Robert Buist wrote: "I have pillars of it twenty feet high, forming, during the month of June, a very attractive object, having a profusion of flowers of the richest shades of crimson; many of them being striped with white. From the base to the pinnacle it is one mass of glowing beauty."[32]

Large, spreading shrubs of 'Russell's Cottage Rose' are often found in old cemeteries. From late May to late June they produce masses of bright magenta flowers that resemble moss roses or ancient gallicas. The fringed stipules are a good clue to the identity of this multiflora rambler.

'RUSSELL'S COTTAGE ROSE' bears clusters of five to seven very full, mauve-red flowers, sometimes two inches in diameter. The petals may be streaked with light pink or white, and their colors change and fade as the flowers age, so that various shades of mauve, red, and pink are common. These large blooms, with a strong fragrance reminiscent of old garden roses, are quartered, and they have button eyes; in this they resemble gallicas, which would support Prince's claim that this is a hybrid China with a French (i.e., gallica) component. The flowers—on short, stiff, glandular, very bristly laterals—have a blooming cycle that can last from late May to late June in the New York City area. Unlike many other densely petaled roses, these set hips. Squat, ovoid, and brilliant orange during the summer and fall, the hips turn black by late winter.

'Russell's Cottage Rose' usually grows slowly as a medium-sized shrub for its first two seasons, sending out only a few four- to five-foot canes from the base. This is the time to start training it, for the early growth is short and easy to manage. As soon as it has become established, however, the bush sends out a multitude of very long canes that have the potential to reach fifteen feet. An untrained 'Russell's Cottage Rose' should be grown as a landscape shrub or used as a hedge; it will overpower a small garden.

You can train this rose effectively on a pillar, fence, or lattice. Just be sure it is in a situation where you will not have to sacrifice too many of its canes to keep it within bounds. Starting while the plant is young, establish the base by removing cluttered and unwanted canes, and tie the young canes to the support. As the plant ages, the canes and laterals become very stiff, and with their long, straight prickles and numerous bristles, they are hard to handle. Training is worth the effort, however, for this rose produces a massive display of wonderfully fragrant blossoms. It is especially attractive when its longest canes are wrapped around a pillar.

'Russell's Cottage Rose' needs little pruning during the early stages of its development—just enough to aid in directing it onto a support if you are training it. Later, however, it will develop many long continuing laterals, some reaching eight feet, and these, together with the long canes from the base, need constant attention if you want a graceful plant. Every year, cut away about one-third of the oldest growth to make room for the new. This can be done right after the rose has bloomed, or you can wait until the hips have turned black. Be sure to remove all the dead wood as well; otherwise this will form a dense mound at the center of the bush. Then, after the old and dead canes have been cut away, train the laterals longer than two feet and shorten the remaining laterals by about two-thirds.

The rough leaves of 'Russell's Cottage Rose' are tinged with red at the edges and have a strong resinous fragrance. Their dark, dusty green color makes them a perfect foil for the mauve-red flowers. The leaves have above-average resistance to diseases, but, like those of R. multiflora and most of its hybrids, they are susceptible to mildew; moreover, they may drop when the weather is hot and dry. During mild winters, the foliage may stay on the bush all year round.

This is a hardy rose, but in extremely cold climates its climbing ability may be limited because the long canes will die back in the winter.

'Russell's Cottage Rose' is very versatile; it's beautiful whether left to follow its naturally uninhibited growth habit in an informal setting or disciplined on a support in a garden. No matter where it is grown, the mystery of its origins adds to its appeal.

'GREAT WESTERN'

Laffay, 1838
'Céline' × a gallica or centifolia

'GREAT WESTERN' is a hybrid Bourbon created by Jules Laffay, one of the preeminent French rose hybridizers of the early nineteenth century. Laffay, who was known especially for his work in creating hybrid Bourbons and hybrid perpetuals, lived in Bellevue, a few miles south of Paris. William Paul described his residence as "a most enviable one; he lives surrounded with Roses and Chestnut trees; and his garden, although not extensive, commands a wide and most agreeable prospect. The soil is a stiff—I had almost said rank—clay, and does not appear to have much labor bestowed on its amelioration."[33] Gardeners can take heart from this. Laffay was responsible for introducing at least thirty-nine new roses, and he is generally credited with having created the hybrid perpetual class—all this in spite of the fact that growing conditions in his garden seem to have been less than ideal.

In his hybridizing efforts, which were directed toward the creation of a rose that would be both hardy and remontant, Laffay often used the Bourbon rose. The original Bourbon was the result of an accidental crossing between a China rose and the European autumn damask, which, until the introduction of the China roses in the late eighteenth century, was the only rose in the West that flowered in the fall as well as in the spring. This crossing took place on the French Ile de Bourbon (now called Réunion) in the Indian Ocean, and after seeds were sent to Antoine Jacques, head gardener at the Château de Neuilly in 1819, the Bourbon rose was extensively cultivated in France.[34] Like the Chinas, the Bourbons are repeat blooming, but the flowers of the Bourbons are larger and more fragrant. Also like the Chinas, they were eagerly seized upon by French hybridizers, who crossed them with many other roses in their attempts to breed the vivid colors and remontancy of the Chinas into European varieties; one result of this was that the rose market in the nineteenth century was flooded with hybrid Chinas and hybrid Bourbons.

With 'Great Western', Laffay was obviously attempting to breed the repeat-blooming characteristic of 'Céline', a now possibly extinct Bourbon with large pink flowers, into a much hardier European rose, probably a gallica or a centifolia. The result was a superior hybrid Bourbon that, like many of his early attempts, lacks remontancy. 'Great Western' resembles its Bourbon parent in many ways, for it has large, shiny green leaves, globular buds, fresh green new canes, and large flowers. The mauve-red flowers, and their tendency to form a button eye at the center, lead one to suspect that the other parent was a gallica hybrid. Laffay created many such hybrid Bourbons and used them in the development of the hybrid perpetuals with which he eventually achieved his goal of remontancy. 'Great Western' played an important role in this process, for it, like 'Malton', was one of the few hybrid Chinas that was fertile.

Thomas Rivers had high praise for 'Great Western', which he said was a well-known rose with a robust habit like 'Céline' and

> has made shoots in one season more than six feet in length, as thick as a moderate-sized riding-cane: its leaves are enormous, and measure from the base to the tip nine inches; and leaflets three-and-a-half by two inches: its large clusters of flowers often contain from ten to fifteen in

each; and as these are generally too much crowded to expand properly, it is better to thin each cluster, removing about half the buds. The flowers of this truly gigantic rose are of a rich red, tinted with purple: they are variable, according to the season, being much more brilliant in dry weather than in moist. Budded on very stout stocks of the dog rose, it will soon form a large umbrageous tree: it will also form a fine pillar rose.[35]

Later he may have felt that he had overrated this rose; when the eighth edition of his book was published in 1863, he replaced it with 'Paul Ricaut'.

Laffay evidently named this rose for the famous transatlantic steamer *Great Western*, which made her maiden voyage in 1838. The name was often mangled in French gardening catalogs; Rivers wrote of his amusement upon finding it listed as 'Grande Wistern'.[36]

'GREAT WESTERN' bears clusters of large, double, fragrant, mauve-red flowers whose color is reminiscent of the magenta gallicas. The two- to three-inch blossoms, frilly and brilliantly colored, are cupped at first; when fully open they appear to have yellow button eyes. They bloom throughout the month of June in the Cranford Rose Garden.

This is a vigorous rose of moderate height with a stiff, upright growth habit. Left on its own, one bush will develop into a spreading shrub, capable of filling an area about six feet square. 'Great Western' does not send up long canes from the base as freely as other climbing roses; its height is due more to a buildup of wood than to the length or flexibility of its canes. In addition, the canes become woody and stiff as they age, which makes them difficult to work with. It is possible, however, to train this rose on a pillar; a beautiful specimen reaches seven feet on a square pillar in the rose garden at Castle Howard in England. It also does well on a low fence, a lattice, or a tripod. If you can secure the canes to the structure while they are young, the following season you will be rewarded with new long growth consisting mainly of continuing laterals that will bear a spectacular display of large clusters of intensely bright flowers.

In warm climates there may be an annual surge of vigorous shoots from the base, and these are easier to train than the other canes. In the North, where there are few of these basal shoots, the older canes make up most of the growth, and as many of them as possible should be saved. Therefore, prune 'Great Western' sparingly. During the winter months, when the plant is dormant, simply shorten the laterals that bore flowers the previous season. If the plant becomes bulky and hard to manage on its support, shorten one or two of the oldest canes.

'Great Western' will not bloom until its second year. After several seasons, there may be a decline in flower production. If this happens, cut back some of the longest canes by about two-thirds in early spring; this will promote new growth that will bloom the following year. Over time, short, unproductive wood from past seasons will build up; remove this as well as any other old, dead, or cluttered canes.

This rose grows well in partial shade. Like most Bourbons, it suffers from mildew and blackspot. Keep this in mind and make sure to provide good air circulation when choosing a site for it.

Long hard to find in commerce, 'Great Western' has recently been reintroduced to the American market and is now available from a few nurseries that specialize in rare plants. A grand old rose with a distinguished history, it merits attention today.

The large, mauve-red flowers of 'Great Western' complement the pink blossoms of 'Christine Wright'. 'Great Western', a hybrid Bourbon, has large, globular buds that are typical of Bourbon roses and flowers that have the rich color of the gallicas.

'COUPE D'HÉBÉ'

Laffay, 1840
A Bourbon × R. chinensis *hybrid*

'COUPE D'HÉBÉ' (Hebe's Cup) is another hybrid Bourbon created by Jules Laffay in his search for a hardy, remontant rose. In this instance he crossed two parents of China ancestry to create an impressive pillar rose from the hybrid Bourbon group.[37] Although 'Coupe d'Hébé' produces only a rare repeat in the fall, it is a superb rose nevertheless, one that was highly praised by nineteenth-century garden writers and horticulturists. Thomas Rivers called it the "gem" of the hybrid Bourbon family, "in colour of a beautiful wax-like pink, and in the disposition and regularity of its petals quite unique; this, like most of the group, soon forms a large bush or tree, and is also well adapted for a pillar rose."[38] In nineteenth-century flower shows this rose was often on the winners' bench; it was also a favorite for forcing in pots for winter bloom.

The name is derived from a classical myth. Hebe (Hebe of the Fair Ankles) was the goddess of youth who served as cupbearer to the gods. Unhappily, she was dismissed and replaced by Ganymede after she fell and indecently exposed herself.

'COUPE D'HÉBÉ' has clusters of fat buds that open to deep pink flowers shaped exactly like a cup. It blooms in early summer and may have an occasional repeat in the fall. With its globular buds and large, wonderfully fragrant, distinctively colored flowers on short laterals, it greatly resembles a Bourbon. The petals of its very double blooms are waxy, and those in the center have a darker color than those on the outside.

This is an extremely versatile hybrid Bourbon. The plant has a lovely shape and is attractive as a free-standing shrub. It can also be used as a climber, for it has long, graceful canes that are easy to wrap around a pillar or a tripod or spread out on a fence. In addition, it lends itself well to pegging.

'Coupe d'Hébé' should be pruned sparingly, especially as the flowers are followed by interesting hips. It is not a rampant grower and will thrive unattended for several seasons. If the center of the plant becomes cluttered, thin it out. This will help the bush keep its graceful shape. It will also promote the good air circulation necessary for the health of this rose, which, like most of the hybrid Bourbons, is highly susceptible to foliage diseases. Do not despair if it does lose some of its foliage, however; new leaves will develop quickly.

'Coupe d'Hébé' is one of the most charming and adaptable of the old-fashioned roses. Whether left on its own or trained as a climber, it adds charm to any garden. It is also a wonderful rose to plant in a pot and force into bloom during the winter months, as was often done in the nineteenth century.

'Coupe d'Hébé' has been called the "gem" of the hybrid Bourbon family. Its name comes from the shape of its flowers, reminiscent of the cup with which Hebe, the goddess of youth, served the gods.

'SPLENDENS'

Known before 1841
A descendent of the Ayrshire roses

ALTHOUGH ITS flowers are not spectacular, 'Splendens' is historically interesting as one of the first climbing roses used on pillars and walls and as a weeping standard. A descendent of the Ayrshire roses, it is also called 'Ayrshire Splendens', and 'Myrrh-Scented Rose', for it belongs to a group of Ayrshire roses that smell like myrrh. It should not be confused with another early nineteenth-century rose called 'Splendens', a hybrid China that is now lost.

Our 'Splendens' is a hybrid distantly related to two wild roses, *Rosa arvensis*, a native of Europe and Great Britain, and *R. sempervirens*, a native of the Mediterranean region. The clustered flowers are creamy white, with traces of red, which may indicate a connection with a China, as well, or a relative of a China—possibly a Noisette, since they too have flowers borne in clusters. As is the case with many of the roses from the early part of the last century, its origins have been the subject of much controversy, and its exact genesis will probably never be known.

The Ayrshire roses from which 'Splendens' was derived have a confusing history.[39] They have been traced back to the late eighteenth century, when seeds from a rose that was probably *R. sempervirens* were sent from North America to the earl of Loudon at Loudon Castle in Ayrshire, Scotland. These seeds, which the earl received because he had helped to fund a plant-collecting expedition to North America, grew into seedlings that were suspected to be a cross between *R. sempervirens* and *R. arvensis* (both of which had apparently been brought to America by the colonists) or *R. sempervirens* and an unidentified garden rose. The offspring of these seedlings were eventually called Ayrshire roses due to the fact that they were extensively hybridized by gardeners in Ayrshire and from there distributed to nurseries in England and elsewhere.[40] One of their many climbing descendants was 'Splendens'.

The growth habit of 'Splendens' and the other Ayrshire roses is similar to that of *R. arvensis*, the field rose, and *R. sempervirens*, the evergreen rose, both of which are vigorous and rampant trailing plants with very long, slender canes, and single, scented, white flowers. *R. arvensis* is noted for its ability to thrive in even the most difficult soil conditions. *R. sempervirens*, the rose Jacques used in the early nineteenth century to create 'Félicité Perpétue' and other hybrids, is called the evergreen rose because in many climates it keeps its leaves nearly year-round.

The Ayrshire roses became famous because of their versatility as well as their hardiness in the English climate. With their long, thin canes they could be used as groundcovers, spread out over walls, fences, and the sides of buildings, trained over arches, doorways, and the roofs of cottages, wrapped around pillars, pulled up into trees, or shaped into weeping standards. William Paul said of the Ayrshires: "The shoots are slender, owing to which the varieties form admirable Weeping Roses when worked on tall

This specimen of 'Splendens', which grows in the Cranford Rose Garden, has small white flowers that open from buds with hints of blush. In England we have seen flowers of this rose that have more blush coloring.

stems: they are also of the best description for planting to cover banks, and rough places in parks or shrubberies, soon converting the dreary waste into a flowery plain."[41] One writer later in the century noted that 'Splendens' and the other Ayrshire roses even had the ability to thrive in the smoke and fog of cities.[42]

'SPLENDENS', which blooms in early summer and is not recurrent, has small, semidouble, creamy white flowers that are tinted with red, especially in the bud stage. The petals form a loose cup around a broad center of orange-yellow stamens. The entire plant is covered with a bountiful display of myrrh-scented blooms usually borne in clusters of ten to thirty on the terminal buds of the canes and the short, wispy laterals that emerge all along the length of the canes. These bright, attractive flowers, which are not long lasting in hot weather, are followed by a few one-inch hips, red at first, turning brown by midwinter.

Like *R. sempervirens*, 'Splendens' has very long, thin, vigorous canes that spring from the base of the plant and creep along the ground. These pliable canes are easy to train, which makes this an extremely versatile rose that can be used as a groundcover or trained in any number of ways, just as it was in the nineteenth century. In the Cranford Rose Garden one plant of 'Splendens' serves two functions, part of it forming a groundcover and the rest winding its way up through the branches of a wisteria tree, where it has reached eight feet after two seasons.

The flower-bearing ability of the canes improves with age, so plant this rose where heavy pruning will not be necessary to keep its vigorous growth from interfering with paths or other plants. Each year the long canes and laterals that formed during the previous season will bear large clusters of flowers at their tips. After they have flowered, or during the winter, shorten the laterals by half their length. When the plant is mature, thin out the oldest and weakest growth, and open up the center to let in light and air.

The small leaves, which are tinted with red along the edges, remain on the plant for a long time, even lasting through most of the winter in protected areas or in mild climates, a characteristic inherited from the evergreen rose. Leaves exposed to freezing temperatures, however, may drop in the fall: before they do, they turn orange-red.

'Splendens' is of questionable hardiness in northern regions. North of New York City its long canes suffer winterkill when it is grown as a climber. This rose is best used as a groundcover in cold climates.

'BLAIRII NO. 2'

Blair, before 1843
'Parks' Yellow Tea-scented China' × *a*
hardy European rose

TWO ROSES named 'Blairii' were raised by a Mr. Blair of Stamford Hill, near London. Both are still available, but 'Blairii No. 2' is by far the more significant.[43] One of the most beautiful of the hybrid Chinas, it was the result of a cross between 'Parks' Yellow Tea-scented China', one of the "stud" China roses, and a hardy European rose. It displays its China heritage in its large, double, rosy blush flowers, which have very substantial petals and display two tones of pink that become increasingly distinct as they age. A clue to the identity of its other parent may lie in the shape of the flowers, which look exactly like cabbage roses just before they are fully open.

It is easy to understand why 'Blairii No. 2' quickly became popular, for it is a magnificent, versatile climber that can be grown as a freestanding shrub, trained on pillars, and shaped into a weeping standard. Its spectacular blossoms won many medals in nineteenth-century flower shows.

'BLAIRII NO. 2' bears large round buds that open to large, two-inch, rose pink flowers, so heavy they nod like tea roses. These very fragrant, globe-shaped, double blooms are borne singly or in clusters, and they are dramatic, for as they age the petals reflex back to display a distinct variation of tone: light pink petals on the outside of the flower, dark pink petals in the center. This rose blooms from late May to the end of June in the Cranford Rose Garden.

Left on its own without support, 'Blairii

No. 2' will form a low spreading hedge, about three feet high. Its stiff and inflexible continuing laterals, which may be as long as twelve feet, can be trained along a fence or on a pillar or a tripod. Even though the canes are at first upright and rigid, at bloom time they are bent down by the weight of the large buds and flowers, and the bush takes on a graceful, weeping shape.

As it ages, 'Blairii No. 2' spreads out, builds up a dense mass of old wood at the center, and begins to look cluttered. After three or four years, removing the old, dead, or crowded canes improves its appearance. Other than this, 'Blairii No. 2' should be very sparingly pruned, as it is the older growth that produces the flowers. Removal of too much wood will create a vigorous bush with abundant new growth that will not flower until the following season. Do not shorten the laterals when deadheading this rose, for after the flowers have faded, new growth starts immediately behind them. Simply pinch off the spent blooms. The tendency for flower production to be inhibited by pruning is

The exquisite pink flowers of 'Blairii No. 2' have two tones, a clue that there is a China rose in its ancestry.

even more pronounced with 'Blairii No. 2' than with 'Malton'.

'Blairii No. 2' starts to bloom in the second season after it is planted. Eventually it will become an immense bush that will be covered with a glorious display of flowers at the height of the rose season, when the modern roses are at their peak.

Because the leaves of 'Blairii No. 2' are susceptible to mildew, plant it in a spot with good air circulation. Even if the bush does lose some of its foliage, it will quickly send out new leaves and recover.

'Blairii No. 2' appears to have above-average hardiness, suffering very little winter dieback in the New York City area. Farther north, the new growth this hybrid China sends out late in the season will die back in the winter, which limits its use as a climbing rose. Nevertheless, it is always worth growing. Even in regions where it remains a low-growing shrub, it is an exceptionally beautiful rose.

Like many hybrid Chinas, 'Blairii No. 2' has long canes that, when trained around a pillar, produce a shower of blooms. The less this rose is pruned, the more it will flower.

'BALTIMORE BELLE'

Feast, 1843
R. setigera × *possibly an unknown Noisette*

AROUND 1836, seeds of *R. setigera* (the prairie rose) that were planted by Samuel Feast of Baltimore, Maryland, produced new setigera hybrids. Unfortunately, Feast was vague about the identity of the roses with which he crossed *R. setigera*, leaving us to speculate about the other half of the parentage.

At the time they were introduced, there was great hope for these setigera hybrids, which were honored with the first medals ever given for new roses in the United States. One of them, 'Queen of the Prairies', received a gold medal from the Massachusetts Horticultural Society in 1846;[44] another, 'Baltimore Belle', received a silver medal from the Horticultural Society of Maryland. Philadelphia nurseryman Robert Buist expressed his enthusiasm for the new roses as follows:

> There is not a rose fancier but will thank him [Samuel Feast] for opening a field for the hybridizer, in which the rose is to be cultivated to admiration, and blooming six months of the year, throughout every state of the Union. These roses will form parents to be impregnated with the more fragrant blooming sorts, such as Bourbon, Tea, Bengal and Noisette. We may therefore, expect from them a progeny perfectly hardy, and blooming at least three or four times during the season. In general, rose-growing is confined to latitudes south of the 41°; the Chinese varieties and their hybrids, that bloom constantly being too tender to bear winter exposure north of that line. When we can produce perpetual blooming hybrids from this Rosa Rubifolia [*R. setigera*], they will withstand every variety of climate, and perhaps may some day be seen covering the frozen hut of the Esquimaux.[45]

Later in the century, another American nurseryman, H. B. Ellwanger, had equally flattering comments. Ellwanger evaluated hundreds of roses in his classic book *The Rose*, first published in 1882. He was a testy critic of roses he considered inferior—and there were a good number of them. But for the new setigera hybrids, which he considered superior to many of the new varieties arriving from Europe, such as the Ayrshires and the *R. sempervirens* hybrids, he had only the highest praise. He felt that it was important to develop further this new class. But *R. setigera* proved to be notoriously recalcitrant in the hands of hybridizers; even Ellwanger had to admit that his own experiments with it were failures.[46]

With the exception of 'Baltimore Belle', the Feast setigera hybrids have all disappeared from commerce. They were widely grown in the nineteenth century, however. 'Baltimore Belle' and 'Queen of the Prairies' were especially popular on pillars and arches. They were also often grown as hedges, and in warm climates they were drawn up into trees. In the late 1800s the Dosoris estate on the north shore of Long Island, the home of Charles A. Dana, the editor and part owner of the New York *Sun*, had an

The offspring of Rosa setigera *and possibly an unknown Noisette, the rambler 'Baltimore Belle' was raised by Samuel Feast of Baltimore, Maryland. Its tiny red buds open to large, pale blush flowers.*

impressive garden that featured a spectacular tunnel formed of grapevines and twenty-four large arches covered with double-flowered prairie roses, probably 'Baltimore Belle' and 'Queen of the Prairies'. For a short time 'Baltimore Belle' was also used as a rootstock; specimens growing wild in old gardens may be the rootstock itself, which has taken over from the budded rose.

'Baltimore Belle' was the most successful and long lasting of Feast's setigera hybrids. Its mystery parent was probably one of the Noisettes, the newly created, cluster-flowered, everblooming roses that became popular during the first half of the nineteenth century. Feast was no doubt attempting to produce a climber that would combine the hardiness of *R. setigera* with the desirable qualities of the Noisettes. 'Baltimore Belle' did inherit the clustered flowers of the Noisettes, but it is not everblooming. Although it is not quite as hardy as *R. setigera*, it can withstand colder climates than the original Noisettes, which, as crosses between Chinas and musks, were not very rugged.

At La Roseraie de l'Haÿ-les-Roses near Paris, France, 'Baltimore Belle' and other Feast hybrids are prominently displayed on arches.

'BALTIMORE BELLE' is an elegant rose with large, drooping clusters of double, blush-colored flowers that open from red-tinged buds, turn shell pink, and fade to creamy white. The translucent petals, wavy at the edges, look like silk. A great favorite when it was introduced, it is still the showpiece of any garden during its two weeks of bloom at the end of June, after the peak season of the modern roses.

The canes of 'Baltimore Belle' are greener and more pliable than those of *R. setigera*, and its prickles are not as menacing; the hybrid is, therefore, easier to train. In addition, it is not as rampant a climber as *R. setigera*, nor is it as expansive or invasive. Its growth habit is like that of a rambler, with new canes, which can grow as long as ten feet in one season, emerging from the base. Unlike the canes of *R. setigera*, these suffer some dieback in the winter because, like the Noisettes, this rose has the tendency to send out late-autumn growth that is killed by cold weather. In northern climates this can be considered "nature's pruning," an advantage because it helps keep the bush controllable.

When 'Baltimore Belle' was first introduced, it was recommended as a vigorous, decorative climber. It soon became popular as a pillar rose as well, for this type of training was very fashionable in the 1840s. It takes skill and patience to contain 'Baltimore Belle's' thick and unruly canes on a single pillar, however, and much of its flowering wood will be sacrificed in the process. An easier, and very dramatic, way to grow 'Baltimore Belle' is to create a free-standing hedge or to train it along a low fence. When planting it this way, allow six to eight feet between the bushes.

The double flowers make a spectacular show, but their beauty is short-lived, for they are easily spoiled by rain and the heat of the sun. This is a rose that should be planted in a spot that gets shade at midday. It also needs good air circulation, for it inherited from its Noisette parent a susceptibility to leaf diseases.

Once established, 'Baltimore Belle' may become quite large, depending on the amount of pruning and exposure to cold weather. The only major pruning it requires is the removal of the old wood to make way for the new. Do not cut away any wood until after its second season, however, or you will sacrifice blooms, for this rose flowers on one-year-old growth. Following the second season, the older canes become thick and less productive than the younger ones. Remove the oldest wood if it becomes invasive.

In spite of the fact that 'Baltimore Belle' is less hardy than its parent, *R. setigera*, it is durable enough to thrive for many years without care, which is why it is sometimes found around Victorian houses and in abandoned gardens. Collectors of old roses have promoted a resurgence of interest in this and the other Feast hybrids. Many of the varieties that have been lost in this country are on display in European rose gardens, such as La Roseraie de l'Haÿ-les-Roses, near Paris, and in the Gardens of the Royal National Rose Society at Chiswell Green, near St. Albans, England.

'PAUL RICAUT'

Portemer, 1845
A Bourbon rose × a centifolia

'PAUL RICAUT' is a hybrid Bourbon that has in recent years been misclassified and sold as a centifolia, probably because its large, many-petaled flowers do, in fact, look like those of the centifolias, or cabbage roses. It was, however, classified as a hybrid Bourbon in the old literature, and it is probably a cross between a Bourbon and a centifolia.[47] 'Paul Ricaut' was introduced in the United States by William Prince, who thought it the most beautiful rose ever produced.

Like 'Malton', 'Mme. Hardy', 'Fellenberg', 'Great Western', and 'Coupe d'Hébé', this rose is a survivor from a period when nineteenth-century French hybridizers were busily crossing hybrid Chinas and Bourbons with old European varieties and turning out a multitude of new variations. 'Paul Ricaut' was the work of M. Portemer, who lived in the small town of Gentilly, just south of Paris. Little is known of this hybridizer except that he introduced his first variety around 1837 and was either deceased or retired when H. B. Ellwanger published the first edition of *The Rose* in 1882.[48] Like Prince, Ellwanger considered 'Paul Ricaut' one of the finest roses ever created, saying that it had "nearly everything that makes a rose valuable save the property of blossoming more than once."[49] In the eighth edition of *The Rose Amateur's Guide*, published in 1863, Thomas Rivers replaced 'Great Western' with 'Paul Ri-

caut', claiming that the latter was one of the best hybrid Bourbons. Shirley Hibberd, in *The Rose Book*, noted that 'Paul Ricaut' was a popular show rose because of its perfect form.

This rose may have been named for Sir Paul Ricaut (or Rycaut), an English diplomat who died in 1700. The name is often spelled 'Paul Ricault'.

'PAUL RICAUT' is a spectacular rose with enormous, very full, mauve-pink flowers that are up to four inches in diameter, cup shaped, and distinctively quartered. These huge, fragrant blooms, borne singly or in clusters on short laterals, are so heavy they hang from the bush. They display their Bourbon heritage in their large, globular buds, which are vivid scarlet as the sepals are opening. The influence of China roses, passed on through the Bourbon parent, is evident in the large, dark green foliage, the vigorous growth habit, and the red stipules. Characteristics derived from the centifolia parent are the quartered blooms with many petals, the rough texture of the foliage, and the prominent prickles. 'Paul Ricaut' blooms for at least a month at the peak of the modern rose season.

This upright, fast-growing rose will reach six to eight feet in one season. Without the aid of a pillar or a fence, 'Paul Ricaut' can grow about five feet high, a good height for a hedge. Unless it is given some kind of manmade support, however, the shrub can become sprawling and hard to manage. The weight of the flowers may even cause it to fall over and become a tangled mess. It is best to train it on a pillar, a high

The hybrid Bourbon 'Paul Ricaut' produces long, arching canes that are laden with enormous mauve-pink flowers. In the Cranford Rose Garden this two-year-old plant shares an eight-foot pillar with the hybrid China 'Fantin-Latour'.

fence, or a tripod, wrapping the canes around the support or spreading them out horizontally as much as possible to increase their blooming potential. Because the blooms nod, try to train this rose so that many of them will be at eye level or higher.

Training should be done when the canes are young, for with age they become stiff and hard to manage. In the Cranford Rose Garden, Stephen wraps two of the longest around a pillar and leaves the shorter, unmanageable ones to fan gracefully out from the base. The canes are wrapped as tightly as possible around the support and tied securely, but the ends are left free, which gives them a chance to display their beautiful arching form. This rose also makes a wonderful effect when it is pegged to the ground. Give it plenty of room, for it will easily cover an area twelve feet in diameter.

'Paul Ricaut' requires very little care other than a light pruning every now and then to improve its shape on the support. Once a year, during the dormant period, remove any old, dead, or invasive wood. After a few years, shorten one or two of the older canes by about two-thirds to encourage new growth that will fill in any bare spots at the base of the plant.

'Paul Ricaut' has no excessive disease problems, and it is extremely hardy. Like all the hybrid Bourbons, it will thrive even when left completely on its own, as evidenced by the many specimens that have flourished for decades in cemeteries and abandoned gardens.

Other Hybrid China, Hybrid Bourbon, and Hybrid Noisette Roses

'Brennus'
'Irwin Lane'
'Fantin-Latour'
'Juno'
'Mme. Plantier'
'Cardinal de Richelieu'
'Variegata di Bologna'
'Variegata di Bologna Rouge'
'Complicata'

'SOMBREUIL'

Robert, 1850
Parentage unknown

THERE IS A great deal of mystery surrounding this rose. Many people feel that the 'Sombreuil' sold by rose suppliers today is not the rose that originated in the nineteenth century. There are several reasons for this skepticism. One is the fact that in 1959 'Sombreuil' was marketed as a new variety of climbing hybrid tea named 'Colonial White'.[50] After this, people become suspicious about 'Sombreuil'. Another cause for uncertainty is that 'Sombreuil', which is classified as a tea rose, is unusually hardy, and hardiness is not a characteristic most people associate with tea roses. After comparing the Cranford Rose Garden specimen of 'Sombreuil' (which was purchased within the past five years) with color plates of this rose in nineteenth- and early twentieth-century rose books,[51] Stephen still has doubts about whether it is the same as the original rose because the early illustrations bear only a distant resemblance to the rose sold by that name today.

'Sombreuil', which is classified in the old literature as a tea rose, was introduced in 1850 by M. Robert of Angers. Robert, who took over the nursery of the famous rose breeder. J. P. Vibert in 1851,[52] was one of the many nineteenth-century French hybridizers who experimented with the Chinas and their progeny. Its hardiness does not disqualify it as a tea rose; rosarians in the nineteenth century noted that "climbing" tea roses were more hardy and vigorous than the "bush" teas from which they were derived. Shirley Hibberd, for example, described 'Sombreuil' as a tea rose, vigorous and hardier than other roses of this class and doing fairly well in his garden even though most other tea roses had to be grown under glass.[53]

The original tea rose, *Rosa odorata*, a form of China rose, is thought to have originated in China from a cross between *R. chinensis* and *R. gigantea*, an extremely vigorous evergreen climber native to Burma and southern China whose canes can reach fifty feet in length. The tea rose was first introduced into Europe in 1810. One theory about the name is that tea roses arrived in Europe smelling like the tea crates in which they were shipped from China. Like the Chinas, they are everblooming, and this characteristic, combined with their delicately colored flowers and remarkable fragrance, made them very popular. Hybridizers soon produced many new cultivars, including 'Gloire de Dijon' (1853), a climbing variety that was so popular rosarians began to think of this type of rose as a separate class of tea rose, the climbing tea rose, a class that had the vigor of *R. gigantea*. Later, other tea roses with a climbing habit, including 'Sombreuil', were also reclassed as climbing tea roses.

One suspected parent of 'Sombreuil' was 'Gigantesque', a rose that early writers described as a tea with very pale rose-colored flowers.[54] H. B. Ellwanger also suggested that 'Sombreuil' has Bourbon influence.[55]

In the old literature there is mention of a completely different rose with a similar name, 'Rose Sombreuil', an alba that had been introduced many years before.[56] In one of the earliest references we have found to our 'Sombreuil' it is listed as 'Mademoiselle de Sombreuil'.[57] This indicates that it was named for Marie-

Maurille Virot de Sombreuil, who saved her father from the September massacres during the French Revolution.

'SOMBREUIL' has globular, pointed, creamy buds that are tinted with yellow and pink. The large, double flowers, white with a peach-pink hue at the center, are flat and quartered and have button eyes. They reveal their tea rose heritage in their nodding demeanor, wonderful fragrance, and pale, two-tone coloring. They are sometimes more than three inches in diameter and are usually borne in clusters of two to four on laterals along the established canes. New canes are produced late into the season, and because clusters of flowers appear at the ends of all the new, young growth, 'Sombreuil' blooms throughout the summer and right up until the first hard frost.

This climbing tea rose is a rampant grower that increases in size by leaps and bounds once it has become established; after two years it can cover an area twelve feet wide and eight feet high. It is an ideal rose for training in a fan shape on a fence, lattice, or wall, especially as the canes do not die back when they are tipped down. It is also attractive covering a pergola or an arch over a walkway where its dense foliage and delightfully scented flowers will form a shady, fragrant bower. Five or six hours of sun a day are sufficient for this rose; in fact, the flowers will last longer in partial shade than in full sun, and their color will be richer. You can expect 'Sombreuil' to bloom during its first growing season.

'Sombreuil' needs very little pruning; simply remove any old or dead wood that interferes with the vigorous new growth. It has dark, glossy, disease-resistant foliage and is fairly hardy, suffering only minimal winter damage as far north as New York City.

This is one of the best climbing tea roses, and one of the most beautiful roses ever created. It makes a wonderful companion for some of the dark red, everblooming climbers, such as 'Don Juan', 'Red Fountain', or 'Climbing Crimson Glory'.

The 'Sombreuil' we grow in America today is not the rose described in nineteenth-century literature. Whatever the true identity of our 'Sombreuil', it is a hardy and vigorous climber, wonderful for any garden.

64

ROSA WICHURAIANA

Discovered in 1861
Introduced into the United States in 1888

OF ALL THE wild roses discovered in the nineteenth century, the two that would prove to be the most important for the future development of climbers were the tough and versatile *R. multiflora* and *R. wichuraiana*. Their long, flexible canes; extreme vigor and hardiness; expansive growth habits; adaptability to all types of soils; luxuriant foliage; and masses of fragrant flowers made them immediately attractive to hybridizers, who sought to breed these characteristics into roses of other classes. The search for the perfect climber, one that would combine all the desirable qualities of the species roses with the large, full flowers, rich colors, and remontancy of many garden varieties, was on.

Rosa wichuraiana, a creeping wild rose native to coastal regions of Japan, eastern China, and Korea, was discovered in 1861 by Dr. Max Ernst Wichura, the German botanist for whom it is named. Early nurserymen often mistook it for two other species roses, *Rosa sempervirens* and *Rosa bracteata*, and the early literature on this rose is rife with confusion. It was introduced into the United States in 1888, when specimens thought to be *Rosa bracteata* were sent from a nursery in Berlin to the Arnold Arboretum in Boston, Massachusetts. When the plants flowered two years later, they were identified as *R. wichuraiana*, and as such they were propagated and sent to American nurseries and botanical gardens and to the Royal Botanic Gardens at Kew in England. *R. wichuraiana* quickly became an important and popular rose

in Europe and the United States; it was slower to catch on in England, probably because it needs a sunny climate to fulfill its potential.

In 1891, shortly after plants of *R. wichuraiana* were received by the Arnold Arboretum, Charles Sprague Sargent, the director of the Arboretum, made the following assessment of the new rose:

> *R. wichuraiana* has been used very largely during the last two years by the parks department of the city of Boston, especially in Franklin Park, for covering rocky slopes, embankments and such spots as it was desirable to clothe quickly with verdure. It appears to be admirably suited for such purposes, and as it grows more rapidly than almost any other vine which has been tried in similar situations, soon making a dense mat over the ground, it seems destined to become a popular plant. Its remarkable habit, its hardiness, the brilliancy of its lustrous foliage, and the beauty of its flowers, which appear when most shrubs are out of bloom, certainly recommend it to the attention of the lovers of hardy plants.[58]

R. wichuraiana was known as the "memorial rose" in the United States because of its popularity as a grave blanket. Its potential as a decorative plant was also immediately obvious, for it offered a fragrant display of blooms much later in the season than most other species roses and was easier to train than *R. multiflora*. It was raised up onto arches, trellises, pergolas, and arbors, even though gardeners realized that it had limitations when grown this way; for once its canes are lifted off the ground, they require protection in cold weather or they will die back. At the turn of the century *R. wichuraiana* was

Rosa wichuraiana is a natural choice for covering a steep incline, especially in a seaside garden.

also frequently grown in pots and forced into bloom for Christmas, Easter, Memorial Day, and other holidays. In addition, it became a valuable understock, and it is still used for that purpose today by a few nurseries.

Because *R. wichuraiana* blooms in midsummer, long after the flowers of most other wild roses have fallen, it has few naturally occurring hybrids. (In this it differs from *R. multiflora,* which blooms at the same time as the majority of other species roses and hybridizes readily in the wild through natural pollination.) Rose growers soon discovered, however, that *R. wichuraiana* is easy to cross artificially with other roses and has great potential as a breeding plant. Initially it was hybridized with other species roses such as *R. setigera, R. sempervirens, R. multiflora,* and *R. rugosa.* Later, crosses were made in which just about all the garden roses known at the turn of the century were used as either seed or pollen parents.

Jackson Dawson, the plant propagator at the Arnold Arboretum, created several wichuraiana hybrids; but the first truly successful crosses were developed by Michael H. Horvath at the Newport Nursery in Rhode Island, which had received some of the original rooted specimens of *R. wichuraiana* sent out by the Arnold Arboretum. Horvath, who was once described by J. Horace McFarland as "that rose wizard," later wrote of his work: "In 1893, while I was employed by the Newport Nursery Co., at Newport, R.I., I first saw *Rosa wichuraiana*. Struck by its beautiful, lustrous, shiny foliage, I thought it was too bad that such wonderful growth and foliage should be topped by the meager little flowers it bore. I decided that it would make a good subject to experiment on, and proceeded to pollinate some of its flowers."[59] Horvath first crossed it with a China

rose and a polyantha, which resulted in four wichuraiana hybrids that were in 1898 and 1899 introduced by the Pitcher and Manda Nursery of South Orange, New Jersey, as 'Pink Roamer', 'South Orange Perfection', 'Manda's Triumph', and 'Universal Favorite'.[60] Another of Horvath's early hybrids was 'Gardenia', a cross between *R. wichuraiana* and 'Perle des Jardins', a yellow tea rose. Introduced by W. A. Manda in 1899, 'Gardenia', like all of Horvath's wichuraiana hybrids, brings out the best of both parents, combining the growth habit and glossy foliage of *R. wichuraiana* with yellow buds and double, creamy white gardenialike flowers that more closely resemble the blossoms of a tea rose than the coarser blooms of the species rose.

'Gardenia' and other wichuraiana hybrids created competition for the many popular multiflora hybrids such as 'Crimson Rambler', which had been introduced in 1893. The wichuraianas were easier to train, their flowers had softer colors, and their foliage was more attractive. Other noted hybridizers such as M. H. Walsh and Dr. Walter Van Fleet produced equally important wichuraiana hybrids. Many hardy modern climbers and ramblers, including two of the most successful climbers of all time, 'Dorothy Perkins' and 'New Dawn', have *R. wichuraiana* in their background.

The offspring of *R. wichuraiana* carry many of its characteristics: clustered flowers, some single like those of the parent, others double; lustrous leaves that are nearly evergreen in certain varieties, and sometimes as small as those of the species; strong prickles; pliable green canes that grow from the base each season; the tendency to root wherever the canes touch the ground; some fragrance; and, in many instances, above-average disease resistance. The canes can be trained in many forms and do not die back at the ends when tipped down.

R. WICHURAIANA is a prostrate, sprawling rose with long, supple, trailing canes. It blooms in midsummer, bearing clusters of small, single, white, very fragrant flowers with glowing yellow centers; the dark, glistening foliage forms a verdant setting for these snowy blossoms. The tiny, dark leaves provide a dense groundcover throughout the year in many climates, remaining green nearly all year round even as far north as New York City if the plant is grown in a sheltered area. In the fall there are small, orange-red hips that last throughout most of the winter before they blacken and fall off. Eventually *R. wichuraiana* loses its foliage, which turns vivid yellow and adds wonderful color to the winter garden before it drops. During the colder months, the canes that are exposed to the elements turn a dusty purplish red, while those that are protected and close to the ground remain green and keep their leaves.

R. wichuraiana can be left to trail along the ground, creep over a wall, cover a bank, or create a natural barrier. It is sometimes trained up through the branches of trees or shrubs; in the Cranford Rose Garden it grows up into a six-foot-high cotoneaster. Do not overlook its many uses as a decorative garden plant; its very long, pliable canes, which can easily reach fifteen feet in one growing season, can be wrapped around any kind of structure.

One way to grow *R. wichuraiana* is with another late-blooming species rose, *R. setigera*. To create a wonderful effect, train setigera specimens on pillars or tripods set about twenty feet apart and fill in at the base with the low-growing *R. wichuraiana*. The two wild roses will bloom at the same time, the fragrant white carpet of *R. wichuraiana* offsetting the massive bright pink display of *R. setigera*.

R. wichuraiana will grow just about anywhere. In the Far East, its native habitat, it grows in the sand right along the seashore. It also thrives on rocky banks and in other places where the soil is poor. Because it grows close to the ground, forming a dense, ivylike mat, it makes an excellent groundcover to hold the soil and improve the appearance of many an otherwise barren spot. It is a rampant grower, so in certain situations it may have to be sheared back frequently to keep it within bounds. Cemetery caretakers must have found this rampant habit tiresome, for it is seldom found covering graves today.

The long canes, which have numerous thin and inconspicuous but deadly hooked prickles, mound up at the center of the plant, eventually forming a heavy underlayer of dead wood that may be two and a half feet high. New growth covers and hides this mound, but when the leaves drop, the unattractive dead canes are exposed. If you are growing the rose for a formal display, remove all the old wood each year after it has bloomed; the plant produces much new growth from the base, so there will always be plenty of young, healthy canes.

Although *R. wichuraiana* may need winter protection in northern climates if it is trained up through trees or on supports, it is generally very hardy when it is allowed to follow its natural habit and remain close to the ground. Its tough foliage is extremely vigorous and disease resistant.

R. wichuraiana is a beautiful and valuable wild rose. Its important role in the development of modern climbing roses should not overshadow the fact that it has many uses as a decorative plant in the garden or the landscape.

'ZÉPHIRINE DROUHIN'

Introduced into France by Bizot, 1873
Parentage and origins unknown

'ZÉPHIRINE DROUHIN' is one of the many Bourbon roses that can be trained as a climber. Little is known about its origins except that it was brought to France in 1873 by Bizot, a rose grower in Dijon, who named it for Madame Zéphyrine Drouhin, the wife of an amateur horticulturist in Semur.[61] The first date of introduction is usually given as 1868, but this is uncertain, especially as it was known by different names in various countries. In Switzerland it was called 'Charles Bonnet'; in England, 'Madame Gustave Bonnet'; and in Italy, 'Ingegnoli prediletta'.[62]

At one time this rose could be found climbing walls, sprawling over arches, and clambering up pergolas in gardens all over Europe. In 1901 its virtues were enthusiastically enumerated by a French writer who praised it for its beautiful pink flowers, long bloom period (which he said lasted from spring through frost), hardiness, and lack of prickles. He recommended it especially for amateur gardeners.[63]

'Zéphirine Drouhin' did not become popular in the United States until many years later. In 1932 J. Horace McFarland wrote that he had just seen at a nursery in central New York "a magnificent late June show of the old Rose Zephirine Drouhin, a Bourbon sent out in France in 1868, and only just now beginning to be really known in America for what it is. In the case I mention, the plant had not been trained as a Climber, but had been allowed to sprawl on the ground, wherefore it was covered with bloom, and the people who grew it insisted that it would keep on blooming now and then all Summer and Fall, thus showing its beautiful light-crimson, fragrant flowers on thornless stems over a very long season."[64] As evidence of its continuing popularity in the twentieth century, the Royal Horticultural Society gave it an Award of Garden Merit in 1969.

In the early literature, this rose is classified as a hybrid Bourbon; but with the exception of its canes, which have no prickles, everything about it is typical of the Bourbons: it has big globular buds, large flowers, and blooms borne in clusters like those of the original Bourbon rose. In 1919 Alex Dickson of the Dickson Nurseries in Ireland introduced a sport of 'Zéphirine Drouhin' named 'Kathleen Harrop', which also lacks prickles but is not as vigorous.

'ZÉPHIRINE DROUHIN' has old-fashioned-looking, semidouble, ruffled, dark satiny pink flowers that fade to a lighter shade as they age. These blooms, borne singly or in clusters on long laterals, are wonderfully fragrant and are excellent for bouquets. Contrary to what early garden writers said, however, it has been Stephen's experience, and that of other northern gardeners, that this rose blooms only once a season, simultaneously with the main flush of the hybrid teas. In England and the warmer regions of the United States, such as Texas and California, it produces a second impressive display in the fall.

'Zéphirine Drouhin' is a very vigorous rose with long, arching canes. Its abundant canes, which are easy to work with because they have

The silver-pink petals of 'Zéphirine Drouhin' fill the air with an exquisite fragrance common to all Bourbon roses.

71

no prickles, can be trained in a variety of ways—coiled around a support, twisted around an arch, wound around a window, or pulled up into a tree. In the Cranford Rose Garden 'Zéphirine Drouhin' makes a stunning display on a white lattice fence. In the Bagatelle rose garden in Paris, a stone wall covered with 'Zéphirine Drouhin' and purple clematis is a special attraction.

This rose is somewhat difficult to contain on a pillar, for many new canes spring from the base; in order to keep the plant under control, this invasive growth should be cut out each year. Additionally, many of these basal canes will bear flowers at the tips, so this pruning may result in the loss of valuable flowering wood. On a lattice, fence, or other broad support, however, the basal canes can be used to good advantage. Like all Bourbons, this is an excellent rose for pegging, because horizontal training induces the development of flowering laterals, especially on the older canes.

At planting time this rose should be given a hard pruning to encourage vigorous new growth. It will not bloom during its first season, and although during the first few years there may be an occasional terminal bud with clusters of blooms, it will be at least three seasons before it produces a substantial display of flowers. Refrain from pruning 'Zéphirine Drouhin' until it is well established. After the third year, remove only the wood that is unproductive or too invasive for the allotted space.

Like most Bourbons, this rose is susceptible to mildew and blackspot. Keep this in mind when deciding where to plant it and choose a spot that has good air circulation.

'Zéphirine Drouhin' suffers very little winter kill in the Cranford Rose Garden; but north of New York City it is of questionable hardiness, and its climbing ability is limited because the canes die back in the winter. However, there have been favorable reports of its hardiness from states in the Midwest, such as Indiana, which is Zone 5.

For those who cherish the rustic charm and wonderful fragrance of old-fashioned roses, 'Zéphirine Drouhin' is ideal. It is also a joy to work with because it has no prickles. The lovely plum-red canes are an additional attraction, especially in winter.

Other Bourbon Roses to Use as Climbers
'Mme. Ernst Calvat'
'Mme. Isaac Pereire'
'Kathleen Harrop'
'Louise Odier'

'CRIMSON RAMBLER'

Introduced into England by Turner in 1893
A R. multiflora hybrid

1893 MARKED A milestone in the history of climbing roses, for this was the year in which 'Crimson Rambler', a climber with brilliant red flowers, was introduced. This extraordinary rose, known in Japan as 'Cherry Rose' and in China as 'Ten Sisters', was observed in a Japanese garden by Robert Smith, a Scottish professor of engineering at Tokyo University. In 1878 Smith sent specimens to Thomas Jenner in Scotland, who called it 'The Engineer' in honor of the professor. In 1889 Jenner gave all his stock of the new rose to John Gilbert, a nurseryman in Lincoln, England, who won a certificate of merit for it at the Royal Horticultural Society the following year. Gilbert thought his nursery too small to market properly such a significant rose, and he sold his stock to Charles Turner of the Turner Nurseries in Slough, England. Turner renamed the rose 'Crimson Rambler' and put it on the market in 1893. Also known as 'Turner's Crimson Rambler', it won a gold medal at the National Rose Society in the same year. In 1895 it was brought to the United States by the firm of Ellwanger and Barry in Rochester, New York.

Until the introduction of 'Crimson Rambler', most of the roses with canes long enough to cover large surfaces had flowers that were colored white, blush, or shades of pink. 'Crimson Rambler', which is thought to be a sport of *R. multiflora cathayensis*, caused a sensation because it has massive clusters of double, bright crimson flowers. As the first hardy red climber on the market, it had a few decades of immense popularity. At the time when it was introduced, most comparable roses were hybrids of *R. sempervirens*, *R. setigera*, and the Ayrshire roses. 'Crimson Rambler' offered exciting new possibilities for decorative effects because it had an abundance of very long, flexible, hardy basal canes that could more easily be trained in a variety of ways. It stood at the head of the group of roses that later became officially classed as ramblers.

When it was introduced into the United States, 'Crimson Rambler' was an immediate and enormous success. It could be found climbing the sides of houses, screening porches, framing doorways, covering arches, pergolas, and trellises, and spilling over stone walls and fences. Room was made for it in even the smallest gardens. People soon discovered that this rose, which roots easily from cuttings stuck in the ground, quickly produces a marvelous display no matter where it is planted. One source documents a hedge one hundred thirty-five feet long that was planted from cuttings in 1896 and the following year produced nearly fifty clusters of flowers a foot.[65] Charles Turner said in 1892, the year before he introduced 'Crimson Rambler', that it was one of the freest roses he knew, blooming carelessly on long, sturdy canes covered with healthy foliage and huge bouquets of compact, blood red flowers.[66] It was popular as a cut flower, providing a beautiful display in which the individual flowers in each cluster open in succession. It was also a desirable potted plant because it could easily be grown from cuttings, trained into a variety of shapes (arches, loops, hoops, pyramids, globes, fans, umbrellas, and even ships), and forced into bloom for holidays.[67]

In spite of its enormous popularity at the time of its introduction, 'Crimson Rambler' has a number of faults, including lack of fragrance,

susceptibility to mildew, a tendency to lose its foliage, and the messy appearance of its fading flowers. These shortcomings were at first overlooked because it was such a novelty, but when the more disease-resistant wichuraiana hybrids 'Dorothy Perkins' and 'Excelsa' appeared in 1901 and 1909, 'Crimson Rambler' fell out of favor. Today, one often finds old specimens of 'Crimson Rambler' around turn-of-the-century houses. One such plant, twelve feet high and equally wide, is in Annville, Pennsylvania, on the campus of Lebanon Valley College, where it stretches to the second story porch of a nineteenth-century house and puts on a spectacular show each year in early June. 'Crimson Rambler' is also frequently found in old cemeteries, for this rose is extremely durable, continuing to produce flowers on stunted canes even after it has been mowed down.

'Crimson Rambler' has a number of hybrids. Its most successful rambler descendants are those that also have R. wichuraiana in their background; two examples are 'Hiawatha' and 'Bloomfield Courage'. One unusual, and apparently extinct, variety was the rambler R. wichuraiana rubra, a cross between R. wichuraiana and 'Crimson Rambler' that looked exactly like R. wichuraiana with red flowers. Other notable offspring of 'Crimson Rambler' are two "blue" ramblers: 'Veilchenblau', introduced in 1909 by J. C. Schmidt of Erfurt, Germany, and 'Violette', introduced in 1921 by E. Turbat of Orléans, France. 'Veilchenblau', called the 'Blue Rose', has clusters of small, semidouble blooms that are a violet blue, fading to mauve. 'Violette' has semidouble flowers of reddish violet,

often with a streak of white on one of the petals; these also fade to mauve.

Because 'Crimson Rambler' was so popular, hybridizers in the United States, Europe, and England were encouraged to cross R. multiflora and other multiflora hybrids with roses of different classes—such as teas, hybrid teas, and hybrid perpetuals—hoping to obtain other equally desirable climbing roses. They also began to look for more species roses that could be used to develop new climbers. As a result, further new classes came into being, the most notable being the polyanthas, the first of which was a cross between R. multiflora and a dwarf China rose. One of the most famous polyanthas ever created was 'Mme. Norbert Levavasseur', whose parents were 'Crimson Rambler' and another polyantha. 'Mme. Norbert Levavasseur', which was also known as 'Baby Rambler', 'Red Baby Rambler', and 'Dwarf Crimson Rambler', was an important ancestor of all our modern cluster-flowered roses; this is the legacy for which 'Crimson Rambler' is best remembered today.

'CRIMSON RAMBLER' blooms in early summer, at the same time as the hybrid teas and other modern roses. It produces large pyramidal clusters of double, scentless, bright crimson flowers that should be removed immediately after blooming as they fade to an unattractive reddish blue; there are few hips, so nothing is lost by deadheading. Unlike other multifloras, 'Crimson Rambler' produces many basal breaks. These and the numerous long, pliable continuing laterals make it an easy rose to train.

'Crimson Rambler', the first hardy red climber on the market, was extremely popular at the turn of the century, when its long, flexible canes were used for creating decorative effects. Here it mounts arches at the Planting Fields Arboretum in Oyster Bay, New York.

There are an unlimited number of ways to use 'Crimson Rambler'. It can screen a porch or the side of a small cottage, smother a fence, envelop a lattice, provide a natural hedge, or furnish cover for a barren plot of ground. Because of its stiff, upright growth habit, it can also be grown as a free-standing bush. It can even be trained into a festoon on a chain or a rope; however, this requires constant pruning of the older canes and laterals, which become less pliable as they age. It also means sacrificing much of the flower-producing wood.

The rules for pruning 'Crimson Rambler' are the same as for other multiflora hybrids. As the canes age over the years, they produce an increasing number of flowering laterals. The older laterals are the most valuable flower producers, especially when they are mature, so they should be preserved as much as possible. Naturally, you will have to remove any canes that are invasive, especially if you are growing this rose as a screen for a porch; but try to limit the amount of wood you remove. Dead wood will probably occur in shaded areas near the center of the plant; remove this as well as any canes that have become crowded. Opening up the center of the plant will improve its appearance and also promote good air circulation, which will inhibit the formation of mildew. Save all the new, long canes for training.

This is a very vigorous rose with long, leathery, light green leaves that are highly susceptible to mildew. It is hardy; the specimen on the two-story porch in Annville, Pennsylvania, is in Zone 6, which is one zone colder than New York City.

'Crimson Rambler' is still on the market. It is a must in any historic collection of rambling roses, and it will always be a beautiful addition to home gardens both large and small.

'ALISTER STELLA GRAY'

Raised by Gray; introduced by Paul and Sons in 1894
Parentage unknown

ALTHOUGH THE EXACT parentage of this pale yellow Noisette is not known, one of its ancestors was probably a tea rose. It was created by an amateur rosarian, Alexander Hill Gray, who was so devoted to tea roses that he moved from his native Scotland to Bath, England, which had a better climate for growing this class of rose.

Soon after the Noisettes were introduced early in the nineteenth century, hybridizers began to attempt to improve them. One of their aims was to create a yellow Noisette, and to achieve this aim they crossed Noisettes with yellow tea roses. As a result, the Noisettes lost some of their original hardiness, but they also gained in vigor, probably because one of the parents of the original tea rose was *R. gigantea*, which is extremely vigorous though not very hardy.

When 'Alister Stella Gray' was introduced in 1894, it was marketed in the United States as 'Golden Rambler', a name designed to take advantage of the demand for yellow climbing roses. Considered by some to rival 'Crimson Rambler' in its ability to produce masses of flowers, it became very popular here and in England.[68] In 1893 the floral committee of the Royal Horticultural Society unanimously awarded it an Award of Merit.[69] It was also successful in France, recommended for planting in beds where it would produce masses of yellow if its canes were arched over and affixed to the ground with hooks.[70]

'ALISTER STELLA GRAY' is a lovely rose with clusters of twelve to fifteen pale yellow flowers that assume different forms as they age. The creamy buds are long and pointed, much like those of hybrid teas; they open to large, multipetaled, apricot-yellow flowers that have quartered centers and resemble dahlias. As the flowers age, they fade to a washed-out yellow, and the petals reflex, leaving the glowing orange anthers completely exposed so that the center of the blossom becomes its dominant feature. After this, the flowers become messy and should be deadheaded to promote the production of new blooms, for this rose, like all Noisettes, repeats continuously all summer, blooming and sending out new growth until late in the season. There is a strong, fruity fragrance. The dark foliage has above-average disease resistance.

'Alister Stella Gray', which has a graceful habit, may reach six or seven feet in height. In warm regions it is very vigorous, and its pliable canes and laterals, which range from six inches to two feet in length, can be trained on tripods, lattices, or even up the sides of houses. After two seasons in the Cranford Rose Garden, this rose has suffered no dieback; in colder climates the long shoots it sends out late in the season suffer winterkill, so its size is more modest and its climbing ability is limited to pillars and short supports. To prevent this cold-weather damage, cover the canes or bury them in the ground before the first hard frost.

With its masses of exquisite, creamy yellow flowers, delicious fragrance, and ability to bloom all season long, 'Alister Stella Gray' is a splendid old-fashioned rose that has been much praised by garden writers. It makes a lasting impression on everyone who grows it.

Following page: *The creamy yellow flowers of 'Alister Stella Gray' have a strong, fruity fragrance. (Photograph by Saxon Holt.)*

'AGLAIA'

Schmitt; introduced by Lambert, 1896
R. multiflora × 'Rêve d'Or'

'AGLAIA' was one of a trio of ramblers raised by Schmitt of Lyon, France, and named for the three Graces of classical mythology: Aglaia, Thalia, and Euphrosyne. It was introduced into England by the German hybridizer, Peter Lambert.[71] The flowers of 'Thalia' are white, and those of 'Euphrosyne' are pink, but 'Aglaia' caused the most excitement when it appeared because it was the first yellow "rambler" on the market.

Ever since the introduction of 'Crimson Rambler' in 1893, hybridizers had been attempting to develop climbing roses that would combine long, flexible canes and strong growth habit with a wide variety of colors, including yellow. The Noisettes, which have a climbing habit, were a logical choice for these hybridizing efforts. But at that time most yellow Noisettes were less hardy than the original roses of this class, such as 'Fellenberg', because they had been weakened by the infusion of tea rose blood. 'Alister Stella Gray', which is vigorous but not hardy, is a good example of this problem. By crossing *R. multiflora*, a hardy wild rose, with 'Rêve d'Or', a Noisette with buff-yellow flowers, Schmitt hoped to add hardiness to the yellow Noisettes.

Although it is actually not very hardy, and its flowers are more white than yellow, 'Aglaia' was at the time of its introduction touted as a hardy yellow-flowered rambler, and for marketing purposes, it was called "the yellow Crimson Rambler" or 'Yellow Rambler'.[72] Nurseries advertised it as the perfect companion for 'Crimson Rambler' and claimed that it was equally versatile; but gardeners in colder regions soon realized that it had neither the vigor nor the hardiness of 'Crimson Rambler'. It was also apparent that the flowers were not as yellow as the catalogs had led people to believe. 'Aglaia' lost its popularity quickly as new ramblers came on the market. Hybridizers saw possibilities in it, nevertheless, and used it to create some important early polyanthas.[73] 'Aglaia' made its greatest contribution to the rose world in 1904, however, when it produced a seedling called 'Trier', which was one of the first hardy ever-blooming climbers.

Apparently it was with the introduction of 'Aglaia' that the term "rambler" began to be used to describe a class of climbers of this type.

'AGLAIA' BLOOMS early in the season, producing large, pyramidal clusters of fragrant, double flowers. Although the buds are yellow, the flowers are such a pale shade that it takes imagination to see them as anything other than white. The plant blooms only once; later there are small orange hips.

'Aglaia' has an awkward and cluttered growth habit for a rambler. Instead of sending out long canes from the base, the plant produces much twiggy growth and many long continuing laterals on its upper parts; in this it is more like the Noisettes, which develop growth everywhere. During its first two seasons it seems to be little more than an unruly shrub with hardly any climbing or rambling ability. By the third season, however, it will easily cover a wall or a fence, or spill down a bank.

This rose is difficult to train on a pillar, a narrow arch, or any structure where its vigorous growth has to be restrained. It is certainly not a rose to plant near a walkway or in a bed with other plants. Rather, place it where its

long canes can follow their natural habit and cascade gracefully out from the plant without interfering with pedestrians or neighboring plants.

Even though the bush needs minimal pruning, you must be conscientious about removing any crowded wood that builds up in the center, as the foliage needs good air circulation. The small, glossy, light green leaves are attractive, but they are susceptible to black spot and mildew.

'Aglaia' is not very hardy north of New York City, but in the South and in California it grows rampantly. It takes at least three seasons to bloom well, but once it is established, the early summer display of cream-colored flowers is impressive, especially if the plant is allowed to grow freely in a natural setting.

The new growth of 'Aglaia' should be tied in place while the plant is in peak bloom, before the canes become too rigid.

'CONRAD FERDINAND MEYER'

Franz Müller, 1899; introduced by Fröbel ('Gloire de Dijon' × 'Duc de Rohan') × R. rugosa 'Germanica'[74]

'CONRAD FERDINAND MEYER' was created by Dr. Franz Müller, a physician in Weingarten, Germany, who began hybridizing roses shortly before his retirement. Introduced in 1899 by the Fröbel Nurseries of Zurich, Switzerland, it was named for the Swiss poet and author, who was born in that city.

This rose is one of the most successful hybrids of *R. rugosa*, an extremely hardy wild shrub rose from the Far East that was introduced into England at the end of the eighteenth century and became naturalized in much of Europe and North America. Because of its ability to thrive in even the most unfavorable conditions, *R. rugosa* was used widely in Europe for hedges. Hybridizers were eager to breed its hardiness, vigor, and disease resistance into garden roses. In the process they often succeeded in tempering some of its coarser characteristics, such as the rather garish magenta color of its flowers, its leathery leaves, and its wicked prickles.

The other parents of 'Conrad Ferdinand Meyer' were the famous old climbing tea rose 'Gloire de Dijon' and a popular hybrid perpetual 'Duc de Rohan'. When these were crossed with a rare rugosa variety, 'Germanica', the result was a beautiful hybrid rugosa with large exhibition-quality flowers.

At the time of its introduction, 'Conrad Ferdinand Meyer' was highly praised for its exquisite blooms, which could be entered in flower shows, and for its versatility, as it could be used for decorating a pillar or creating an impenetrable hedge. It is still a great favorite today. With its long canes and smooth foliage, inherited from 'Gloire de Dijon', it looks very different from the shrubby, rough-leaved species *R. rugosa,* and it remains one of the few rugosa hybrids that can be trained as a climber. The British hybridizer David Austin is developing a new class of roses called "English Roses," using 'Conrad Ferdinand Meyer' as a parent.

In 1907 a sport of 'Conrad Ferdinand Meyer', 'Nova Zembla', was introduced. This rose has flowers that are a paler pink than those of its parent, but otherwise it is exactly the same.

IN THE CRANFORD ROSE GARDEN 'Conrad Ferdinand Meyer' is one of the earliest of the large-flowered roses to come into bloom, sending out its first heavy flush in late May. Mature bushes continue to bloom, though less profusely, throughout the summer and until the first frost. The enormous, silvery pink flowers are borne in clusters or, on occasion, singly. Like 'Gloire de Dijon', they have a marvelous old rose fragrance, and while they are opening they exhibit perfect hybrid tea form. When the twenty-four to thirty petals are fully unfurled, the flower takes on a looser, cupped shape, more like a tea rose. These old-fashioned-looking blooms are often as large as four inches in diameter, and in 1899 flowers of such size on a tall growing rose were a novelty.

'Conrad Ferdinand Meyer' has a tall, stiff growth habit and can easily fill a space twelve

The rugosa hybrid 'Conrad Ferdinand Meyer' makes a beautiful cut flower.

feet square. During its first year it bears flowers at the ends of its long canes, which often become top-heavy with blooms. As they mature in the second and succeeding years, the canes produce many long, flower-producing laterals. Once the plant is well established it may send out as many as five canes from the base each season, and these can be fanned out on a fence, lattice, or wall, or wrapped around a tripod. It is important to keep the canes in a horizontal position as much as possible, for this induces the development of new, long laterals, which result in continuous and abundant flower production. The long canes can also be pegged along the ground, although they are stiff, and so the job is not easy. Bend them down as far as possible and fasten the ends to stakes. Untrained, the bush tends to become leggy and top-heavy, and it will not produce much new growth from the base.

Several bushes of this rose can be used to cover a four-post arch. To create the support, drive iron posts straight into the ground at the corners of an eight-foot square and connect them at the top with iron rods that meet in the center. Plant a specimen of 'Conrad Ferdinand Meyer' at the base of each post and train the stiff canes to grow up and over the top. The result will be a shady green kiosk covered with fragrant, silvery pink blooms.

Because it has a multitude of small, densely packed and extremely fierce prickles, inherited from *R. rugosa*, 'Conrad Ferdinand Meyer' is difficult to work with. These prickles make the rose a menace even to itself, as on loose canes blowing in the wind they can tear the foliage.

This rose does not set hips, and the faded flowers are messy. Deadheading keeps the plant looking neat and also encourages good repeat bloom. When removing the spent blossoms,

shorten the laterals that bore the flowers by two-thirds, or until there are two or three bud eyes left.

Let the canes of 'Conrad Ferdinand Meyer' grow for two seasons before doing any pruning other than deadheading and removing dead wood. Once the plant is established you can prune after the first flush of bloom. Cut out crowded canes that are at least two years old, remove all the old wood, and open up the plant; this will induce new basal growth during the summer. Be careful not to cut away healthy wood, for as the canes age they turn a grayish brown; before cutting anything out, scrape away a bit of the outer bark to see if there is live green tissue underneath.

In northern regions, do not prune or deadhead 'Conrad Ferdinand Meyer' after the middle of August. Pruning encourages new growth, and like many hybrids that have tea roses in their heritage, the plant will send out new shoots so late in the season that they will not have time to harden off before the first frost. Do not prune during the winter except to remove dead wood. Otherwise, if there is a winter thaw, the plant will send out new growth that will die back when cold weather returns.

This rose tolerates drought and grows well in all kinds of soil. However, it is not as hardy as some other rugosa hybrids; it suffers winter kill in climates where temperatures fall below −20 degrees. It is also subject to black spot and mildew because its foliage is more like that of a tea rose than a rugosa.

'Conrad Ferdinand Meyer' is an exceptionally beautiful and popular climber with large, finely colored flowers that stand out against its lovely, dark, smooth foliage. It is very effective when planted as a companion to its sport, 'Nova Zembla'.

Other *R. rugosa* Hybrids to Use as Pillar Roses

'Nova Zembla'
'Ruskin'
'Dr. Eckener'
'Vanguard'
'Sarah Van Fleet'
'Thérèse Bugnet'

Recent Roses Created by David Austin Using 'Conrad Ferdinand Meyer'

'Cressida'
'Sir Clough'
'Tamora'

'ALBÉRIC BARBIER'

Barbier, 1900
R. wichuraiana × *'Shirley Hibberd'*

THE WORK OF Michael H. Horvath with *R. wichuraiana* inspired René Barbier of the firm of Barbier et Compagnie in Orléans, France, to use this species rose in his hybridizing efforts. A member of Barbier's firm had visited Horvath at his experimental grounds in Glenville, Ohio, and he returned to Orléans with encouraging reports of the new wichuraiana hybrids.[75] When Barbier later noticed a cluster of flowers on a young plant of *R. wichuraiana* he had received from America, he decided to try his own experiment with this rose. He fertilized the flowers with the pollen of roses of several other classes. This work resulted in five hybrids, one of which, a cross with the yellow tea rose 'Shirley Hibberd', was the rambler 'Albéric Barbier'.[76]

Barbier subsequently produced twenty-three climbers using *R. wichuraiana* as the seed parent. Unlike American hybridizers such as Horvath and Walsh, who used hybrid perpetuals and other relatively hardy roses in their wichuraiana crosses, Barbier used many tea roses, which were common in French gardens, as the pollen parents, no doubt attempting to combine their flowers with the growth habit of *R. wichuraiana*. He also experimented successfully with Noisettes, Chinas, and early hybrid teas. All of his hybrid wichuraiana climbers combine flowers that resemble those of the pollen parent with the extreme vigor and disease resistance of the species rose. (One of his more unusual roses is 'Wichmoss', a climbing moss rose whose parents were *R. wichuraiana* and 'Salet', a moss rose; 'Salet' repeats its bloom, but 'Wichmoss' does not.)

Barbier's wonderful climbing roses inherited varying degrees of hardiness, and some of them, especially 'Albéric Barbier', are extremely disease resistant. Thirteen of the roses, including 'Albéric Barbier', are still available today, seven from North American nurseries. A nearly complete collection of his climbers grows in the gardens at La Roseraie de l'Haÿ-les-Roses, near Paris.

THE FLOWERS of 'Albéric Barbier' are often described as yellow, but that is an exaggeration dating back to the turn of the century when the writers of garden catalogs were eager to fulfill public demand for a satisfactory yellow climber. Although the tightly closed buds are yellow, the flowers are creamy white. These semidouble blooms, two or three inches in diameter, are borne in clusters on short laterals, and they look and smell very much like tea roses. They bloom at the peak of the hybrid tea season and do not repeat.

This is a vigorous rose that sends out new, red growth early in the spring and grows quickly, producing canes as long as twenty feet in one season. The pliable canes are easily trained on a pillar, a pergola, a screen, a wall, or an arch. When 'Albéric Barbier' is trained as a weeping standard, the canes make a fountain of flowers that cascade right to the ground. Like other wichuraiana ramblers, it often produces

Glossy, dark green foliage is a distinctive characteristic of the elegant and versatile white rambler, 'Albéric Barbier'.

many canes that grow straight out from the base; this prostrate habit makes it suitable for a groundcover. When young, these canes are easily wound around a pillar. However, as the plant ages they resist being turned away from their natural growth habit; because of this, an untrained specimen of 'Albéric Barbier' can become invasive in a small space.

This rose requires little pruning if it is grown in an area that can accommodate its abundant growth. If space is limited, the long canes and their laterals can be shortened. After a few seasons, remove some of the older wood to make room for the vigorous new shoots. It is not necessary to deadhead.

The leaves are extremely glossy, disease resistant, and long lasting, sometimes remaining on the bush even after frost. J. H. Nicolas noted that this was one of several roses that are especially interesting because of their foliage: "Dark, bronzy foliage and purple wood, in very harmonious combination. Trained on pillars, they are highly ornamental, indeed. Two or three shoots are tied up to a stout pole, and from these will grow slender laterals, drooping or 'weeping' gracefully, that give the plant an artistic effect that cannot be obtained with any other climbing shrub, and with but a few Roses, as the habit of sending runners from old wood is a rare one."[77]

'Albéric Barbier' thrives in partial shade. Its tea rose heritage serves it well in the hot, dry climates of countries like Bermuda, where it survives long periods of drought much more successfully than many other modern climbing roses. It is not, however, as cold hardy as the American wichuraiana hybrids, for it sends out shoots so late in the season that they do not have time to harden off before the first frost. In colder regions it is best grown as a groundcover or in a protected spot—perhaps against a wall or in some other location where there is a good wind break.

René Barbier was renowned for the climbers he created in the early part of the century. The beautiful and versatile 'Albéric Barbier' is one of his best, a very decorative rose that puts on a marvelous display of creamy white flowers at the beginning of the summer and then adorns the garden with its dark, shining foliage for the rest of the growing season.

Barbier Hybrids

'Albertine'
'Alexandre Girault'
'Auguste Gervaise'
'Paul Transon'
'Jacotte'
'Wichmoss'
'Cramoisi Simple'
'François Juranville'

'DOROTHY PERKINS'

Jackson and Perkins, 1901
R. wichuraiana × *'Mme. Gabriel Luizet'*

'DOROTHY PERKINS' was the first truly successful rambler. The offspring of *R. wichuraiana* and 'Mme. Gabriel Luizet', a pink hybrid perpetual introduced in 1877, it is a vigorous, hardy rose with attractive, shiny leaves; long, flexible canes; and glorious masses of fragrant pink flowers. Until the introduction of 'Dorothy Perkins' no climber with such abundant blooms would thrive in northern climates; suddenly houses and porches all over New England were swathed with its canes and enveloped with clouds of its flowers. The canes of this rose can be trained in just about any shape imaginable, and in the public gardens that were just getting established in the United States, it was prominently displayed on arches, pergolas, trellises, and other structures to show its versatility. Some of the most dramatic plantings were at Elizabeth Park in Hartford, Connecticut (America's first municipal rose garden, established in 1904), where 'Dorothy Perkins' covered long arches throughout the garden. The plant was enormously popular in other countries, as well. One rosarian said that it had "changed and added to the brightness of every village in England."[78]

'Dorothy Perkins' was considered a great improvement over the once all-popular 'Crimson Rambler' because it was more resistant to mildew. It set the standard for wichuraiana ramblers, which came to be known as 'Dorothy Perkins' types, and it marked the high point of an era in which hybridizers were actively crossing *R. wichuraiana* with roses from other classes in the search for the perfect climber.

This superstar was developed by E. Alvin Miller, foreman and plant propagator at Jackson and Perkins, and it was named for the granddaughter of the founder of the company. From the time of its introduction until the shift to large-flowered, everblooming climbers in the 1930s, 'Dorothy Perkins' was the most popular climbing rose in America, if not the world. It contributed much to the phenomenal success of the rapidly expanding Jackson and Perkins Company. In 1930 Bobbink and Atkins had this to say in their catalog about the pink rambler that had become ubiquitous in the American landscape: "One of the best, and much too popular to need recommendation." Its use was so widespread that eventually people tired of it, and although it is still grown, it has lost out in popularity to other, large-flowered climbers. Old abandoned bushes of 'Dorothy Perkins' can be seen all across the country, often thriving despite years of neglect.

'Dorothy Perkins' was instrumental in the creation of early floribundas, which were known as hybrid polyanthas. 'Ellen Poulsen' and 'Johanna Tantau' are two examples.

EVEN TODAY, many people feel that no other rambler can surpass the beauty of 'Dorothy Perkins', and, indeed, there is no sight more pleasing than an arch enveloped by its enormous clusters of small, frothy, shell pink flowers. This rambler blooms for three to four weeks in midsummer, beginning when the hybrid teas are at their peak. The one-inch flowers, borne in immense clusters on extremely long laterals, are small but very full, with ruffled petals that reflex to expose a button eye. They hold their color and make excellent bouquets, filling a vase with a mass of pink, although they provide little fragrance.

Occasionally 'Dorothy Perkins' repeats its bloom in the fall, especially after droughts or other periods of stress. The second blooms, which are sparse and not as clustered, are borne on the same laterals that bloomed earlier in the season. This should be taken into account when pruning; if you are hoping for a second flush, shorten the laterals back by only two-thirds so that some of the old flowering wood remains.

'Dorothy Perkins' is one of the easiest ramblers to grow. It prefers full sun, but it also tolerates partial shade; and it thrives in all types of soil. Like *R. wichuraiana*, it is especially well adapted to the sandy soil of the seashore. It thrives and is vigorous even in cold climates, although if newly formed canes do not have time to harden off, the tips will die during the winter. It actually does best without winter protection, seeming to benefit from exposure to cold. The best time to plant it is in the fall. Like other wichuraiana hybrids, it should be given an initial hard pruning, down to four inches. A fast-growing plant, it will bear flowers the second season after it is planted, a trait inherited from *R. wichuraiana* and common to all ramblers of this type.

One of the characteristics that endeared 'Dorothy Perkins' to the public was its adaptability to training. Although the numerous strong, hooked prickles make winding hazardous, the long flexible canes, which can reach fifteen feet in one season, are so pliable that they can be intricately wrapped around just about anything—pergolas, arches, tripods, screens, fences, lattices, porches, doors, and windows. The ends don't die back when tipped down; therefore the canes can be trained up, twisted, looped, and turned back down again, with no ill effects. They can be shaped into tunnel forms or trained as weeping standards, in which case their heavy clusters of flowers will hang gracefully from the ends of the long laterals, creating a fountain of bloom. 'Dorothy Perkins' can also be grown free form, trailing down a hillside, covering a bank, or climbing a wall. Spaced four feet apart, several bushes planted together will, after a few years, mound up to five or six feet and form a free-standing hedge or fence. The only restriction is that 'Dorothy Perkins' must not be planted close against a wall or other solid structure, for it is susceptible to mildew and needs good air circulation.

'Dorothy Perkins' is a rampant rose that produces abundant new growth after blooming. As it ages, the bush seems to lose some of its ability to develop numerous basal shoots, producing instead a multitude of extremely long continuing laterals. This is especially true under less than ideal growing conditions. These secondary canes may be the only new canes a bush will generate, so if you are attempting to rejuvenate this rose, inspect it carefully before cutting out any of the main canes. To restore a bush that has been reduced to a single, woody cane, wait until after it has bloomed and then cut the entire plant back to four or six inches from the ground. This will force it to start producing new basal shoots. You may lose a season of bloom, depending on how long it takes these new shoots to develop.

Grown as a groundcover, 'Dorothy Perkins' requires no care at all; grown as a hedge, it demands only a little work. To keep the plants looking neat, remove the faded flower clusters

The canes of an old specimen of 'Dorothy Perkins' have worked their way through the cracks of an abandoned barn in Natchez, Mississippi.

and cut out the older wood to provide good air circulation. If you want to make life easy for yourself (and avoid the horrible hooked prickles), simply shear the plants down to a height of three feet immediately after they bloom. They will look forlorn for a while, but they will grow quickly for the rest of the season and bloom again the following summer in all their glory.

If you grow 'Dorothy Perkins' on a pergola or an arch, more work and fortitude are necessary. Cut to the ground all the wood that has bloomed, or as much as you need to make room for any new growth. The new canes will already be sprouting from the base or at various points along the older wood by the time the flowers are fading; tie these young canes to the support. The old canes should be removed eventually in any case, because with age they lose their flexibility and ability to bear flowers; the newer canes are the best flower producers. 'Dorothy Perkins' will survive even if you do nothing with it; but a little pruning will extend its life and keep it free from the mite and mildew problems that will certainly develop if the wood is allowed to become crowded.

In addition to its other virtues, 'Dorothy Perkins' is extremely easy to propagate. Cuttings root easily, and new plants can also be produced by layering—tipping the ends of the canes down and burying them in the ground, where they will root, a trait inherited from *R. wichuraiana*. In the early days of its popularity, rooted cuttings of 'Dorothy Perkins' were sold in two-and-one-quarter-inch pots.

The glistening foliage is very attractive, especially before flower production begins, when it densely covers any structure on which it is grown and highlights the curve of an arch or the outline of a pergola. Once the flowering laterals develop, the heavy clusters of buds hang gracefully.

'Dorothy Perkins' was the prototype for many subsequent wichuraiana ramblers. They are all similar in growth habit and foliage, and they are all extremely easy to grow. 'Minnehaha', 'Lady Gay', and 'Debutante' are just a few examples. There are several sports. One of these, 'White Dorothy Perkins', also called 'White Dorothy', is just like its parent, but snow white and with a bit more fragrance; it was introduced in 1908 by B. R. Cant and Sons of Essex, England. Another sport, 'Lady Godiva', was also introduced in 1908 by Paul and Son, of Cheshunt, England. Its flowers, which have no fragrance, are in tighter clusters than those of 'Dorothy Perkins' and are a softer color. Each flower is half pink and half faded pink, eventually fading to white.

'FRAU KARL DRUSCHKI'

Lambert, 1901
'Merveille de Lyon' × *'Mme. Caroline Testout'*

'FRAU KARL DRUSCHKI' is a pure white hybrid perpetual that can be grown as a climber. It was developed by Peter Lambert of Trier, Germany, and introduced in 1901. Lambert was not seeking a climber when he crossed 'Merveille de Lyon', a light pink hybrid perpetual, and 'Mme. Caroline Testout', a medium pink hybrid tea. Rather, he was caught up in the rage for hybrid perpetuals—hardy shrubs with enormous, fragrant, many-petaled flowers that were popular in Victorian flower shows. His cross produced a hardy, perpetually blooming rose with large, scentless, snow-white flowers. The new creation, which was unofficially called 'Snow Queen', instantly charmed the rose world with its pure white blooms. Its other noteworthy characteristic was only discovered a few years later, when growers found that this hardy hybrid perpetual was vigorous enough to use as a climber. As all hardy climbers up to that time had small, nonrepeating flowers, Lambert's achievement opened up exciting new possibilities for gardeners.

When this rose was exhibited in Berlin in 1901, it was honored with the name of the wife of the president of the Association of German Friends of Roses, Frau Karl Druschki. During the First World War, when German names were out of favor, it was renamed 'Snow Queen' in England, and it became known as 'White American Beauty' in the United States and 'La Reine des Neiges' in France. The whitest of all roses, it was described in the 1923 Bobbink and Atkins catalog as "the most popular rose in America."

'FRAU KARL DRUSCHKI' is as popular today as when it was first introduced. Throughout the summer it produces large, pointed, rose-pink buds that open to enormous, pure white flowers. (With the advent of cool weather in fall, the buds become dark pink.) While the buds are opening, they are high centered, like hybrid teas; but when all the petals have gently unfurled, the flowers are free form and cup shaped. Sometimes they keep their pointed centers, the innermost petals remaining curled around the stamens and pistils. The flowers are produced on sturdy laterals—some as short as six inches, others as long as six feet—that spring from all parts of the plant. Deadheading is not necessary, but new blooms will appear more quickly if you shorten the laterals back by two-thirds. These fantastic blooms have only two faults: they lack fragrance, and like many other white roses, they may become spotted and look bedraggled after a cold rain.

'Frau Karl Druschki' has dark green but not glossy leaves that are notoriously susceptible to mildew, less so to black spot. It is a very woody shrub with a few strong basal canes that support a thick canopy of growth above. Left on its own, this vigorous and invasive rose becomes unwieldy, developing into a huge mass of thick, tangled canes with much dead wood in the center. It can cover an area twelve feet square, providing a glorious, free-form display of enormous white flowers, but smothering everything in sight.

Today, when there are so many hardy, large-flowered climbers available, the climbing ability of 'Frau Karl Druschki' is often overlooked.

Many gardeners treat it like other hybrid perpetuals, pruning it back severely to a height of two or three feet at the beginning of the season. This is an easy way to deal with its rampant growth while having as little contact as possible with its brutal prickles. If you are more courageous, however, you can prune it selectively and induce it to take on the characteristics of a climber. First, cut out the older wood and open up the center to let in the air. Then shorten the longest canes back to the point where they are a half-inch in diameter and prune any laterals back to four inches. Now you will have manageable canes that you can work with.

If you train the young canes horizontally, you will induce vigor in the plant, causing the canes to grow as much as eight feet high and twelve feet wide—enough to cover a fence or the sides of a tripod. Because of the weight of its aging canes, it is difficult to keep 'Frau Karl Druschki' on a single, upright support, such as a pillar or post. However, if you have limited space, it is worth the trouble to train a plant this way. Keep it under control by cutting out the older wood and training only the new, long canes.

When 'Frau Karl Druschki' is used as a climber, it must be pruned annually in late winter or early spring to remove the oldest wood and make room for the rampant new growth. Preserve as many of the year-old canes as possible, for they produce the best bloom. Canes that are less than a half-inch in diameter and too short for training should be treated like laterals and cut back to two or three bud eyes.

This rose does not have a creeping habit, but it can be made into a groundcover if it is pegged. This is done by arching the canes down and tying the ends to stakes in the ground. As horizontal training creates abundant bloom, the pegged canes will become a series of flowering mini-arches. It can also be used as a hedge, where its fierce prickles will make an intruder-proof barrier.

'Frau Karl Druschki' is very hardy, but in the coldest climates it may fare better as a shrub than as a climber because its long canes will suffer winter kill if they are not protected. One way to take advantage of its climbing ability in regions with severe winters is by pegging; trained this way, the canes will escape harsh winter winds because they are close to the ground.

No matter where or how 'Frau Karl Druschki' is grown, it is an exceptional rose, still as desirable as it was in 1937 when J. H. Nicholas said of it, "the greatest white rose ever produced, or would be if it was perfumed."

Other Hybrid Perpetuals to Use as Climbers

'Eugène Fürst'
'Earl of Dufferin'
'Ulrich Brunner Fils'
'Baronne Prévost'
'Gloire de Ducher'
'Heinrich Münch'
'Hugh Dickson'

If 'Frau Karl Druschki' is grown as a climber, the long arching canes must be securely tied to the support. Here the weight of the large white blooms has pulled the rose from its pillar. 'Silver Moon' grows on the lattice in the background.

'AMERICAN PILLAR'

Van Fleet, 1902; introduced by Conard and Jones, 1908
(R. wichuraiana seedling × R. setigera) × a red hybrid perpetual

'AMERICAN PILLAR' is the creation of one of America's foremost rose breeders. Dr. Walter Van Fleet was originally a medical doctor, but he left the medical profession for his real love, plant hybridizing. Working at the Bureau of Plant Industry in the Department of Agriculture, he developed blight-resistant chestnuts and improved varieties of strawberry, gladiolus, canna, corn, gooseberry, and other plants. He also published several books on plant breeding. Today, however, he is most remembered for his wonderful climbing roses.

Dr. Van Fleet felt that American gardeners wanted a special kind of rose that did not need the "incessant coddling" required by the new hybrid teas being introduced from Europe and England. He worked for many years to develop what he called "dooryard roses," roses with beautiful flowers, luxuriant foliage, colorful hips, disease resistance, and the ability to thrive in even the harshest climates. To create these, he crossed many types of garden roses with hardy species roses. In 1922, three of his climbers, 'Dr. W. Van Fleet', 'Silver Moon', and 'American Pillar', were called "the three greatest climbing roses of the new world—roses which . . . have been sold by the carload and planted by the hundred thousands."[79]

Dr. Van Fleet raised 'American Pillar' in 1898 at his home in Little Silver, New Jersey. He said of its origin: "The American Pillar Rose was raised by me in 1898 from seed of a Wichuraiana-setigera cross-pollinated with a bright red Remontant Rose seedling, that had a touch of Polyantha or rather Rosa multiflora in its make-up. It thus contains the blood of four Rose species, but I regard it as essentially a Wichuraiana-setigera hybrid."[80] The exquisite new climber that resulted, therefore, had in its heritage *R. wichuraiana*, *R. setigera*, *R. multiflora*, and the chinas and other old garden roses (by way of the red remontant rose). And despite the great variety of its heritage, the flowers of 'American Pillar' most closely resemble those of *R. setigera*. With the exception of 'Baltimore Belle' and a few other setigera hybrids developed in the mid-nineteenth century by Samuel Feast and Joshua Pierce, most crosses with *R. setigera* had produced very unattractive offspring, as Van Fleet himself was well aware. 'American Pillar', one of his most beautiful roses, is especially noteworthy because it is a highly successful setigera hybrid.

The firm of Conard and Jones, which introduced this and many other Van Fleet roses, first proudly displayed 'American Pillar' on the estate of Pierre S. Du Pont in Kennett Square, Pennsylvania.[81] This estate is now the site of the famous Longwood Gardens, and specimens of 'American Pillar' still grow there, covering metal arches that enclose a small courtyard. This rose also decorates long arches over the main walkways in the Elizabeth Park Rose Garden in Hartford, Connecticut. At the Cranford Rose Garden it spans twenty feet on the lattice-

The Van Fleet hybrid 'American Pillar' is still a popular rose in Europe. At the Bagatelle rose garden in Paris it frames an entranceway.

work fence that frames the collection. But, except for the specimens in these gardens, 'American Pillar' is not often grown in this country today. In Europe, however, it graces almost every major rose collection, usually trained to make a magnificent rose tunnel.

'AMERICAN PILLAR' is a once-blooming climber that bears enormous clusters of as many as thirty-six single, bright pink blossoms. The flowers look like those of *R. setigera* except that the pink is softer and the centers are more distinctively white. The yellow stamens are prominently displayed, giving the dainty blossoms a sunny appearance. Like *R. setigera*, 'American Pillar' blooms late in the season, after the peak of the modern shrub roses, and the flowers are followed by quantities of bright red hips that are irresistible to birds. With its beautiful scarlet hips and large, glossy leaves that turn purple and red in the fall, this rose is an attractive plant in the garden for much of the year.

'American Pillar', which grows eight feet high and twenty feet wide in the Cranford Rose Garden, is a vigorous rose with thick, sturdy canes and very long, stiff laterals that can be trained on chains, ropes, and all kinds of arches. Despite its name, however, this rose is not the best choice for a pillar; it is too rampant, and its canes are too heavy.

A typical *R. wichuraiana* hybrid, 'American Pillar' sends up many new canes from the base each year, and in most cases these do not produce flowers until the following season. It also develops many continuing laterals. The one-year-old canes, which produce the best bloom, are also the most pliable; so when pruning, sacrifice the older canes in favor of the new ones. After the plant has bloomed, shorten the flowering laterals; if you want to preserve the hips, prune in winter or early spring. During the summer, remove older wood to make room for the younger canes that are developing. If you are growing 'American Pillar' in a confined space where it has to be heavily pruned—over an arch or a doorway, for example—it is best to remove as much of the old wood as possible after the blooms have faded, even though this means sacrificing the hips.

'American Pillar' has disease-resistant leaves; nevertheless, it should be grown in a well-ventilated spot. It can tolerate partial shade but not dry weather, when it tends to drop its foliage. It is so vigorous that it often suffers winter damage because it sends out new canes so late in the season that they do not have time to mature and harden off before the first frost.

'American Pillar' is a wonderful rose that does not deserve the neglect it has suffered in recent years. Its massive clusters of delicate flowers make a bold display in early summer, and its hips and leaves provide interest and color for the rest of the season. It is a showpiece in any garden.

'SILVER MOON'

Van Fleet, 1902; introduced by Peter Henderson, 1910
(R. wichuraiana *seedling* × *'Devoniensis')* × Rosa laevigata

'SILVER MOON' was raised by Dr. Van Fleet at his home in Little Silver, New Jersey, and introduced along with 'Dr. W. Van Fleet' by the firm of Peter Henderson and Company in 1910. According to Van Fleet, "Silver Moon is the offspring of Cherokee rose pollen on the stigmas of a cross between Wichuraiana and Devoniensis, the latter a strong-growing Tea rose, possibly having traces of the Indian *Rosa gigantea* in its composition."[82] If this is the case, 'Silver Moon' is one of the few successful hybrids of the Cherokee rose (*R. laevigata*), a vigorous wild climber native to China and Formosa that is notoriously resistant to hybridizing. As Van Fleet himself wrote: "Countless attempts have been made to blend it with the choicer garden roses, but failure has been so constant that Cherokee rose-breeding has been pronounced impracticable. The writer has squandered whole seasons of work on the Cherokee, and has little to show for it except Silver Moon and a bushy seedling producing apple-blossom-pink, semi-double blooms, of exquisite fragrance but of little garden value."[83]

Many rosarians question whether Van Fleet, who was apparently not the best of record keepers, remembered accurately the parentage of 'Silver Moon', for while it is not a rose that will thrive in the coldest climates, it seems far too hardy to have *R. laevigata* and 'Devoniensis', both of which are extremely tender roses, as its parents. *R. laevigata*, for example, will not survive in the New York City area. Neverthe-

less, the large white flowers of 'Silver Moon', whose broad petals encircle bright yellow stamens, are what one might expect from such a cross. *R. laevigata* has large, white, broad-petaled flowers characterized by prominent yellow stamens, and the large, double flowers of 'Devoniensis', a vigorous tea rose, are also white.

When the American Rose Society conducted a poll in 1922 to determine the favorite roses of its members, 'Silver Moon' was rated the most popular climber in the southern states, and it came in second in New England and the middle, central, and western states, where it was surpassed only by 'Dr. W. Van Fleet'.[84]

'SILVER MOON' was one of the first truly satisfactory large-flowered white climbers. It blooms in early summer, with clusters of pointed, pale yellow buds that open to large, semidouble flowers whose white petals seem suffused with the golden glow of the conspicuous yellow stamens. These flowers, on long, erect laterals, are fuller than those of *R. laevigata* because they have about twenty petals; nevertheless they have a wild rose appearance. Unlike the flowers of *R. laevigata*, they are not very fragrant. The leaves are large, glossy, and long lasting on the bush, a trait inherited from *R. wichuraiana*. They are also extremely disease resistant.

This rose is a very vigorous, rampant grower that often attains eighteen or twenty feet in one season. In the early part of the century it was often used as a hedge, but it can be trained in a variety of other ways—on a wall, fence, wide archway, or any structure that will accommodate its vigorous growth. The canes of 'Silver Moon' can become very cluttered; the center of a mature bush is often nothing more than an ugly mound of tangled wood, surrounded by green, young growth. To keep the plant neat, thin out the old wood during the winter.

This rose is not reliably hardy in northern climates. New growth is especially susceptible to cold, so do not prune in late summer because this encourages the canes to send out young shoots that will be killed by the first frost. Wait until spring to shorten the laterals, which in colder climates will die back in any case. In some regions the whole plant needs winter protection. Release it from its support, bury it in the ground, and cover it with mulch.

'Silver Moon' remains a popular climber. It is especially delightful when combined with another old-fashioned-looking rose that blooms at the same time, 'Zéphirine Drouhin', whose dark, satiny pink flowers make a perfect foil for its elegant, creamy white blooms.

'Silver Moon', a Van Fleet hybrid of uncertain parentage, has glossy foliage and bright white flowers with golden centers. Here the blossoms poke through a holly hedge in Central Park in New York City.

'DR. W. VAN FLEET'

Van Fleet, 1902; introduced by Peter Henderson and Company, 1910
(R. wichuraiana *seedling* × *'Safrano'*) × *'Souvenir du Président Carnot'*

'DR. W. VAN FLEET' is the third and most important of Van Fleet's famous trio of climbers ('American Pillar' and 'Silver Moon' being the other two). This rose also has *R. wichuraiana* in its heritage. Van Fleet crossed a seedling from *R. wichuraiana* with 'Safrano', an old-fashioned tea rose with creamy apricot-yellow flowers, and fertilized the resulting seedling with pollen from 'Souvenir du Président Carnot', a hybrid tea with flesh pink flowers. The new rose was a vigorous climber with unusually large, soft pink blossoms. Van Fleet later wrote: "The result practically places the highly finished Carnot blooms on a rampant hardy climber, from which buds with 18-inch stems may be cut by the armful in its season of bloom."[85] One of the best assessments of this rose was made by G. A. Stevens, who, though not enthralled with the color of the flowers, was well aware of the importance of their size, a significant departure from what he called the "fussy little cluster-flowered ramblers. . . . Here was an heroic rose, of noble size and perfect form, borne on a rampant plant, first of the new race of climbers."[86]

This extraordinary rose, voted America's favorite climber by the members of the American Rose Society in 1927,[87] was raised by Van Fleet in 1899, and it was only through a stroke of good luck that it was not lost. When the original seedlings bloomed in 1901, Dr. Van Fleet thought them promising enough to deserve a name, and he called the new rose 'Daybreak'. He sold the plants to the firm of Peter Henderson and Company in New York, where they were put into a hothouse and forced into bloom instead of being propagated slowly in a coolhouse, as he had instructed. When they produced flimsy and unimpressive flowers as a result of this treatment, the plants were banished to a garden in New Jersey, where they all died because they were too weak to withstand the winter cold. Fortunately, Van Fleet had kept one plant for himself, and for the next five or six years, while he waited for Peter Henderson and Company to put 'Daybreak' on the market (he had not been told their plants had died), he watched his rose grow into a healthy, beautiful climber. When he learned what had happened, he cut an armful of 'Daybreak's pink flowers and took them, along with flowers of a new, white rose, to Henderson, who bought them both on the spot for $100. Henderson introduced the two roses in 1910: he called the white rose 'Silver Moon' and the pink 'Dr. W. Van Fleet', even though the doctor, an extremely modest man, had wanted it to have its original name, 'Daybreak', rather than his own.[88]

The importance of 'Dr. W. Van Fleet' extends far beyond its claim as one of the first large-flowered climbers. Even though it blooms only once, for a long period at the peak of the hybrid tea season, and therefore did not immediately fulfill the hybridizer's desire to create an

The creation of the large-flowered climber 'Dr. W. Van Fleet' was a major breakthrough in the history of climbing roses.

everblooming climber, in 1930 it produced a remarkable sport that does have the ability to bloom profusely all season long: 'New Dawn'.

THE NODDING BUDS of 'Dr. W. Van Fleet' resemble those of tea roses, a characteristic inherited from 'Safrano'. The large, blush-colored flowers, however, are more like those of the hybrid tea parent, 'Souvenir du Président Carnot', at least until they are fully open. These three- to four-inch blooms have a distinctive fragrance, a combination of the scents of tea and damask roses as well as *R. foetida*. Some gardeners find that their pink lacks intensity, but this may be the result of poor or shady growing conditions. In bud form this rose has warm blush tones that make it a very popular cut flower. As they age, the flowers turn almost white and then fall immediately before they become messy. The size of the flowers made this rose extremely appealing at a time when people were tiring of climbers with clusters of small flowers.

'Dr. W. Van Fleet' produces wonderful, large, orange-red hips that last through the winter. Therefore, do not deadhead the bush. When the canes are young, they are plum-red; but when mature, they are dark green and quickly become heavy and woody—unlike the earlier wichuraiana ramblers. In late winter or early spring, neaten the bush by cutting out dead, crowded, or invasive canes. The best blooms occur on the old wood, however, so do not cut out too much. The rule for this rose is, the less pruned the better. The same is true for 'New Dawn' and many of its progeny.

This is an enormously vigorous rose that grows at least twelve feet in one season, a superb example of the dooryard roses Dr. Van Fleet worked so hard to create. In two years it easily covers the side of a house, and at one time it enveloped doorways, porches, brownstone fronts, and farmhouse walls all across the country. It is much too rampant to be confined to an arch or a pillar, but it can be trained along a fence or a wall, shaped around a door or a window of a house, left to grow free form as a hedge, or used as a groundcover on a steep slope. Just be sure to keep it away from paths and walkways, for it is extremely aggressive.

'Dr. W. Van Fleet' has vigorous canes with huge prickles and many long continuing laterals, traits inherited from *R. wichuraiana*. It is a very hardy rose with large, glossy leaves that are free of mildew and other diseases.

'Dr. W. Van Fleet' is such a beautiful and important climber that even if Van Fleet had never created another rose, it would have made him famous. It marked a milestone in the development of large-flowered climbers and continued to influence the history of this class of rose when it later produced its phenomenal everblooming sport, 'New Dawn'.

Other Van Fleet Climbers

'Alida Lovett'
'Bess Lovett'
'Breeze Hill'
'Glenn Dale'
'Mary Wallace'
'Philadelphia'
'Ruby Queen'

'TRIER'

Lambert, 1904
Seedling of 'Aglaia'

THE MULTIFLORA RAMBLER 'Trier' was one of the first truly hardy, perpetually blooming rambling roses. It was introduced by Peter Lambert, who named it after his native city, Trier, Germany. Lambert said that 'Trier' was a cross between 'Aglaia' and a rosy pink hybrid perpetual, 'Mrs. R. G. Sharman-Crawford'. A chromosome count has revealed, however, that this is not possible, and it is now generally agreed that 'Trier' is simply a seedling of 'Aglaia'.[89] Its heritage can be traced back through 'Aglaia' to the Noisettes and the musk rose. Of the many important roses that Lambert created, 'Trier' was perhaps the most significant, for at the time of its introduction it was the only hardy, everblooming climber. It became popular as a rose that would cover a pillar or a wall with white blossoms all summer.

When Lambert subsequently crossed 'Trier' and other Noisette-related roses with tea roses, hybrid teas, dwarf polyanthas, and *R. foetida bicolor*, he developed the original hybrid musk roses.[90] These hybrid musks were, in fact, first introduced in Germany as Lambertianas. Later, the Reverend Joseph Pemberton in England produced many hybrid musks, all of which have 'Trier', or a seedling of 'Trier', as one parent.[91]

'TRIER' has pink buds that open quickly to small, cup-shaped flowers with twelve to fifteen creamy white petals that retain only a trace of pink. There is a hint of yellow at the base of each petal, and this, together with the bright-yellow anthers, gives the flowers a distinctly golden-centered look. These one-inch, semi-double blooms are arranged in clusters of five or more on a lateral, but the clusters do not have the pyramidal form that one would expect from a descendant of *R. multiflora*. They do, however, have the characteristically sweet multiflora fragrance. 'Trier' starts blooming in late May, continues its lavish display through June, flowers sporadically during the summer, and then puts on another generous flush that lasts from October until the first frost. After the flowers are gone there are many hard, round hips.

Given its heritage, it is no surprise that 'Trier' is a vigorous climber. In two years it can grow ten feet high and twelve feet wide. It has a twiggy growth habit, very much like that of a Noisette, or at least a rose with China influence. It also has the multiflora trait of sending out many long, continuing laterals and a few basal canes. The young canes are smooth and plum-colored, like those of the variety of multiflora that has no prickles. This coloring makes them attractive in the winter garden.

'Trier' is vigorous enough to surmount a seven-foot lattice. When it reaches the top, the canes continue to grow and they arch over, sending down a cascade of fragrant blooms. Other arching canes develop all over the plant, especially in the middle section. The bush becomes very wide and spreading, so in spite of the fact that it was originally considered a pillar rose, that is not really the best way to grow it, because you will have to cut away many of the beautiful canes and much of the flowering wood to keep the plant under control. 'Trier' is more suitable for a lattice or other wide support, which it will cover with dense foliage. As the plant grows, it becomes rather rigid and stiff, so it is important to tie the new canes securely to a support as soon as they are long enough. Once the bush is established, the center becomes dense with old dead wood and must be thinned annually.

The light green leaves resemble those of the wild *R. multiflora* in their large size and their elongated, pointed shape, but they are more attractive because they are smoother, like those of the Noisettes. The foliage has above-average disease resistance and is long lasting, holding onto the bush well into the cold of the winter.

This is a very hardy rose that suffers little winter dieback. At the time of its introduction, it was extremely popular and was considered the ideal rambler because of its ability to bloom all season. While we might consider such praise excessive today, when there are so many other fine everblooming climbers on the market, 'Trier' represents an important stage in the history of this type of rose. Its major significance, however, is its role in the development of the hybrid musk class.

Throughout the month of June the delicate blossoms of 'Trier' cover a twelve-foot section of lattice fence in the Cranford Rose Garden.

'HIAWATHA'

Walsh, 1904
'Crimson Rambler' × *'Paul's Carmine Pillar'*

'HIAWATHA' was created in 1904 by Michael H. Walsh, an Englishman who came to this country in 1868 and eventually took charge of the estate of Joseph S. Hay in Woods Hole, Massachusetts. Roses were Walsh's main interest, and by 1906 he was growing and hybridizing them extensively. His first introduction was a hybrid perpetual, 'Jubilee' (1897), but he did most of his work with climbers, conducting many successful experiments in which he used species roses to create hardy varieties. At the time of his death in 1922, he had produced thirty-eight new ramblers.[92]

'Hiawatha' was once sold as part of a quartet of Walsh ramblers that included 'Evangeline', 'Milky Way', and 'Paradise'. 'Milky Way', which has pure white flowers, and 'Paradise', whose flowers are white tinged with rose, were described in the 1930 Bobbink and Atkins catalog as "the finest small-flowered climbers in commerce." They are no longer available. 'Hiawatha' and 'Evangeline', both named for characters in Longfellow poems, are still in commerce.

As a cross between 'Crimson Rambler' (a *R. multiflora* hybrid) and 'Paul's Carmine Pillar' (a *R. wichuraiana* hybrid), 'Hiawatha' is an important rose, one of several ramblers descended from these two influential species roses. In the early part of this century it was widely grown. Many bushes have outlasted the gardeners who planted them, and homeowners who inherit them often do not know what they have. The multiflora characteristics passed on to 'Hiawatha' through 'Crimson Rambler' can help in identifying it: pyramidal clusters of flowers, distinctively fringed stipules, and resinous glands on the pedicels. The prickles are like those of *R. wichuraiana*, but because it has so many obvious multiflora traits, it is usually classed as a multiflora hybrid.

At the time of its introduction, 'Hiawatha' was much praised for the color of its flowers. In a French journal, for example, they were described as "un joli rouge brilliant,"[93] and in the 1930 Bobbink and Atkins catalog this rose was called "the most dazzling red of all climbers. . . . Most successful for a smashing color effect." Its color, however, does not always seem so "brilliant" or "dazzling" today. In the Cranford Rose Garden the flowers of 'Hiawatha' appear soft and muted compared with the more vivid reds of many modern roses. Perceptions change over the years, and color descriptions in old books and catalogs are often outdated.

In 1931 Conard-Pyle introduced a new, apparently remontant, form of 'Hiawatha', a rambler known as 'Hiawatha Recurrent', which was created by a French hybridizer, J. Sauvageot. It was a cross between 'Hiawatha' and 'Maman Levavasseur', a polyantha descended from 'Crimson Rambler'.

The Walsh rambler 'Hiawatha' makes a spectacular weeping standard. After the flowers fade, the old canes should be removed, leaving only the new, long canes that emerge from the bud union. To encourage a weeping form, small fishermen's weights can be attached to the ends of these young, pliable canes.

IN MID-JUNE, the laterals of 'Hiawatha' are profusely covered from base to tip with large, loose, open panicles of small, dainty, five-petal flowers. The petals are soft red with white at the base, so that the flowers appear to have small white eyes. These one-inch blooms, which close at night, are cupped, and they look a bit like anemones. They have very yellow anthers and a light, pleasant fragrance. There is sporadic rebloom in autumn on current laterals that have been shortened.

'Hiawatha' is extremely vigorous, often spreading to a width of fifteen feet in one season. Like many ramblers, it can mound up to four or five feet in the center and needs a large space. It looks its best when allowed to spill down a bank, clamber over a stone wall, or climb up through the branches of an evergreen tree. Its rampant growth is also effective on a series of arches, a white fence, or any other broad support. This is not really a rose for a tidy formal garden, but if you are willing to work with it, you can adapt it to a restricted area. In the Cranford Rose Garden it grows on a post in one of the beds. To confine it to a post, an arch, or a pillar, cut out all but three of the canes, wrap them around the support, and every year thereafter remove all the unnecessary new growth. As with all ramblers, this rose sends out many young shoots while it is blooming; rejuvenate the plant periodically by cutting out the old, less-trainable canes and replacing them with new ones.

Like many wichuraiana hybrids, 'Hiawatha' sometimes sends up long shoots from the base, but it is less apt to do this than some other ramblers. Most of the seasonal growth consists of long continuing laterals emerging from the older wood. After the plant has finished blooming, keep it tidy by shortening all the laterals to about one inch. As it does not have an outstanding display of hips, nothing will be lost.

'Hiawatha' is an extremely hardy rambler. Its small, glossy leaves (inherited from *R. wichuraiana*) are sometimes marred by mildew, but on the whole they are quite disease resistant. Like other multiflora ramblers, this rose loses foliage as the growing season progresses, a condition not related to disease. New leaves eventually appear. The bush has an open, airy look, and it tends to fade into the background when it is planted with ramblers that have larger, denser foliage and more conspicuous double flowers.

While it is not a climber for every garden, 'Hiawatha' is the perfect choice for a landscape planting, a casual corner in a cottage garden, or any informal setting that suits its loose, uninhibited growth habit and its small, old-fashioned-looking flowers.

'EVANGELINE'

Walsh, 1906
R. wichuraiana × *'Crimson Rambler'*

'EVANGELINE' is another vigorous Walsh rambler that has both *R. wichuraiana* and *R. multiflora* in its heritage. As with 'Hiawatha', the multiflora characteristics predominate: pyramidal clusters of flowers; distinctively fringed stipules; and resinous glands on the pedicels, petioles, and sepals. Its beautiful, large, glossy, light green leaves, which are susceptible to mildew, resemble those of 'Crimson Rambler'. From *R. wichuraiana*, it derived extreme hardiness, a late bloom period, pliable basal shoots, and deadly hooked prickles.

Early in this century, 'Evangeline' was a very popular rose. It was often referred to as the only rambler that had a distinctive fragrance, and it was described in the 1930 Bobbink and Atkins catalog as "one of the most charming and airily graceful of climbing roses." Today it is not known as well as some of the more dramatic, large-flowered, repeat-blooming modern climbers, but it is still popular. In old seaside gardens specimens are often found scrambling up into trees.

IN THE NORTHEAST, 'Evangeline' is one of the last ramblers to come into bloom, flaunting its clusters of deliciously scented flowers in mid- to late June, just a bit earlier than *R. wichuraiana*. In the colder regions of New England, it may bloom as late as mid-July. The large, single, rosy white flowers, which look like apple blossoms, are borne in heavy, hanging, long-stemmed clusters that seem to be a larger, more decorative version of the panicles of *R. multiflora*. The prominent, yellow anthers attract bees and are easily pollinated. Later, many small red hips cover the bush. These make lovely fillers in floral arrangements, but on the bush they become unsightly after the first frost.

'Evangeline' is an old-fashioned-looking rose that needs a large space. Although it used to be popular in England as a weeping standard, this is not a practical way to grow it, nor is it a good choice for a small garden or any spot where it has to be kept neat and confined. Even more difficult to restrain than 'Hiawatha', it can in one season produce canes as long as twelve or fifteen feet, and it develops vigorous new growth from base to tip on every bit of old wood. Spilling out energetically in all directions, it soon becomes unruly unless the oldest growth is removed. It is also unpleasant to work with because it has very strong, hooked prickles, inherited from *R. wichuraiana*. In its natural state it has a beautiful shape, and rather than try to tame it, many people prefer to let it follow its own wild habit and spill over a bank, climb up a lattice into a tree (its prickles help secure it to the branches), or form a forbidding hedge. This way, it doesn't have to be pruned, and the laterals can be left to display their wonderful hips.

If you want to grow 'Evangeline' in a garden, to keep it from becoming invasive you must remove the older wood each year and sacrifice some of the current continuing laterals. If you do not want to spend too much time pruning it, plant it in the background—on a lattice at the rear of a bed or along a fence. If you are willing to put in a lot of extra effort, you can train it on a pillar, a chain, or an arch; several bushes can even be used to form a fragrant tunnel spanning a walkway. In the Cranford Rose Garden two specimens of 'Evangeline' are grown on two pillars that are spaced twelve feet apart and connected at the top with chains. By the second season, the canes covered the pillars, extended out along the chains, and met in the center. To train the roses, it was necessary to cut out all the excess growth, no matter how healthy, so that only the three longest canes remained on each. Then these canes were wrapped as tightly as possible around the pillars and coiled around the chains. After flowering, the long laterals hang down into the beds below; to keep them from smothering the other roses, they are shortened to within two or three inches of the main cane.

At the same time, the abundant new growth that springs from the bases of the plants or develops along the current season's canes must be kept under control. Most of the new shoots are too short to use for training on the pillars, and they are simply eliminated, as they would otherwise become very invasive in such a restricted space. Every year all the old wood is cut out and replaced with a few of the new canes that are long enough to train.

'Evangeline' flourishes in full sun or partial shade, but like 'Crimson Rambler', it is very susceptible to mildew. Because of this, it should not be grown on a wall, for its dense foliage mildews rapidly when good air circulation is lacking. Its leathery green multifloralike leaves turn orange-yellow at the end of the season, adding fall color to the garden.

This is a very hardy rose. Its informal, old-fashioned appearance makes it ideal for a cottage garden or any rustic spot. It grows happily in sandy soils, and so is a good candidate for seaside gardens. In addition, it blends in well with the foliage of trees, other shrubs, and species roses. Because of its vigorous growth habit, 'Evangeline' is best used in the background. It makes a pleasing companion for 'Hiawatha'; flowering just after the peak bloom period of modern roses, these two ethereal ramblers make a lovely show in mid-June, the pinkish-white blooms of 'Evangeline' complementing the soft red of 'Hiawatha's' gossamer flowers.

The deliciously scented flowers of 'Evangeline' resemble apple blossoms. This rose was very popular when it was first introduced in 1906.

'TAUSENDSCHÖN'

Kiese; introduced by Schmidt, 1906
'Daniel Lacombe' × 'Weisser Herumstreicher'

'TAUSENDSCHÖN' ('Thousand Beauties') is a rambler created in 1906 by Hermann Kiese, head gardener at the firm of J. C. Schmidt in Erfurt, Germany. In the old literature, Schmidt is usually given credit for this rose, but he was the introducer, not the hybridizer.

The seed parent of 'Tausendschön' was 'Daniel Lacombe', a multiflora rambler with large, pinkish blooms that Kiese used to create two other ramblers, 'Rubin' and 'Leuchtstern', while he was with Schmidt; both of these were also originally attributed to Schmidt. In 1908 Kiese established his own firm, and there he developed many other cultivars—hybrid teas, hybrid perpetuals, and polyanthas as well as ramblers. Most of his hybrids are rare today, but 'Tausendschön' remains a celebrated rose for its spectacular trusses of flowers that undergo various color changes throughout their life.

The pollen parent of 'Tausendschön' was 'Weisser Herumstreicher', a large-flowered rambler with pure white flowers that is a cross between 'Daniel Lacombe' and 'Pâquerette'. 'Pâquerette' is an important rose that was introduced in 1875 and is generally considered the first representative of the polyantha class. 'Tausendschön' subsequently played an important role in the development of the polyanthas. In some cases it was crossed with other varieties to create new polyanthas, one of which was 'Louise Walter'. The major contribution of 'Tausendschön' to the polyantha class, however, was its sport 'Echo' (also called 'Baby Tausendschön'), introduced by Peter Lambert in 1914. 'Echo' produced many other polyanthas, a number of which were sports. It was also a parent of one of the earliest and most influential floribundas, 'Smiles'.

Two other sports of 'Tausendschön' were significant. 'White Tausendschön', a rambler discovered by William Paul in 1913, has white flowers but is otherwise identical to its parent. It fell out of favor because the petals of its flowers become spotted and muddy looking as they age. 'Roserie', discovered in 1917 by R. Witterstaetter of Cincinnati, Ohio, is a vigorous rambler that is also exactly like its parent except that its flowers remain a constant pink.

'TAUSENDSCHÖN' has enormous clusters of large, double flowers that open in succession and change color as they age; at any one time a cluster will have eight to ten flowers in various shades of pink, lavender, blush, and white—an impressive display that led one rosarian to describe each truss as "a bouquet in itself."[94] The individual flowers appear white eyed because the petals, which are loosely cupped and wavy, have white at the base and converge on a center of exposed golden yellow stamens and pistils. This rose, which is only slightly fragrant, reaches peak bloom at the same time as the modern shrub roses and does not repeat.

'Tausendschön' is not as vigorous as the rampant wichuraiana ramblers such as 'Dorothy Perkins', but it produces enough growth to be trained on an eight- to ten-foot pillar. Its long, pliable canes are a pleasure to work with. They

'Tausendschön' sends masses of flowers spilling over a fence in Quincy, Massachusetts.

have no prickles and are easy to wrap around a support. It puts on an outstanding show when it is planted against a six-foot-high fence. (However, it needs good air circulation because the long, glossy leaves are susceptible to mildew.) Tie a few of the canes to the fence and the rest will cascade out gracefully, bearing clouds of multicolored blooms.

'Tausendschön' should be pruned sparingly. Each year, immediately after the plant has flowered, cut back a few of the oldest canes to the point where the most vigorous continuing laterals begin, usually about halfway up the cane. Do not prune late in the season, as this will cause the plant to send out new growth that will not have time to harden off before frost.

'Tausendschön' is a very hardy rose. Soon after its introduction, a German rosarian noted that it had survived two severe winters in Zwittau, protected by only a light covering of pine twigs.[95] In England it was said to need no winter protection at all.[96] In this country we have seen specimens thriving north of Boston. It does, however, have a tendency to send out vulnerable new growth during any unseasonably warm spell that occurs during the winter.

At the time of its introduction, gardeners raved about 'Tausendschön', claiming that 'Thousand Beauties' was the perfect name for a climber with such a profusion of large, multicolored flowers. Specimens from the early part of the century are often found in abandoned gardens. Today, when there are so many modern climbers on the market, 'Tausendschön' is often overlooked, but it deserves to be more widely grown, for it is a magnificent rose.

'EXCELSA'

Walsh, 1909
R. wichuraiana × *an unknown polyantha*

'EXCELSA', a rambler introduced in 1909, is M. H. Walsh's most famous rose and one of the most important of all the wichuraiana hybrids. Through its polyantha parent, it has some multiflora in its heritage (probably from 'Crimson Rambler'), but its wichuraiana characteristics predominate. Like 'Dorothy Perkins', with which it is almost identical except for its crimson red flowers, it set a standard for wichuraiana ramblers. Originally it was marketed as a red sport of 'Dorothy Perkins', and it is sometimes mistakenly called 'Red Dorothy Perkins', but these two roses are not related. In 1914 it won for its creator the prestigious Gertrude M. Hubbard Gold Medal, awarded by the American Rose Society once every five years to the raiser or originator of the best American rose introduced during the previous five years.

Until 'Excelsa', the only cold-hardy red climbing rose available was 'Crimson Rambler', which is notoriously susceptible to mildew. 'Excelsa' also suffers from mildew and mites, but to a much lesser degree; at the time of its introduction, it was the healthiest rambler on the market. Gardeners were clamoring for a new red climber, and it became immensely popular. Recently, an elderly gentleman in New York City wrote that he remembered riding the old elevated railway north out of Manhattan on summer days when the conductor would stop the train in the Bronx to pick blossoms of 'Excelsa' from bushes growing in profusion beside the tracks. Even today, specimens of 'Excelsa' planted in the early part of the century can be seen along railroad rights of way, on old estates, in abandoned gardens, and around old graves.

In spite of its early success, 'Excelsa' has its faults. Its mildew problem, though not as severe as with 'Crimson Rambler', was soon recognized, as was its tendency to fade to a pinkish red in bright sun. Also, like 'Dorothy Perkins', it was so widely used that people became bored with it and stopped using it when large-flowered red climbers came on the market.

'EXCELSA' blooms later than most ramblers, enlivening the landscape from mid-June to mid-July with cherry red flowers that hang in immense, heavy clusters on its flexible laterals. The flowers, double and pom-pomlike, have no fragrance and seldom repeat their bloom during the season, although there may be few rare blossoms in the fall. The subdued red is uneven, and even though in old garden catalogs it is often described as a brilliant crimson, it is not always particularly bright. This inconsistency has confused many people in their attempts to identify abandoned bushes or specimens that they acquire along with a home built in the early part of the century. Sometimes the color is a deep pink, sometimes an intense red (especially in shaded areas); in either case it fades to a lighter hue in full sun and as the flowers age. Some people like this muted, variable red because it is easier than solid red to mix with other colors in the garden.

The canes of 'Excelsa' are very long, often reaching fifteen feet in one season. Because many of these prostrate canes grow from the base, 'Excelsa' makes a good groundcover; in this regard it differs from 'Dorothy Perkins', which is more like modern climbers, developing over the years one or two main canes that produce long continuing laterals on the upper parts of the plant. 'Excelsa' is also useful as a hedge. The prolific basal growth eventually forms a high mound of wood at the center;

because it is shaded, much of this central growth dies. The canes have large, prominent prickles, so pruning is difficult (and dangerous). If you choose to grow 'Excelsa' as a groundcover or a hedge, plan on leaving it to its own devices.

When it was first introduced, 'Excelsa' was often chosen over 'Crimson Rambler' for embellishing arbors, arches, posts, and chains, as well as for other decorative purposes because, in spite of their prickles, its long, thin canes are more pliable. In modern gardens in the United States it has given way to the repeat-blooming climbers. The Europeans still know how to use it to good advantage, especially in display gardens. They draw the canes over the curves of arches, fashion them into tunnels, shape them into weeping standards, and drape them into magnificent festoons. At La Roseraie de l'Haÿ-les-Roses, near Paris, magnificent long tunnels of 'Excelsa' provide shade from the sun.

One of the best ways to use this rose is to wrap the younger canes around a post and along connecting chains. To keep it neat, groom the bush at the end of the blooming season by pruning it back severely and removing all the old flowering wood. Leave the new basal growth, which is always so prolific that there is plenty to replace what has been cut away.

'Excelsa' can also be used as a background plant, and like 'Dorothy Perkins' and 'Crimson Rambler', it is good for forcing in pots. There are some ways, however, it should not be grown: up the side of a house, against a wall, or crowded in with other plants in a small garden. Good air circulation is an absolute must; otherwise its glossy foliage will be covered with mildew. But in an airy spot 'Excelsa' holds its foliage well and is less prone to mildew than many other ramblers. It is also very hardy and thrives in all types of soils. One often sees specimens of 'Excelsa' planted in the coastal regions of New England; many of these were planted by local garden clubs to honor Walsh, who lived in Woods Hole, Massachusetts.

'Ivy Alice', a sport of 'Excelsa' introduced in 1927, is a very vigorous climber that is exactly like 'Excelsa' except for the blush pink color of its huge clusters of flowers. These double, cupped, antique-looking blooms, which have a slight fragrance, come on long stems and are good for cutting. When 'Excelsa' and 'Ivy Alice' are planted together, their flowers harmonize beautifully; if the canes are intermingled, the flowers all appear to come from the same plant. 'Ivy Alice' sometimes sports back to 'Excelsa'. When this happens, sections of its soft-pink petals are dramatically stained with red.

'Excelsa' is still very much worth growing, for it has numerous decorative possibilities in the garden. This rambler and its sports can be used in combination with many other ramblers; they go especially well with 'Dorothy Perkins' and its sports.

Other Walsh Ramblers

'Lady Gay'	'Galaxy'
'Minnehaha'	'Debutante'
'Milky Way'	'America'
'Paradise'	

Three canes of the Walsh rambler 'Excelsa' are wrapped tightly around a chain connecting two pillars in the Cranford Rose Garden. The result is a festoon of red blossoms.

119

'CHRISTINE WRIGHT'

Farrell; introduced by Hoopes, Brothers and Thomas Company, 1909
An unamed wichuraiana seedling × 'Mme. Caroline Testout'

'CHRISTINE WRIGHT'—like 'American Pillar', 'Silver Moon', and 'Dr. W. Van Fleet'—was one of a new breed of wichuraiana hybrids that resulted from the search by hybridizers for a hardy, repeat-blooming, large-flowered climber. It was developed by James A. Farrell, assistant superintendent at one of the nurseries belonging to the firm of Hoopes, Brothers and Thomas Company of West Chester, Pennsylvania. In *The American Rose Annual*, Farrell described the process by which he hybridized this rose under the guidance of Josiah Hoopes, who was a botanist as well as a nurseryman. His account gives insight into the complicated process by which new roses are created:

> Aside from his wonderful knowledge of conifers and other ornamental trees, Mr. Hoopes was a great lover of the rose, and under his instructions in the year 1898 I fertilized *Rosa wichuraiana* with pollen from several tea and hybrid tea roses, resulting in the production of four distinct varieties. Three of these were named Edwin Lonsdale, Prof. C. S. Sargent, and Robert Craig. The fourth was a large single pink variety, which I crossed with American Beauty, producing the rose named and disseminated as Climbing American Beauty. This same pink seedling was again crossed with Mme. Caroline Testout as pollen parent, and there resulted four fertile seeds from this cross, all of which germinated and grew. One, when it bloomed, produced a flower similar to La France in color, but with so many petals that it did not properly open, wherefore it was discarded. Of the other three seedlings, one has been named Christine Wright, another Columbia, and the third Purity.[97]

By crossing a seedling of *R. wichuraiana* with 'Mme. Caroline Testout', a very popular hybrid tea, Farrell created a rose that was in its day considered one of the best climbing or pillar roses, a sister to the popular 'Climbing American Beauty', another wichuraiana hybrid he developed under the supervision of Hoopes. Because 'Christine Wright' has large flowers and perfectly formed buds, it is often classed as a climbing hybrid tea.

'CHRISTINE WRIGHT' is one of the earliest modern climbing roses to come into bloom, sometimes starting to flower two or three weeks before the peak of the hybrid tea season. Its old-fashioned-looking pink blossoms are three-and-a-half inches in diameter and are usually borne in clusters, although they sometimes occur on single stems. The flowers are at first cupped, but they open quickly. Their twelve to sixteen solid pink petals assume a starburst form around a yellow "eye" of prominent stamens. From 'Mme. Caroline Testout', its hybrid tea parent, this rose inherited a strong, musky, old-rose scent, a delicate pink color, and large flowers. From *R. wichuraiana* it

Blooming at the end of May, 'Christine Wright' is often the first large-flowered climbing rose to come into bloom in the Cranford Rose Garden. The large blooms have an old-fashioned look, reminiscent of Victorian hybrid perpetuals.

The large, heavy flowers of 'Christine Wright' hang over the top of a high fence.

derived glossy, dark foliage along with the ability to climb. The flowers are good for cutting only while they are in the early, cupped stage; after that they age rapidly and soon lose their petals. Even though individual flowers are not long lasting, new blooms are produced in abundance over a period of about three weeks. Occasionally there will be a few repeat blooms in the fall, usually after an Indian summer. This rose sets lovely hips, so do not deadhead spent flowers.

'Christine Wright' can be grown on a fence, lattice, tripod, or wall. It is also beautiful scrambling up into a low-growing tree or a shrub. In the Cranford Rose Garden it is trained up through the branches of a wisteria. This rose is not suitable for a pillar, however, because it sends out so many new canes from the base that in order to keep it tidy you would have to cut away much of its valuable flowering wood.

When newly planted, 'Christine Wright' should be severely pruned, as this encourages the production of vigorous new canes to train during its first season. The following year the bush will start to bloom, producing flowers at the ends of long laterals that develop off the canes that were trained the previous year.

Since this is essentially a nonrepeating rose, the oldest wood can be pruned out as soon as the plant has finished blooming. Remove only as much as is necessary to keep the plant within bounds. In late winter, shorten all the laterals that bloomed during the previous season; this encourages strong flower production on the remaining parts of the laterals.

The leaves of 'Christine Wright' are dark and shiny and provide a wonderful backdrop for the satiny pink flowers. The foliage appears very early in the season (by mid-April in the Cranford Rose Garden) and is extremely disease resistant. Like many of the large-flowered wichuraiana climbers, this rose is quite cold hardy. It tolerates some shade and does best when planted away from the hot midday sun.

This early-blooming climber with its large, fragrant, old-fashioned-looking flowers is a wonderful rose to have in the garden. It blooms at just the right moment to provide a transition between the fleeting glory of the old garden roses and the summer pageant of the later-blooming modern varieties.

122

'CLYTEMNESTRA'

Pemberton, 1915
'Trier' × *'Liberty'*

'CLYTEMNESTRA' is a hybrid musk, created by the Rev. Joseph H. Pemberton, a British curate who was a noted rose hybridizer and the author of the classic book, *Roses: Their History, Development and Cultivation*, published in 1908. In his attempts to create perpetually blooming pillar roses, Pemberton worked exclusively with 'Trier' or seedlings of 'Trier'. By mating this early multiflora rambler (which is distinctly related to the musk rose through its parent 'Aglaia') with hybrid teas, Pemberton developed a type of small-flowered, perpetually blooming shrub rose with a vigorous habit. He called his creation the hybrid musk, even though *R. moschata* is actually very far back in its family tree. The importance of the twenty-three hybrid musks Pemberton created lies not in their remote musk rose heritage, but, rather, in the fact that in them the blood of *R. multiflora* (inherited from 'Aglaia', the parent of 'Trier') is combined with that of modern garden roses. Pemberton's success inspired other hybridizers, most notably Wilhelm Kordes in Germany, to develop hardy, remontant shrub roses.

'Clytemnestra' is a cross between 'Trier' and 'Liberty', a hybrid tea with fragrant, velvety crimson flowers. Although it is only a distant relative of *R. moschata*, it has a distinctive musk rose fragrance.

'Clytemnestra' had its greatest popularity in the 1920s and 1930s, when it was grown extensively as a pillar rose. In 1936 concentric rows of it were planted as free-form shrubs in the Rose Arc section of the Cranford Rose Garden, where their apricot-pink blooms are still reflected in a shallow pool. Large displays of this rose are rare in the United States today, however. Visitors from England, where Pemberton's roses are a familiar sight, are often pleasantly surprised to find it prominently displayed in an American garden.

'Clytemnestra' was frequently confused with 'Cornelia', another Pemberton hybrid musk; the two are almost identical except for subtle differences in the shape and color of the flowers, those of 'Cornelia' being a consistent pink, without the apricot shades that characterize 'Clytemnestra'. As climbers with larger blooms came on the market, these two hybrid musks were forgotten. Nurseries eventually lost track of which was which, and 'Clytemnestra' went out of commerce altogether. Within the past few years it has become available again, and its identity has been verified by comparison with the rare specimens in the Cranford Rose Garden.

'Clytemnestra' was, like many of Pemberton's roses, named for a heroine in classical mythology. One of his earliest hybrid musks, it was also one of his most successful; in 1914 it won the British National Rose Society Gold Medal.

'CLYTEMNESTRA' puts on an amazing show of blooms in June, repeats sporadically during the heat of the summer, and sends out another abundant flush in the cooler weather of autumn. It was very popular at the time of its introduction because of the unusual color of its flowers—a delicate blend of creamy peach and apricot that was novel in a perpetually blooming pillar rose. These blooms start out as fiery-orange buds, and as they open, their ruffled petals immediately reflex back, taking on a loose starburst appearance. The stamens and

pistils protrude, casting a yellow glow on the pale apricot petals. These unusual-looking flowers, borne in panicles typical of the multiflora hybrids, have the sweet scent that characterizes all the hybrid musks, a subtle and elusive fragrance unlike that of any other rose. Pemberton called it "a delicate and refined perfume, suggestive of heather and lime blossom."[98] In the Cranford Rose Garden, this fragrance is particularly delightful on a cool evening.

The growth habit of 'Clytemnestra' is like that of 'Trier', as it tends to sprawl, sending out three- or four-foot-long continuing laterals and eventually becoming a large, spreading shrub. In warm climates it grows rampantly and can easily cover a fence five feet high and fifteen feet long. It is not as vigorous as 'Trier', however, and in cool climates it will grow to only five or six feet, an ideal height for a pillar.

Left on its own, 'Clytemnestra' is an attractive and graceful shrub. It usually has one or two sturdy main canes, plum-colored like those of 'Trier', which thicken and darken with age; from these spring numerous continuing laterals that develop curved prickles as they mature. When it is grown as a shrub, the only pruning required is the removal of old, cluttered, or dead wood, especially from the center of the bush so the plant will keep its graceful form.

When pruning out dead wood, be sure to inspect the canes carefully before you cut; the older, gray-brown canes tend to look dead when they are not.

When it is trained on a pillar, 'Clytemnestra' requires constant attention to keep its lovely shape. Each winter, remove all the dead wood. During the growing season, prune away any old wood that is unproductive or too heavy for the pillar; in warm climates this will have to be done frequently.

The plum-colored canes of 'Clytemnestra', which have few prickles, can also be pegged to the ground, where they will root easily and produce laterals with masses of exquisite blooms.

The foliage is dark, glossy, and very disease resistant. During dry spells some of the leaves may drop, and they may also suffer from mite damage if the canes grow too close to a surface that reflects heat, such as brick, concrete, or gravel. North of New York City, this rose is not hardy; it might grow as a shrub, but it will never be tall enough to be used as a climber.

'Clytemnestra' is an elegant rose that is once again becoming popular. There are many ways to grow it. Our favorite is as a free-form shrub planted by a pool that will reflect the pink flowers sweeping gracefully toward the water on the long, arching, continuing laterals.

The hybrid musk 'Clytemnestra' was introduced in 1915 by the Rev. Joseph Pemberton. The color of its flowers, a blend of creamy peach and apricot, makes this one of Pemberton's most unusual roses.

'MARY LOVETT'

Van Fleet; introduced by Lovett, 1915
R. wichuraiana × 'Kaiserin Auguste Viktoria'

THE CLIMBER 'Mary Lovett' is a lovely rose that produces hundreds of large, double, snow-white blooms. An early creation of Walter Van Fleet, it is also known as 'White Dr. Van Fleet'. Its parents were *R. wichuraiana* and 'Kaiserin Auguste Viktoria', a superbly fragrant white hybrid tea introduced in 1891 by Peter Lambert of Trier, Germany.

For many years 'Mary Lovett' was out of commerce, and rosarians considered it lost. Even the plant that was included in the original plan of the Cranford Rose Garden had died. In 1989 a mystery rose sent by Heritage Rose Gardens in California to the Cranford Rose Garden for identification proved to be a specimen of this once-popular rose.

'MARY LOVETT' blooms from the end of May to the end of June. The pointed buds open to clusters of three or four flat flowers with twenty-five to thirty petals and exposed stamens. These clusters are borne mostly at the ends of laterals, each at least a foot long, although some of the laterals produce only a single bloom. The flowers are very fragrant, a characteristic inherited from their hybrid tea parent. In the Northeast they do not repeat their bloom; repeats occur rarely in other parts of the country. The flowers wilt quickly, especially in full sun, and the spent blooms hang on for a long time, looking dusty and messy. They set only a few orange-red hips, one-half inch across, so it is best to deadhead frequently.

This rose is a vigorous grower. Although it sends up only one or two main canes from the base, these produce many laterals that in three years can easily fill an area twelve feet high and twenty-four feet wide. It will cover a tall fence or the wall of a two-story house. In the Cranford Rose Garden 'Mary Lovett' has grown so large that it has invaded a wisteria on the other side of the latticework fence that surrounds the garden. This is not a rose for a small space. Because its flowers are so white, they look best against a dark background, such as a dark lattice or a hedge of evergreens.

The laterals and canes of 'Mary Lovett' are covered with hooked prickles. Not much pruning is required; shorten the laterals to get rid of spent flowers and cut out new, long invasive laterals.

'Mary Lovett' has glossy, dark green foliage that is highly disease resistant, a characteristic inherited from *R. wichuraiana* and common in Van Fleet's roses. The leaves do yellow slightly before they drop off in the fall.

In the 1930 Bobbink and Atkins catalog, 'Mary Lovett' was described as follows: "large, handsome flowers of pure, waxy white, sweetly scented, broad petaled, and of open form, borne singly and in sprays upon a strong-growing plant well furnished with heavy glossy foliage." This is an apt description of a wonderful rose whose rediscovery should delight gardeners everywhere.

'Mary Lovett' was the creation of Dr. Walter Van Fleet. After its introduction in 1915, it went out of commerce and was considered lost until a mystery rose with snow white flowers that was sent to the Cranford Rose Garden proved to be a specimen.

'THISBE'

Pemberton, 1918
Possibly a sport of 'Daphne'

'THISBE' is a hybrid musk of uncertain parentage. It may be a sport of 'Daphne', another Pemberton hybrid musk, which was introduced in 1912. The connection with *R. multiflora* is more obvious in 'Thisbe' than in some of the other roses of this class, for it has distinctly fringed stipules.

Most of Pemberton's hybrid musks have white, pink, or apricot flowers, but those of 'Thisbe' are unusual because they are yellow. It probably inherited this color from its very distant ancestor, 'Rêve d' Or', a yellow Noisette. It is also possible that Pemberton used a yellow Noisette or a yellow tea rose to create this hybrid.

One of the hardiest and most vigorous of the hybrid musks, 'Thisbe' was extremely popular when it was introduced because true yellow flowers were rare in hardy climbers at that time. In England and Europe it was widely grown on pillars and fences. In the United States, where nurseries were slow to realize its potential, it was used mainly as a free-growing shrub.

'THISBE' is a vigorous, bushy rose that blooms profusely from late May through June, slows down during the heat of high summer, and picks up again in September. The flowers, which have a sweet, fresh scent, are borne in clusters of three to five. They start out as flat-topped, urn-shaped, yellow-orange buds and open to full, rosette-shaped, very pale yellow blooms—no more than two inches in diameter and each having thirty to thirty-five petals. The outer petals reflex back immediately, exposing a button eye. The flowers fade and fall quickly, and the second bloom occurs on the ends of the new growth. This rose does not set hips.

Of all the Pemberton hybrid musks, 'Thisbe' is the most difficult to train. It spreads naturally to become a large bush. Many people choose to grow it this way because its mature canes are very stiff and they have a multitude of dangerous prickles. If you are courageous, however, you can train it. Start while the canes are young and force them to grow upright by tying them to a pillar. The canes are long, and if you can manage to wrap two of them around the pillar, you will be rewarded with a fountain of flowers, for they will arch out from the support, bearing small blooming laterals all along their length. This rose can also be used to cover a high fence or a wall; it is less interesting treated this way, but it is easier to handle.

'Thisbe' has elongated, dark green foliage with good disease resistance, but the leaves mature so early in the season that many of them drop during the summer, a trait common in a number of the earlier yellow roses. It requires little care, being both hardy and vigorous. Deadheading is not needed for repeat bloom, and the only pruning necessary is the removal of invasive, old, or dead wood that interferes with the vigorous new growth.

'Thisbe' is hardier than most of Pemberton's other hybrid musks and deserves to be better known. The exquisite creamy yellow flowers on long, arching canes are proof that Pemberton's dedication to the development of this type of rose was justified.

The long canes of Pemberton's 'Thisbe', a yellow hybrid musk, can be wrapped around a pillar to make a beautiful display.

'PENELOPE'

Pemberton, 1924
Suspected to be a cross between 'Ophelia' and 'Trier'

'PENELOPE' is a hybrid musk with flowers that are larger and more double than any of the other Pemberton roses of this class. Its seed parent, 'Ophelia', was an early hybrid tea of unknown parentage and the progenitor of many roses, sometimes through its sports, sometimes through hybridization, as with 'Penelope'. In 1925 'Penelope' won the Royal National Rose Society Gold medal.

'PENELOPE' has clusters of as many as twenty long, fat, peach-pink buds that open to two-inch, antique white flowers. The twenty to twenty-five wavy petals are loosely cupped around a glowing center of prominent golden stamens. The creamy blossoms, which have a sweet honeysuckle fragrance, bloom all season long, but they are most abundant in cooler weather.

This is a vigorous pillar rose with a graceful, arching habit; like 'Clytemnestra' and 'Thisbe', it naturally grows to be a handsome shrub. In cool climates 'Penelope' acts like a large-flowered climber, but it will not have the same vigor because it is not as hardy. It will reach about six feet, becoming a small shrub with canes that will cover a pillar but not a taller support. In warmer regions it grows larger and can be trained on an arbor or a pergola. A series of these roses can be used to make a deliciously fragrant tunnel. Like all hybrid musks, 'Penelope' is a good rose for pegging.

The flowers are borne on laterals ranging in length from six inches to two feet. Other than deadheading, it needs only minimal pruning to remove dead, cluttered, or invasive wood.

This rose is of questionable hardiness north of New York City. Unlike other Pemberton hybrid musks, which have not suffered during the winter in the Cranford Rose Garden, 'Penelope' dies back in freezing weather unless it is protected.

Other Pemberton Hybrids to Use as Pillar Roses

'Pax'
'Moonlight'
'Danaë'
'Prosperity'
'Cornelia'
'Felicia'
'Francesca'
'Kathleen'
'Nur Mahal'
'Robin Hood'
'Vanity'

Pemberton's hybrid musk rose 'Penelope' has large, two-inch flowers that are especially abundant in cool weather.

'BLOOMFIELD COURAGE'

Thomas, 1925; introduced by Bobbink and Atkins and Howard and Smith
A R. wichuraiana hybrid

'BLOOMFIELD COURAGE' is a rambler that was created in 1925 by Captain George C. Thomas, Jr., who named it after his family estate, Bloomfield, in Chestnut Hill, Pennsylvania.[99] Thomas began hybridizing roses in 1912, attempting to create hardy, everblooming climbers for the Philadelphia area. His work was interrupted by the First World War, during which he served as an aviator in France. In 1919 he moved to Beverly Hills, California, where he continued to grow and hybridize roses. He wrote in 1927 that he had accomplished the task of breeding hardiness and recurrent bloom into his climbers, and that the work was now to improve the blooms. At the time of his death he had introduced thirty-nine new roses, many of them with 'Bloomfield' in their names. He also wrote two important books about roses: *The Practical Book of Outdoor Rose Growing* (1914), and *Roses for All American Climates* (1924).

'Bloomfield Courage' is a combination of two historically important roses, *R. wichuraiana* and 'Crimson Rambler', a multiflora hybrid. Of all the attempts that have been made to combine the characteristics of *R. wichuraiana* and *R. multiflora*, only two have resulted in successful and enduring varieties: 'Hiawatha' and 'Bloomfield Courage'. These two roses are often confused with each other but are easily differentiated because 'Bloomfield Courage' has almost no prickles, a trait found in many multiflora hybrids.

THIS DAINTY rose has small, single, dark velvety red flowers with bright white centers. They bloom in graceful, open clusters of up to twenty-five blossoms that cover the bush with a solid mass of red. Nevertheless, this rose has an airy look and can easily fade into the background if it is planted with other ramblers that have larger, more showy flowers. By itself, however, on a strong arch, pergola, or any structure that can accommodate its vigorous growth, 'Bloomfield Courage' is a valuable addition to a garden because it is one of the first ramblers to come into bloom. In the Cranford Rose Garden it starts its display in early June and continues for nearly a month. It sets many beautiful red hips that look like those of *R. multiflora*—they make a good winter display.

'Bloomfield Courage' is a vigorous rambler that needs a lot of space because, like all multifloras, it tends to produce excessively long canes off its old wood and relatively few basal breaks. It grows rapidly, easily attaining twenty feet in one season, and can quickly get out of hand on a pillar or an arch. It is well suited for a fence because it will cover an area twelve feet wide. Like all ramblers, it can be used as a groundcover and is also ideal for training up through trees. Old specimens can be found climbing into trees in abandoned gardens.

This rose is a joy to work with because its long, pliable canes, which have hardly any prickles, are easy to train. In the Cranford Rose

'Bloomfield Courage' is often confused with another rambler, 'Hiawatha'. Both roses have single red blooms, but the canes of 'Bloomfield Courage' are nearly free of prickles.

133

Garden it is grown in three ways. In one location, it is trained on a lattice; it scales this and makes its way up into the trees on the other side of the garden. The lattice, which is white, sets off the crimson of the flowers; it faces west so that the setting sun highlights their white eyes. Because the canes are trained close together, the leaves densely cover the lattice and the flowers make a bold display. On a large support like this, there is plenty of room for the expansive growth.

'Bloomfield Courage' is also trained on a pair of wide arches over a walkway in the garden. Here it is pruned constantly to keep it from interfering with the path and the beds As soon as it has finished blooming, many of the old canes are removed, and the new canes are tied in to replace them. Invasive laterals are also shortened, but as much of the blooming wood as possible is left so that there will be a good display of hips.

In another part of the Cranford Rose Garden, bushes of 'Bloomfield Courage' are trained on a series of single, thin arches where they create a backdrop for beds of modern roses. Here they must be kept especially neat, and this necessitates severe pruning. Each summer, after they have flowered, the plants are reduced to two or three canes for next year's bloom; these canes are wrapped tightly around the arches.

Except in situations like these where its vigorous growth must be restrained, 'Bloomfield Courage' needs little pruning. When it is grown on a bank or used as a groundcover, it can simply be sheared back to the desired size. On a fence or in any carefree situation, just remove some of the old wood to make room for the new. Be careful, however, not to cut out any canes that will not be replaced by new growth. It is best not to deadhead, as that will remove the wonderful hips, although in places where the growth has to be restrained, this will be unavoidable.

The foliage of 'Bloomfield Courage' is dark and disease resistant. But this rose has the multiflora tendency to drop its leaves throughout the growing season, and so it does not form a dense cover unless the canes are kept close together.

'Bloomfield Courage' is a beautiful rose that is easy to grow. Its canes will quickly cover any structure on which they are trained. It makes a wonderful show when placed in a spot where it is not overpowered by roses with bolder flowers. It is very hardy, suffering only minimal dieback in the winter.

Other Thomas Hybrids to Use as Climbers or Pillar Roses

'Bloomfield Dainty'
'Captain Thomas'
'Dr. Huey'

'NEW DAWN'

Discovered by Bosenberg; introduced by Dreer, 1930
A sport of 'Dr. W. Van Fleet'
Plant Patent No. 1

'NEW DAWN' is a sport of 'Dr. W. Van Fleet', the climber created by Dr. Walter Van Fleet in 1902. It was discovered by Henry F. Bosenberg of New Brunswick, New Jersey, a landscape gardener who had bought a number of 'Dr. W. Van Fleet' roses to use in his work. Bosenberg noticed that one of the roses appeared to be everblooming. After testing it for four years, he decided that it would retain its ability to bloom continuously from the middle of May up until frost. The new rose—the first hardy, large-flowered climber that blooms all season long—was introduced by Henry A. Dreer.

'New Dawn' holds the distinction of being the first plant in the world to be patented. In 1930, the year of its introduction, Congress passed the Plant Patent Act, which granted to anyone who discovered or hybridized a new plant the exclusive right to determine for seventeen years who would propagate and sell it. Up until that time, any plant that went on the market became common property. The creator usually realized very little financial reward. As J. Horace McFarland, the guiding light of the American Rose Society, wrote in 1920, "the hybridizer of garden Roses has to be content with deposits in the Bank of Glory. . . ."[100] 'New Dawn' was the first of the dozens of new roses that are now patented each year.

Except for its everblooming quality and the fact that it is not quite as vigorous, 'New Dawn' is almost exactly like its parent, 'Dr. W. Van Fleet'. Both are rampant growers with large, blush pink flowers, very long canes, fierce prickles, and extraordinarily disease-resistant foliage, characteristics derived from their common ancestor, *R. wichuraiana*. 'New Dawn' has been used to create many other hardy, vigorous, and disease-resistant roses, including climbers such as 'Inspiration', 'Coral Dawn', 'White Cockade', 'Parade', and 'Dream Girl'.

'NEW DAWN' is a superb everblooming climber that produces masses of fragrant, blush-colored flowers from early summer through late autumn. These semidouble, medium-sized blooms, on single stems or in clusters of three to five, open from plump, rose pink buds and turn delicate creamy pink as the petals unfold. The elegant blossoms, which resemble old-fashioned roses, make excellent cut flowers, often lasting a week or more. They have a wonderful, old-garden rose fragrance that combines the scent of damasks, teas, and *R. foetida*. In addition, 'New Dawn' has beautiful, glossy, emerald green foliage that remains lush and healthy throughout the summer and turns an attractive yellow in the fall.

'New Dawn' is one of the easiest climbers to grow. It resists diseases and insects, is hardy in all climates, and will thrive in any region of the United States. In hot, dry areas—such as Texas, Arizona, and Georgia—flower production may be sporadic during the summer, but in cooler climates, one bush of 'New Dawn' will be covered with hundreds of flowers throughout the growing season. 'New Dawn's only fault may be that it can quickly outgrow any space allotted to it; this is not a rose for small gardens. In a private garden in Atlanta, Stephen recently saw two four-year-old plants that had completely enveloped a pergola twenty-five feet long, six feet wide, and eight feet high. In full bloom during the second week in May, they created a massive canopy that left not a spot uncovered on the support.

'New Dawn's canes become stiff, extremely prickly, and very long, often reaching fifteen feet. New canes develop constantly throughout the growing season, springing from the base of the plant as well as along the already existing canes. Although some flowers develop at the ends of the primary canes, most of them are borne on the laterals springing from the main canes; it is the latter that produce the first flush of blooms.

The effortless way to grow 'New Dawn' is as a groundcover on a sunny bank or steep incline, where it needs no care and can be left to follow its own spreading habit. With its dense foliage and large curved prickles, it will quickly form an intruder-proof barrier. More commonly, however, this rose is trained on walls and fences, or coiled around pillars, posts, and arches. It can also be guided up through the branches of a tree or shaped into a hedge. Training 'New Dawn' requires work but is worth the effort, for a specimen in full bloom scrambling up a wall or spilling over an arch is a glorious sight.

Ideally, 'New Dawn' should be planted in full sun, but it will also thrive on as little as four or five hours of sunlight a day. If you have a shady terrace or backyard, you may still be able to grow this rose; if there is sun above, it will stretch up to it and form a lush canopy overhead. This climber is also well suited to breezy terraces, balconies, and penthouse gardens, for its sturdy leaves are not desiccated by wind. The only special care it needs in these places is attention to its water supply, as wind quickly dries out the soil in containers or small raised beds. In addition, if you plant 'New Dawn' in a small space, you will have to cut it back severely to keep it within bounds, and in doing so, you will prune away most of its flowering wood.

If you want to train this rampant grower on a pillar, a post, or an arch, you must limit the number of canes. Choose four young canes (with age they become too stiff to train) and, as soon as they are long enough, start spiraling them around the support. With soft twine, fasten them to nails driven into the support, or tie them directly to it. Continue training these canes as they grow longer. Cut all the other canes back to the ground, and as new canes develop at the base of the plant, remove these as well. You will also find secondary canes shooting off from the canes that are trained around the support; if these are in the way, cut them back to two or three inches from the main cane. When you train 'New Dawn' on pillars, posts, and arches, you must cut back intrusive canes every year or the plant will quickly grow out of bounds, becoming too crowded on its support or filling an archway so that no one can walk through it.

After its third season 'New Dawn' will become crowded and dense with old wood, which should be thinned out to promote good air circulation and to make room for the vigorous new canes that grow up from the base. When the plant is dormant, remove up to one-third of the oldest growth by cutting dead and old canes down to the ground. On canes that have both

The beautiful blush pink flowers of 'New Dawn' cover a pergola in Atlanta, Georgia. This rose has been the best-selling climber ever since its introduction in 1930.

old and new growth, remove the oldest parts—those that are no longer producing the valuable continuing laterals. 'New Dawn' spreading freely on a bank or hillside will survive without this pruning, but it will be healthier and more attractive if after a few seasons some of the woody, dead undergrowth is removed.

Most everblooming climbers should be pruned during the growing season, just after the first flowering, when their laterals are cut back by two-thirds to encourage good rebloom. Treat 'New Dawn' and its progeny differently from other climbers, however. The new buds on these roses develop immediately behind the fading flowers, and you may destroy them if you cut the laterals back too far. Therefore, simply pinch off the spent flowers, leaving as much of the lateral as possible. If you do this throughout the summer, you will have a profuse display of blooms all season long. Near the end of the season, about a month before the first predicted frost, you may wish to stop deadheading. 'New Dawn' sets hips, and if you leave the spent flowers, you will have an attractive display of these orange hips along with the creamy pink blossoms that the plant will continue to produce right up until winter.

'New Dawn' is very hardy, needing no winter cover in most parts of the United States. In the northern Midwest and the colder regions of New England, however, some of the valuable flowering wood may die during harsh winters. New growth will still spring from the base of the plant the following year, and this will produce a few flowers; but the best blooms develop on older wood, and the bush will flower abundantly only if these older canes survive. You may wish to protect the canes by removing them from their supports, tying them together, laying them on the ground or in a trench, and covering them with a mulch of compost or straw.

If properly grown and pruned, 'New Dawn' is practically disease free. You may find small patches of mildew on the leaves in cool weather, but these will not do any serious damage. During very hot and humid summers, the older foliage may develop black spot. If this becomes a serious problem, remove some of the older wood to promote good air circulation. 'New Dawn' has no insect problems. Its worst enemy is lack of water, which will cause it to lose some of its leaves and delay the blooms. If you grow it in a tub, in a raised bed, in a penthouse garden, or on a windy terrace, water it frequently.

When 'New Dawn' was first introduced, its performance was considered disappointing. This is probably because it bears only a few flowers at the tips of its young canes for at least one season after it is planted. By its third year it starts to bloom abundantly and it continues to do so. Over the years 'New Dawn' has proved to be ideal for anyone who wants to grow a spectacular rose with little effort.

'BLAZE'

Kallay; introduced by Jackson and Perkins, 1932
'Paul's Scarlet Climber' × 'Gruss an Teplitz'
Plant Patent No. 10

WHEN JOSEPH KALLAY of Painesville, Ohio, applied for a patent for this rose in March 1931, he stated that until then its everblooming quality had been unknown in hardy climbers. He was probably unaware of 'New Dawn', the first hardy, large-flowered, everblooming climber, which would be granted plant patent number one in August of the same year. 'Blaze' was, however, the first hardy everblooming *red* climber, and that made it a popular companion for 'New Dawn'.

Although there has been confusion about the origins of 'Blaze', Kallay stated in his patent application that the parents were 'Paul's Scarlet Climber', a once-blooming, large-flowered climber, and 'Gruss an Teplitz', an everblooming Bourbon. There is no reason to doubt this. Until the appearance of 'Blaze', 'Paul's Scarlet Climber', introduced in 1916, had been the most sought-after red climbing rose, surpassing even 'Excelsa' in popularity because it had larger flowers. 'Blaze' quickly usurped its place, for it retained all the best qualities of both parents. It is not as fragrant as 'Gruss an Teplitz', but it has more scent than either 'Excelsa' or 'Paul's Scarlet Climber'. 'Blaze', which won a certificate as the best climbing rose at the *Concours International de Roses Nouvelles de Bagatelle* in 1933, was soon ubiquitous on white picket fences and around doorways all across America. For many people this red climber brings back special memories of childhood. It was Stephen's introduction to the world of roses, for each summer he had the task of deadheading the 'Blaze' that grew on his aunt's white picket fence in New Jersey. He was specifically instructed to cover the wound after each cut with a heavy application of lipstick as a precaution against invasion by insects and diseases.

'BLAZE' bears clusters of fifteen or more bright red flowers. Most of these clusters occur on very short laterals, but blooms may also be found at the tips of new basal canes and at the ends of longer continuing laterals. The buds, which are large and ovoid, much like those of Bourbon roses, open to two-inch flowers that are cupped and rather loosely formed. The scarlet petals have a bit of white near the base, a characteristic that many modern red roses inherited from the red China roses. In the case of 'Blaze', the closest link to the Chinas is 'Gruss an Teplitz'. As the flowers age they take on a bluish tint, an unfortunate trait in numerous modern red roses. There is a faint, rather musky, old rose fragrance.

'Blaze' may at first disappoint the inexperienced gardener, for it needs at least one season of growth before it starts producing its profuse red blooms. To encourage the new growth necessary for abundant flower production in succeeding years, prune back the bush by at least half its height when you plant it. During the first year there will be much shrubby growth, consisting of canes averaging five or six feet in length, and a few long basal breaks, some of which will reach fifteen feet. A few flowers may appear at the ends of the canes during the first summer, but this first year's growth does not become productive until the following year, when it will send out flowering laterals and

longer continuing laterals that will add to the height of the plant. After the hard pruning at planting time, do not prune again until the beginning of the third season. During the first two years, simply remove faded flowers and watch for new canes, which can be tied into place on a support. Keep the canes horizontal as much as possible, for this encourages the development of flowering laterals the following season; fan them out along a fence or any other horizontal structure. In the Cranford Rose Garden the canes of one specimen of 'Blaze' are wrapped around the window of a pavilion so that the opening will be framed with red blossoms.

Beginning the first season, prune 'Blaze' during the summer, shortening the laterals by two-thirds as soon as the flowers have faded. New, strong, flower-bearing laterals will emerge right behind the cut. Once the plant is established, many long canes will also emerge from the base of the plant. After three growing seasons, start pruning during the winter, when the plant is dormant. Remove about one-third of the canes,

beginning with the oldest. Tie the remaining canes to the support, fanning them out as much as possible. Repeat this procedure every winter.

The canes of 'Blaze' are too stiff to be wrapped around a single pillar. The easiest way to train them is on a fence, a wall, or a tripod. In Europe some creative gardeners manage to train 'Blaze' as a weeping standard. To do this, they attach the canes, which are too rigid to cascade on their own, to an umbrella-shaped wire form.

'Blaze' is fairly disease resistant, but it may be affected by black spot and mildew. It is quite hardy, and it has an amazing tolerance for adverse growing conditions. We have seen it in southern New Jersey surviving in an area that is flooded every year with brackish water. It is often found covering ugly wire fences, along highways, and in industrial parks. Even though it was once overused to the point of boredom, this is one of the grand old climbers that will always be part of the American landscape.

Because of its everblooming habit, 'Blaze' became the most popular red climbing rose when it was introduced in 1932.

141

'CLIMBING SUMMER SNOW'

Couteau; introduced by Jackson and Perkins, 1936
A 'Tausendschön' seedling × unknown
Plant Patent No. 400

'CLIMBING SUMMER SNOW' has for many years been incorrectly classified as a climbing floribunda, and the erroneous classification is only part of the confusion surrounding this rose. When it was originally marketed in 1936, it was sold as a climber called 'Summer Snow'. But some gardeners who tested it for the "Proof of the Pudding" in the 1930s soon realized they had acquired something that did not climb. J. Horace McFarland summed up the situation in the 1940 issue of *The American Rose Annual*: "Reports on these roses are all mixed up as there is a dwarf type which can be considered a Polyantha and there also is a Climber or Rambler type. . . . As far as we can figure out, the dwarf is an important free-blooming white Polyantha, while the Climber is moderate growing and blooms but once. The Climber is the original and entitled to the name Summer Snow; the Polyantha is a sport and should have been given a distinct name."[101] No wonder gardeners were perplexed. There were, in fact, unknown to Jackson and Perkins, two different roses, both of which they had introduced in 1936 as one variety called 'Summer Snow'. The polyantha bush type, introduced by mistake in 1936, was actually a sport of the climber, which had been developed by Alphonse Couteau of Orléans, France. In the 1940 patent application for the

Polyantha bush type, Jackson and Perkins acknowledged it was a different rose (a sport of the climber), but they added to the confusion by classifying it as a floribunda and keeping the name 'Summer Snow'.[102] Unfortunately, even though McFarland insisted that the polyantha sport should be given a new and distinctly different name, this never happened. The two are simply differentiated as 'Climbing Summer Snow' and its bush-type sport, 'Summer Snow'. (Just to add to the confusion, 'Climbing Summer Snow' often sports to a pink form.) The term floribunda, questionable enough in the case of 'Summer Snow', should not be applied to 'Climbing Summer Snow' since the climber is not a sport of the bush.

In 1936, the year of its introduction, the rose we now call 'Climbing Summer Snow' was described as a seedling of 'Tausendschön'.[103] In the 1940 patent application, the breeder called it a climber of the polyantha class resulting from a cross between a white polyantha and an unknown seedling. He also noted that its growth habit was quite similar to that of 'Tausendschön' and that its big clusters of large white flowers and its stems, almost devoid of prickles, made it different from other polyanthas. It is very possible that the unnamed white polyantha was a seedling of 'Tausendschön'.

'CLIMBING SUMMER SNOW' has hanging clusters of fifteen to twenty semidouble, cupped white flowers with eighteen to twenty wavy petals. These blooms, about two inches across, are borne on short laterals, and they have a fragrance like that of *R. foetida*, reminiscent of

'Climbing Summer Snow', for many years incorrectly classified as a climbing floribunda, will envelop a pillar or column with a wealth of white blooms.

linseed oil. In cool weather they take on a peach-pink tint. Although the bush rose sport, 'Summer Snow', is remontant, 'Climbing Summer Snow' puts on just one luxurious display in June; after that, there are only rare repeats. It does not set hips. The blooming potential of 'Climbing Summer Snow' improves with age.

This rose is not a vigorous climber. It will cover an arch about eight feet wide, but because it does not have a spreading growth habit, the best way to train it is on a pillar. The canes, which have no prickles, are easy to handle. Throughout the season, tie into place the new continuing laterals (both long and short) that develop along the older wood.

The amount of growth varies from plant to plant; some bushes send up two or three eight-foot canes from the base, while others produce very little new growth. Older plants tend to become very woody and do not have many basal shoots; much of the growth originates from higher up on the plant. Sometimes a plant will reach a certain height and then start spreading out rather than continuing to grow taller.

After several years, depending on how much space you have, remove the older, less productive wood; this rejuvenates the plant and encourages the development of new canes. Otherwise, do not prune this rose heavily. Simply deadhead and cut out invasive, untrainable growth right after it has finished blooming; then leave the plant alone. If you prune it later in the summer, it will send out new growth that will be killed by frost. Like 'Tausendschön', 'Climbing Summer Snow' is very hardy but quick to break bud during a winter thaw, which often results in damage to the plant.

The leathery, glossy, light green foliage is fairly disease resistant, although it is somewhat susceptible to mildew. The new green leaves appear very early in the season, at the beginning of April in the Cranford Rose Garden.

'Climbing Summer Snow' will ascend a pillar and, true to its name, cover it from bottom to top with pure white blooms. This spectacular rambler is the ideal rose for a small garden where a column of flowers adds beauty while saving space.

'CHEVY CHASE'

Hansen, 1939; introduced by Bobbink and Atkins, 1939
R. soulieana × 'Eblouissant'
Plant Patent No. 443

'CHEVY CHASE' is a red-flowered rambler that was developed by Niels J. Hansen and introduced by Bobbink and Atkins in 1939. Hansen was an amateur hybridizer from Washington, D.C., who created several recognized hybrids; 'Hon. Lady Lindsay' and 'Chevy Chase' are still in commerce. Hansen raised 'Chevy Chase' in the garden of Dr. Whitman Cross in Chevy Chase, Maryland; hence its name.

'Chevy Chase', which won for its hybridizer the American Rose Society Dr. W. Van Fleet Medal in 1941,[104] is a cross between *R. soulieana*, a wild rose from southwestern China that was discovered in 1895, and 'Eblouissant', a polyantha introduced in 1918. *R. soulieana* has white flowers, small, gray-green leaves, and canes that may reach eight feet in one season. It is not hardy much farther north than Washington, D.C., but it is exceptionally disease resistant and has, therefore, been considered a good candidate for hybridizing. 'Eblouissant', which has dark to medium red flowers, has a crimson China, 'Cramoisi Supérieur', in its background[105]; this is probably the source of the vivid red of the flowers of 'Chevy Chase'. 'Chevy Chase' is, however, very different from its parents. Its distinction at the time of its introduction lay in its superior disease resistance—much greater than the earlier red rambler 'Crimson Rambler', which is notoriously mildew prone, and better than 'Excelsa', which is resistant but not immune to this problem. When it was introduced, 'Chevy Chase', which suffers from no disease problems at all, was marketed as a much improved 'Crimson Rambler'.

'CHEVY CHASE', like its polyantha parent, has heavy, erect clusters of vibrant, cherry red blossoms. The individual flowers—short stemmed, double, each with from sixty to seventy tightly grouped petals—are small. The flower clusters, which resemble pom-poms at the ends of very stiff, long laterals, have so many blooms (from six to thirty-six) that they themselves look huge. The overall effect is of masses of color, not small flowers. This small-flowered climber became popular even at a time when large-flowered climbers were all the rage. One of these clusters on its upright and sturdy lateral makes an instant bouquet. The only fault one might find with this rose is that it is unscented.

'Chevy Chase' blooms at the peak of rose season, when the hybrid teas are in full flush. It does not repeat. After flowering, the blossoms dry on the laterals, often hanging there until autumn, turning brown and brittle but not setting hips. The spent flowers should be cut off, or the entire cane can be removed; it is not necessary to be fussy about pruning because this rose puts out so much new growth that all the wood that has bloomed can be cut away and there will still be plenty left. The abundant new continuing laterals that develop rapidly before the old wood has finished blooming are very invasive, growing so vigorously that they spill over into beds and walkways if they are not immediately pruned back or trained. In the Cranford Rose Garden, 'Chevy Chase' continues to put out new growth to the end of October.

Its canes are stiff and thicker than those of wichuraiana or multiflora ramblers, and this makes 'Chevy Chase' difficult to train. Given enough room, it can be left to grow on its own, spilling down an embankment or adorning a stone wall or a fence. It is much too vigorous and unruly for a pillar or a chain, sending out an enormous amount of new growth, all of which is fiercely armed with prickles. It can, however, be trained to grow horizontally on a wide arch over a walkway or on a low fence. It can also be fanned out on a lattice, where it will easily cover an area ten feet high by twenty feet wide. The canes have a distinctive gray-green color, like those of *R. soulieana*. In the winter, the leafless canes fanned out on a lattice or wrapped on a low fence along a walkway make very strong visual lines in the garden.

Many new canes develop from the base of the plant. These canes, which have strong, hooked prickles, are stiffer than those of most other ramblers; they become very long, averaging eight feet, and sometimes even reaching fifteen feet, in one season. Rather than shooting straight up, they have a horizontal or arching habit; left on its own, the plant will form a six-foot-high arching bush that will spread outward with the weight of these canes. 'Chevy Chase' will fill a space twelve feet wide and eight feet high in one season and can easily grow larger.

Wherever you plant 'Chevy Chase', make sure it is accessible, for you have to keep after it—pruning out excess growth and old wood—all the time. Its menacing prickles make it hard to work with, and it should not be grown as a groundcover or in any situation where thinning out old wood from the base will be difficult. One easy way to deal with it is to grow it as a hedge and simply shear it back to the desired height every year; however, constant removal of new laterals depletes the flowering wood.

'Chevy Chase' has, like its parent *R. soulieana*, small, gray-green leaves that are light in color. It has no disease problems, and it is hardy, suffering no winter dieback in the New York City area.

'Chevy Chase' in bloom makes an incredible display. No matter how you train it—on a fence, a tripod, a wide arch, or a wall—keep the vivid red of its flowers in mind, for it can clash with other colors. It is hard to combine with 'Excelsa', for example, but it looks wonderful on a white lattice or picket fence.

The brilliant red rambler 'Chevy Chase' was developed by an amateur hybridizer in Chevy Chase, Maryland.

'THOR'

Horvath; introduced by Wayside Gardens Company, 1940
'Alpha' × 'President Coolidge'
Plant Patent No. 387

WHEN M. H. HORVATH first came to the United States from Hungary in the late nineteenth century, he was employed by the Newport Nursery Company in Newport, Rhode Island, where he did important work with *R. wichuraiana*. In subsequent years, especially after 1920 when he retired as the landscape architect in charge of the design and construction of the Cleveland park system,[106] he created many other outstanding roses. Working at his home in Mentor, Ohio, he concentrated on winter-hardy, large-flowered climbers for northern gardens. As he put it:

> In my locality, the 1907–1908 winter put the Wichuraiana hybrids to a really hard test. That was followed by another sub-zero period during the winter of 1917–1918. At exposed places Wichuraiana hybrids froze to the ground. Thenceforth I decided to enlist a different and hardier species as a foundation stock to work on; a stock which will withstand the midwestern cold blasts and be more likely to give us varieties with which we might push the rose-zone farther north. Having experimented with several native species with which the results were very unsatisfactory, I decided that *Rosa setigera*, regardless of its peculiarities as a prospective parent, including such undesirable attributes as flat flowers and a weak, hinged neck, still had possibilities. Strong habit and hardiness were

present, and also a strong constitution. With my new candidate I hoped I had found the key to hardy roseland![107]

One of the new roses Horvath created was a pink seedling named 'Alpha', a cross between *R. setigera* and *R. sempervirens*. 'Alpha' had little value as a garden rose, but it was important as the progenitor of many other Horvath hybrids. In 1925 he crossed it with 'Château de Clos Vougeot'—a fragrant, deep red hybrid tea that resembles a hybrid perpetual—to create 'President Coolidge'. Later he crossed 'Alpha' with 'President Coolidge' to create 'Thor'. From 'Alpha' (the offspring of two hardy species roses), 'Thor' inherited excellent disease resistance and a fair degree of cold hardiness; from 'Château de Clos Vougeot' by way of 'President Coolidge', it derived large flowers with an amazingly vibrant, deep red color. 'Thor' lacked the ability to bloom all season long, but it was nevertheless a great improvement over other large-flowered red climbers of the time, such as 'Blaze'; its blooms are more beautifully formed, and instead of fading and becoming unattractive with age, their color actually intensifies the longer they stay on the plant.

'THOR' has large, globular buds that open to deep scarlet and multipetaled flowers with a rich and spicy, but not particularly strong, fragrance. The velvety red petals of the three- to four-inch flowers surround exposed yellow pistils and stamens. While the blooms are opening, they look like hybrid teas, but once all fifty to sixty petals are exposed, they resemble cabbage

'Thor', which is difficult to find in commerce, puts on a stunning display of bright red flowers throughout the month of June, here in Brooklyn, New York.

roses. In fact, one specimen of 'Thor' in the Cranford Rose Garden was for many years mislabeled simply 'Cabbage Rose'. These large flowers are borne on single stems or in clusters of three to five. The flowering laterals may be short or up to two feet long. In peak bloom the bush looks especially full because it is loaded with blossoms on many levels. The height of its flowering period occurs a little later than that of the modern shrub roses and lasts for about four weeks.

'Thor' is an extremely vigorous rose whose canes may grow ten to fifteen feet long in one season. A mature plant can cover an area twelve feet high and twenty-four feet wide. One way to train it is on a single pillar. Plant a lower-growing white or light-pink shrub rose at the base, and you will have an unusual and elegant display. Because of its vigorous growth habit, however, 'Thor' is difficult to contain on such a support. A simpler solution is to plant it against a fence or a wall that can accommodate its expansive growth. It is especially effective on a white lattice, interwoven with other climbers such as 'American Pillar' or 'Evangeline'.

Many new canes, some as long as ten or fifteen feet, spring from the base each year, but most of the growth consists of four- to six-foot continuing laterals that develop from the older wood. When training 'Thor', fan the canes out as much as possible so they will produce the maximum number of these long canes and laterals for flower production the following season.

Unlike many other climbers, 'Thor' builds up very little dead wood as it ages. The only pruning it requires is the removal of a few old or crowded canes. The best time to prune it is just after it has flowered so that the plant will immediately produce new growth to fill in any bare spots. If necessary, cut out about one-third of the oldest wood. During the winter, or in early spring, shorten the laterals as well as any canes that are too long or invasive.

'Thor' will thrive almost anywhere, but its flowers will be longer lasting if it is situated in a slightly sheltered spot where it receives two or three hours of shade a day. It rarely blooms during its first year. This rose has large, dark, glossy foliage that provides a wonderful foil for its scarlet red flowers. The leaves, which are absolutely disease free, remain beautiful throughout the summer and into the fall. It is hardy as far north as New York City.

'Thor' lost popularity as more everblooming climbers were introduced. But it is still one of the best red climbing roses created, well worth having in any garden. Some small specialty rose nurseries still stock it.

Other Horvath Climbers and Ramblers

'Doubloons'
'Hercules'
'Long John Silver'
'Mabelle Stearns'
'Manda's Triumph'
'Mercurius'
'Pink Roamer'
'South Orange Perfection'
'Universal Favorite'

'DREAM GIRL'

Jacobus; introduced by Bobbink and Atkins, 1944
'New Dawn' × 'Señora Gari'
Plant Patent No. 643

'DREAM GIRL' is a large-flowered climber that was introduced by the firm of Bobbink and Atkins. The hybridizer, Martin R. Jacobus of Ridgefield, New Jersey, began breeding roses as a hobby, and the results of his efforts include such distinguished creations as 'Oratam', a shrub rose; 'New World', a floribunda; 'Temptation', a climber; and 'Inspiration', a climber that is often considered a sister to 'Dream Girl' because of its similar growth habit and bloom cycle.

In the patent application for 'Dream Girl', Jacobus made a clear statement about the objectives of his hybridizing efforts. He wanted to produce "a hardy, everblooming, fragrant, large-flowered climbing rose variety characterized by a color or combination of colors never before seen in any class of climbing rose." 'Dream Girl' brought him very close to this goal. From 'New Dawn' it inherited vigor and hardiness; from 'Señora Gari', a hybrid tea, it derived large, salmon pink flowers with a hybrid tea form and a memorable fragrance that was described by Jacobus in the patent application as "spicy and penetrating." Like both its parents, 'Dream Girl' blooms abundantly throughout the season; it produces an especially copious display in the fall.

Although this is a hardy and disease-resistant rose, it lacks the phenomenal vigor of 'New Dawn'. It seems to have inherited some of the characteristics of its more distant ancestor, *R. wichuraiana*. When it was first introduced, Bob-bink and Atkins marketed it as a good sprawler as well as a climber, suitable for covering steep banks and rocky walls. People who bought it as a climber were disappointed to find that for the first few years after it was planted it acted more like a shrub rose, and in the "Proof of the Pudding" there were a number of negative comments concerning its growth habit. After several seasons, however, it shows its true nature and becomes large enough to cover a pillar or a fence.

Inexplicably, 'Dream Girl', an exceptionally beautiful rose, is sold today only by a few small nurseries in the United States and England. Many older rosarians remember it with nostalgia because of its remarkable fragrance.

'DREAM GIRL' is an old-fashioned-looking rose that produces large, urn-shaped buds singly or in clusters at the ends of unusually long laterals of twelve to eighteen inches. These buds, whose outer petals are apple blossom pink, open slowly to become large, double, extremely fragrant flowers, salmon pink with apricot overtones and yellow at the base of the petals. As the flowers mature, their petals reflex, eventually exposing the yellow filaments and red anthers. Each flower has fifty-five to sixty-five petals, and there may be as many as eight of these very full blooms on a stem. With their strong, vibrant color, which becomes more intense in full sun, they put on a lavish show all season long, filling the air with a spicy tea scent. The flowers, which can fill a whole room with their fragrance, are also excellent for cutting because they open slowly and last for a long time.

For the first few years after it is planted, 'Dream Girl' acts more like a low shrub than a climber. It often blooms during its first season.

Many gardeners, however, remove the first year's buds before the flowers form, as this makes the plant more vigorous. After three or four years the bush will become large enough to envelop an eight- to ten-foot pillar or cover a fence ten to twelve feet wide. If you want to train 'Dream Girl' on a pillar, start working with the canes as soon as they are long enough to wrap, for with age they become stiff and hard to manage. An even more effective way to display this rose is on a wall or a fence, spread out in fan shape to show off its extraordinary blooms to the best advantage. Train the canes horizontally as much as you can to increase the production of flower-bearing laterals.

'Dream Girl' will bloom prolifically throughout the summer and then put out an even more magnificent flush in the fall, largely due to the fact that it produces strong basal shoots and new continuing laterals that bear terminal blooms. To encourage this autumn extravaganza, lightly prune the flower-bearing laterals as soon as each flower has faded, shortening them by about one-third. Any flowers left on the bush will set hips for a winter display.

Most of the new climbing growth throughout the growing season consists of long continuing laterals. Train these laterals, which may be as long as twelve feet, into place as soon as they develop. As they often bear flowers at their tips, you may want to let the ends hang down or treat them in some other decorative manner that will show off the beautiful blooms. If they get too long, prune them back.

Over the years the plant will become crowded with old canes that must be removed. This can be done immediately after the first flush of flowers has faded or during periods of heat or drought, when flower production slows. The pruning will encourage new growth and abundant flowers in the fall. If large quantities of wood must be cut away, wait until the plant is dormant. After cutting out all the old wood, shorten one or two of the remaining canes by about two-thirds so they will put out new growth to fill in any bare spots at the base of the plant.

'Dream Girl' has very glossy, dark green foliage that is exceptionally disease resistant; in the Cranford Rose Garden, Stephen has never had to spray it for leaf diseases. It is hardy as far north as New York City; in colder climates, the new growth at the ends of the canes may die back in winter.

A wonderful rose that provides exquisite color and fragrance in the garden all season long, 'Dream Girl' should be better known today, for it is one of the best climbers ever created.

'Dream Girl' has large pink flowers with a memorable fragrance unlike that of any other pink climber.

153

'CITY OF YORK'

Tantau; introduced into the United States by Conard-Pyle, 1945
'Professor Gnau' × 'Dorothy Perkins'

THE DISTINGUISHED HYBRIDIZER Mathias Tantau, Sr., of Uetersen (Holstein), Germany, created this large-flowered climber before World War II; it was introduced to the Bagatelle rose garden in Paris in 1938. Originally it was called 'Direktor Benschop', but German names were anathema to Americans in 1945, the year it was introduced here by Conard-Pyle, and it became 'City of York'.[108] The name honors the city of York, Pennsylvania, which adopted it as its official flower on June 2, 1945.[109] For many years it continued to be known in Europe as 'Direktor Benschop'; today the name 'City of York' seems to be universally accepted.

Mathias Tantau, Sr., who founded the Tantau nursery in 1906, began to specialize in roses shortly after World War I.[110] His hybridizing efforts, which resulted mostly in polyanthas and floribundas, were directed toward the creation of roses that would be cold hardy, disease resistant, and perpetually blooming. 'City of York', his only commercially successful climber, does not bloom steadily all season long, but it more than adequately fulfills the other two aims, for it is extremely hardy and disease resistant thanks to its *R. wichuraiana* hybrid parent, 'Dorothy Perkins'. Its other parent, 'Professor Gnau', was also created by Tantau; this hybrid tea is a direct descendant of the old garden roses, which accounts for the old-fashioned-looking flowers and fragrance of 'City of York'.

'City of York' is a hardy, vigorous rose with excellent disease resistance and large, fragrant, creamy white flowers that produce an impressive display in the spring and a second autumn flush in all but the coldest climates. It soon eclipsed 'Silver Moon' as the most popular large-flowered white climbing rose in America, gaining some of the highest grades ever attained in the "Proof of the Pudding" ratings. It even received favorable reports from Wyoming and Minnesota, where it was recommended as a pillar rose. In 1950 it won the American Rose Society National Gold Medal.

THIS FANTASTIC rose produces massive clusters of seven to fifteen antique white blossoms that glow yellow because of their exposed stamens and give off a wonderful wild rose fragrance. Opening from yellow buds, the flowers, on single, short stems, are large, semidouble, and cupped, and their fifteen petals are neatly and compactly arranged. 'City of York' blooms profusely from late May through June and occasionally repeats during the summer. When the weather turns cooler, it often puts on another display, especially after an Indian summer followed by cool rains. This rose sets large hips that turn orange in the fall.

This is a fast-growing rose with glossy, dense, long-lasting foliage that is thick enough to make an outstanding canopy over a walkway. Because its canes are very pliable and may be

The large-flowered climber 'City of York' is a favorite in many European gardens. Here it is seen in the Bagatelle rose garden in Paris, where its creamy white blossoms are festooned on chains. Originally introduced in Germany in 1945 as 'Direktor Benschop', the name was changed in America to honor the city of York, Pennsylvania.

turned down at the tips with no ill effects, they can easily be fanned out on a fence or a lattice; wrapped around a pillar, an arch, or a tripod; or shaped to the curve of a window. 'City of York' also makes an excellent groundcover. It is often found in older public gardens, shaped as a weeping standard or covering arches and fences. In the famous Bagatelle gardens in Paris, it decorates low-hanging ropes and chains.

The autumn flowers bloom on the same laterals that produced the spring display, so as soon as the first flowers have fallen, cut the laterals back by two-thirds to encourage rebloom, even though this means sacrificing the hips. Meanwhile, new canes will spring up from the base, and other long continuing laterals will develop higher up along the older wood. All this new growth will bloom the following year.

During the growing season this rose produces a prodigious amount of new growth, sending out numerous basal canes that quickly become twelve or fifteen feet long. These canes stay close to the ground, rooting wherever they touch it, a trait of most wichuraiana hybrids. With so much new growth, it is often difficult to decide what to remove when pruning. If you do not mind a wild-looking rose, wait until winter to prune; this way you will have the best possible display of repeat blooms in the fall. If you are growing 'City of York' on an arch over a path or in any other situation where its rampant growth has to be restrained, at midseason remove most of the wood that bore the flowering laterals, even though this means losing the hips and repeat blooms. Use the new growth to fill in the spaces on the support where the old wood has been cut away. If there is any old wood left behind, shorten its laterals by two-thirds.

'City of York' is one of the most disease-resistant and winter-hardy roses. Its popularity waned for a while, but now more and more nurseries are offering it for sale again. We consider it the best white, large-flowered climber on the market today.

'INSPIRATION'

Jacobus; introduced by Bobbink and Atkins, 1946
'New Dawn' × 'Crimson Glory'

'INSPIRATION', a large-flowered climber, is another highly successful rose created by Martin R. Jacobus and introduced by Bobbink and Atkins. As he had with 'Dream Girl', Jacobus used 'New Dawn' as one of the parents. The other parent was the once-popular 'Crimson Glory', a dark red hybrid tea with a damask fragrance that was introduced in 1935 by Wilhelm Kordes. The combination of these two roses produced an everblooming climber that combines the best qualities of both: the glossy foliage, extraordinary vigor, and excellent disease resistance of 'New Dawn', and the superbly formed, deliciously scented flowers of 'Crimson Glory'. 'Inspiration' is an improvement over 'New Dawn' because it is hardier, and it bears flowers that are longer lasting and have a more substantial color—a deep, vibrant pink. 'Inspiration' was never patented, but unlike its "sister," 'Dream Girl', it has remained very popular.

AT THE HEIGHT of the bloom season, one bush of 'Inspiration' can explode with more than two hundred large pink flowers, a spectacular display it continues throughout the summer and fall. The buds are high centered, like those of exhibition-quality hybrid teas. They open to semidouble flowers that have an old-fashioned look because of their ruffled and irregularly arranged petals. The outer petals are a deeper pink than those toward the center, which adds to the informal look. These large, richly colored flowers rarely look washed out in full sun.

In the spring the flowers are borne singly or in clusters on short laterals that grow from the canes of the previous year. As this first flush is fading, long new canes begin to develop from all parts of the plant. By the time the hips of the first flowers start to turn orange, the rampant new growth will be loaded with blooms. This cycle repeats throughout the summer. The later blooms have long stems and are especially good for cutting. Toward the end of the summer, the combination of mature orange hips and pink flowers is beautiful, so you may not want to deadhead. If you do, take off only the spent blossoms, for the buds of the new flowers are right behind them.

'Inspiration' has large, dark, glossy leaves that are faintly edged in red. It is an excellent rose to use in the background because, unlike some other climbers, it does not lose its lower leaves but remains full and dense down to the ground throughout the summer. In the North the leaves turn bright yellow toward the end of the season, adding color to the fall garden. Like its parent 'New Dawn', 'Inspiration' is exceptionally disease resistant.

As the weather turns cool in the fall, all parts of the plant put out new growth. The numerous basal shoots, which are bright red, are very stiff and must be trained early to prevent them from becoming invasive. Cut them back after they bloom.

Like most climbers, 'Inspiration' does not reach full vigor or produce plentiful blooms its first year. In fact, this climber is similar to 'Dream Girl' in that it seems to take a long time to come into its own. For this reason, it did not become popular until several years after it appeared on the market. Many of the rose growers who evaluated it for the "Proof of the Pudding" were skeptical at first, giving it low

marks for growth and bloom. Typical comments were "hasn't been inspired yet" and "no blooms, no growth, out it goes!" A few years later, however, the same gardeners wrote "better each year," "improves with age," and "went to town in growth; a fine everblooming climber." So give 'Inspiration' time to get established, and it will, as one gardener put it, "become a star."

Because it can reach a height of at least eight feet and spread horizontally to cover an area twenty-two feet wide, 'Inspiration' should be grown where it can stretch out, such as on a fence or a broad lattice. You can also let it grow without support; it will become a large shrub whose canes will spill over a wall or make a dense barrier replete with forbidding prickles. Do not confine 'Inspiration' to a small garden or a pillar, for in order to keep it within bounds, you will have to prune off much of the vigorous, flower-producing new growth during the growing season.

In the right place 'Inspiration' requires minimal pruning. As with all climbers, shorten by two-thirds the laterals that are not long enough to be trained. When the plant is dormant during the winter, remove the unproductive older wood to make room for the new.

'Inspiration' blooms in full sun or partial shade. It is an excellent background rose for a bed with other flowers that have only one bloom period, such as old garden roses. If unconstrained, its canes will extend out into the bed, filling in bare spots with their luxuriant foliage and producing abundant flowers for color all summer long.

This climber has above-average hardiness, but in regions with extremely severe winters, such as Minnesota, it needs protection during the colder months.

With its masses of large, continuously blooming pink flowers, thick, dark foliage, and beautiful orange hips, 'Inspiration', a true everblooming climber, is the ideal rose for any spacious, informal setting.

'Inspiration', a true everblooming climber, produces a spectacular display of large pink flowers all season long.

'HIGH NOON'

Lammerts; introduced by the Armstrong Nursery, 1946
'Soeur Thérèse' × *'Captain Thomas'*
Plant Patent No. 704

'HIGH NOON', a large-flowered climber, is the result of a cross between two hybrid teas. 'Soeur Thérèse', an important modern yellow rose, and 'Captain Thomas', a fragrant, single, yellow climbing variety. The hybridizer was Dr. Walter E. Lammerts, director of research at the Armstrong Nursery of Ontario, California, until 1940. After Lammerts left Armstrong, his position was taken over by Herbert Swim, who carried on his predecessor's work and raised a number of the roses Lammerts had developed, one of which was this yellow climber. In 1948 'High Noon' was an All-America Rose Selections winner.

In his application for a patent for this rose, Lammerts emphasized the brilliant yellow of its flowers, stressing that such a deep and stable yellow was unknown in continuously blooming roses of this type. He also pointed out that, unlike other yellow roses, the flowers of 'High Noon' do not fade. Another important characteristic was its high degree of resistance to mildew.

Like all modern yellow roses, 'High Noon' has in its ancestry the first yellow hybrid roses, 'Soleil d'Or' and 'Rayon d'Or', which were created in 1900 when the renowned French hybridizer Joseph Pernet-Ducher crossed a red hybrid perpetual, 'Antoine Ducher', with a yellow wild rose from western Asia, *R. foetida persiana* ('Persian Yellow'). The roses that descended from this crossing, long known as Pernetiana roses, have beautiful flowers, but they are all susceptible to black spot, and 'High Noon' is no exception. 'High Noon' also shares the tendency of Pernetiana roses to drop their leaves in midsummer and to bloom most prolifically at the beginning and end of the season.

'HIGH NOON' is a magnificent rose with fiery orange, urn-shaped buds that open to brilliant lemon yellow flowers whose glowing petals are tinged with red. These double, medium-sized flowers, redolent of spice, are loosely cupped and have a starburst effect because of their exposed stamens and pistils. Their formal, hybrid tea look is enhanced by having only one flower on each long stem. They hold their color well, fading only slightly in hot weather. They make good cut flowers even though they tend to disintegrate quickly, not holding the perfect form expected of exhibition quality hybrid teas. The heady perfume of a single bloom can fill a room for days.

This climber has light green leaves that are large, leathery, and glossy, but sparse, especially at the bottom of the plant. This trait, which goes back to its wild ancestor, 'Persian Yellow', is found in all Pernetiana roses. It seems the leaves have a very short life cycle, maturing so early in the season that they drop before the summer is over. 'High Noon', therefore, should be grown together with other plants that will hide the sparseness of its foliage. Do not place it against a wall; it is susceptible

'High Noon' was the first successful everblooming yellow climber. Its fragrant flowers are excellent in bouquets.

to black spot and other foliage diseases and needs good air circulation. It has better disease resistance than many Pernetiana roses, however, and it often recovers from these problems as the season progresses. In addition, it withstands mildew.

'High Noon' is a vigorous, upright climber that easily reaches eight feet high and twelve feet wide. Most of its new canes develop off the main cane, but there are also sporadic basal breaks that grow rapidly to eight or ten feet. Left on its own, the bush becomes messy and cluttered with dead wood, and, like all Pernetiana roses, it needs support. The canes are so stiff and woody, however, that there are a limited number of ways to use them. If you catch them early, while they are still pliable, you can train them on a high fence, a lattice, or a wide arch. But they are much too inflexible to be wrapped around a pillar. When training the canes, try to position them horizontally as much as possible; this stimulates new growth and profuse bloom. Be careful not to tip them down because that causes them to die back at the ends.

'High Noon' blooms best on its older wood, repeating on the same laterals that produce the first flush of flowers. You may not want to deadhead, as that will remove the beautiful hips. If you do, be careful to snip off only the spent flowers, for the new blooms usually occur near the first or second nodes behind the old ones. Otherwise, the only pruning necessary is the removal of old dead wood that builds up and gives the plant an unkempt appearance.

This climber does best in an area that is sunny but not too hot. A spot that gets morning sun and some afternoon shade is ideal. In full shade it will reach for the sun and produce all its flowers out of sight at the tips of the long canes.

'High Noon', which performs best in mild climates, is especially well suited to the Pacific coast. In northern cities, such as Minnesota and Montana, it will thrive if it has good winter protection. In hotter regions, such as Texas, its buds and flowers are small, and they lack the strong, fruity fragrance.

'High Noon' was the first successful everblooming yellow climber. It never caught on in other countries, but in the United States and Canada, gardeners treasure it for its luminous, golden yellow flowers and its wonderful spicy fragrance.

'ALOHA'

Boerner; introduced by Jackson and Perkins, 1949
'Mercedes Gallart' × 'New Dawn'
Plant Patent No. 948

'ALOHA' is a large-flowered climber, developed by Eugene Boerner, who was the director of the hybridizing program at Jackson and Perkins from 1927 to 1966.[111] In his application for a patent for this rose, Boerner stated specifically that it was a pillar plant. Writers of nursery catalogs, however, preferred to emphasize its climbing ability. This—together with their descriptions of its abundant, large, everblooming, apricot-pink flowers—led gardeners to believe that it combined spectacular flowers with a tall growth habit, and they were disappointed when they realized that it actually never grew taller than pillar height. After the initial excitement, its "Proof of the Pudding" ratings went steadily down.

'Aloha' is actually a superior rose that often acts just like climbing hybrid teas, which have flowers resembling those of hybrid teas but not the large, spreading growth habit one usually associates with large-flowered climbers. The true climbing hybrid teas are climbing sports of hybrid teas, but 'Aloha' is a cultivar resulting from a cross between 'New Dawn', a wichuraiana hybrid with a tea rose in its background, and 'Mercedes Gallart', a pink climber with two hybrid teas and several hybrid perpetuals (including 'Frau Karl Druschki') in its heritage. 'Aloha' is not a rampant climber like 'New Dawn'. It has a growth habit more like that of its other parent, 'Mercedes Gallart'. In fact, some growers think that in growth habit and flower size it is more like a vigorous hybrid perpetual than a climber. Its flowers often go through various shades of pink as they mature, a trait they probably inherited from China ancestors with flowers that have yellow and apricot blends.

'Aloha' became very popular once it was accepted as an everblooming pillar rose. It seems to have the ability to sport, or at least to produce blooms that differ greatly in color—some in shades of pink, others orange. Several nurseries in the United States and England are currently propagating promising sports of this rose. It is also being used in breeding programs. David Austin in England has recently used it to produce a new shrub rose, 'Abraham Darby', which is suitable for training on a pillar.

'ALOHA' has very large (four- to five-inch) flowers composed of nearly sixty petals in various shades of pink, sometimes with a hint of orange. These exhibition-quality blooms are borne either in clusters or on long stems and have a strong tea fragrance. Just before they open, the large, tight buds have dark, flat, ruffled tops; they look as though they have been chewed by caterpillars. They unfold to perfectly formed flowers, however. As they mature, the petals, which may be darker on the reverse than on the inside, slowly reflex. Bloom continues well into late fall; the autumn buds are larger than those produced earlier in the season. As the weather turns cool, the flowers take on a quartered appearance; if the days are damp as well as cool, blooms tend to ball. There are a few small hips.

'Aloha' is a fine rose for a pillar. Because it has stiff and erect canes, this rose is often grown without support as an upright shrub. Sometimes it is even planted in beds and pruned back like floribundas. Stephen has had good

luck with it as a climber. With the right kind of pruning it can reach a height of twelve feet or more, and the long continuing laterals that spring from the base and center may give it a spread of at least five feet. In the Cranford Rose Garden one of the oldest specimens, which was sent by the Jackson and Perkins Company in 1949, is fifteen feet high and almost as wide. Trained on the pavilion, it arches around a window and out over a walkway.

'Aloha' becomes woody at the base, with only a few basal breaks. The plant on the pavilion has one or two long main canes and a number of very stiff, medium-length canes that fill in its otherwise bare middle section. Laterals develop on all parts of the older, established wood. Over the years Stephen has encouraged it to reach its large size by selective pruning that induces it to produce long, vigorous shoots. First he removes or shortens by two-thirds all the old, unproductive wood. Then he shortens the laterals on the upper parts of the plant by two-thirds. He is careful to train the canes horizontally, as this encourages the production of the flower-bearing laterals and the long continuing laterals that add height.

It is important to remember not to tip the canes down when you train this rose, as that will inhibit their flower production. The canes quickly became stiff as they mature, so train the longer ones into place while they are growing. Without support the canes tend to arch over when they reach six feet.

'Aloha' blooms continuously throughout the season, but the largest and most beautiful flowers appear in early summer and in the fall. The faded blooms look messy, so snip off the spent flowers at the first node; they will bloom again from this point on the lateral.

'Aloha' is often found on the awards bench in rose shows. If you want exhibition-quality flowers in late winter shorten all laterals that are less than two feet long by about two-thirds. This should be done again after the first flush of bloom if you want larger flowers for an autumn flower show. On the other hand, if you are growing this rose to produce a continuous display in the garden throughout the summer and right up to the first hard frost, just give the laterals minimal pruning.

'Aloha' has very glossy, dark, leathery leaves. The foliage has good disease resistance, but it does suffer some defoliation early in the season. It is healthiest when the plant is grown in a moist area that receives a lot of sunlight.

This is a lovely and surprisingly versatile rose that can be used in a variety of ways. It may not be as tall as other climbers, but it makes up for its lack of height by putting on a glorious show all season long.

The glossy foliage of 'Aloha' forms a rich backdrop for its flat-topped buds and old-fashioned-looking pink flowers.

'TEMPTATION'

Jacobus; introduced by Bobbink and Atkins, 1950
('New Dawn' × 'Crimson Glory') × 'Dream Girl'

FROM 1939 TO 1955 Martin R. Jacobus created roses exclusively for the firm of Bobbink and Atkins, which was located in Rutherford, New Jersey. Of the five climbers he produced, only two, 'Dream Girl' and 'Inspiration', are still in commerce. It is unfortunate that 'Temptation', another large-flowered climber, is no longer available, for it is a marvelous rose. In 1954 one gardener who rated it for the "Proof of the Pudding" described it this way: "For those who incline toward the old-fashioned types . . . this is a winner. A loose rumpled double bloom with exquisite fragrance, shows a dark lavender-pink in spring, almost flesh-pink in summer, and refulgent rose-red in the fall . . . a constant bloomer."[112]

As he had with 'Inspiration', Jacobus used 'New Dawn' and 'Crimson Glory' to create 'Temptation'. This time, though, he first fertilized 'New Dawn' with the pollen of 'Crimson Glory', and then crossed a resulting seedling with 'Dream Girl'. As he had stated in his patent application for 'Dream Girl', Jacobus's aim in hybridizing was to create superior climbing roses that would be everblooming, hardy, fragrant, and have large flowers with unusual colors. Although the color of 'Temptation' is not as unusual as that of 'Dream Girl', it is beautiful. In addition, this rose combines the vigor of 'New Dawn' with the exceptional fragrance of 'Crimson Glory'.

'TEMPTATION' is a stunning rose that blooms prolifically all season long, producing clusters of large, double, sweetly fragrant, carmine red flowers. Borne in clusters of three to five at the ends of long laterals and stems, these flowers, which open from bright red, ovoid buds, have fifty tight petals, the inner ones faintly striped with white. As the heavy blooms open, their petals overlap; later they become flat. Eventually they reflex completely, so that the yellow stamens stand out against the red petals.

Although it is always in bloom, this rose is not a vigorous grower. As it matures, it may spread out to about twelve feet and reach a height of about six feet, becoming taller in warmer climates. Throughout the season there will be new growth from the base and numerous stiff, very long continuing laterals that grow straight out at right angles to the bush and bear large clusters of blooms at their tips. Because of its moderate height and spreading growth habit, 'Temptation' is best used as a cover for a low fence. Its height is adequate for a pillar, but its canes are too heavy and stiff to be wrapped easily around a single support, especially as they are armed with large, wicked prickles. If trained while they are young, the canes can be adapted to a tripod.

As the plant matures, it sends up much growth from the base, and the canes each year produce an increasing number of laterals, some of which will be four to six feet long. As you

'Temptation' is a modern climber with beautiful red blooms that are reminiscent of old garden roses. Unfortunately, this Jacobus cultivar is difficult to find today.

will need all of this wood for training, keep pruning to a minimum. Simply remove any crowded or otherwise undesirable canes. This pruning should be done during late winter or early spring, so as not to interfere with the continuous summer bloom. Deadhead cautiously; like all the offspring of 'New Dawn', 'Temptation' bears its new blooms right behind the old ones, so if you cut the laterals back too far, you will lose the next flowers. If you must remove spent blossoms, just pinch them off.

Like Jacobus's other climbers 'Temptation' blooms throughout the season, even in the first year. It puts on especially copious displays during periods of cool weather. In the fall it will often resume blooming during warm spells following frosts.

'Temptation' has large, glossy leaves that are very disease resistant. It is also very hardy, with high tolerance for poor growing conditions. This is one of many beautiful old roses that over the years have disappeared inexplicably from nursery catalogs. It deserves to be brought back into commerce, for it can provide wonderful color and fragrance in the garden all summer long.

'PARADE'

Boerner; introduced by Jackson and Perkins, 1953
A 'New Dawn' seedling × 'Climbing World's Fair'
Plant Patent No. 1253

'PARADE', a large-flowered climber with deep rose pink flowers, has a distinguished pedigree. From 'New Dawn' it derived outstanding vigor and disease resistance, and its charmingly old-fashioned-looking flowers are probably also due to this famous parent, which had as one of its ancestors the tea rose 'Safrano'. The other parent of 'Parade' was 'Climbing World's Fair', a sport of an important floribunda, 'World's Fair'. 'World's Fair' was the offspring of a damask-scented hybrid tea, 'Crimson Glory', and this accounts for 'Parade's distinctive old rose fragrance.

Eugene Boerner's beautiful everblooming climber was an immediate success, receiving high marks in the "Proof of the Pudding" ratings. Its wonderfully scented and richly colored flowers, reminiscent of Bourbon roses, have long stems, which make them good for cutting. Its foliage is remarkably healthy, and it blooms continuously, sometimes even during its first season. The only gardeners who were disappointed with it were those who expected a descendant of 'Dr. W. Van Fleet' to be a more vigorous climber.

In England and on the Continent, where it was used as a pillar rose and also trained on wires to create hedges, 'Parade' was one of the most highly praised American climbers. Ever since its introduction in 1953, it has been part of the Bagatelle rose garden in Paris.

THE BUDS of this rose look like those of Bourbon roses, and they open to very large, cupped, intensely pink flowers that have a strong damask fragrance. Adding to its old garden rose character are its occasional button eyes and a tendency to quarter in the cool weather of autumn. The three- to four-inch blooms, borne on long, single stems or in clusters of as many as ten, are composed of sixty-five to seventy luminous pink petals; those at the center of the flower are more darkly colored than those toward the outside. Contrary to what one might expect from a rose with such large, multipetaled flowers, there is never a problem with balling. In cool weather the pink turns toward mauve, and later there are large orange hips that make an attractive winter display.

For several years after it is planted, 'Parade' may act more like a shrub than a climber. Eventually it will grow to about eight feet high and twelve feet wide, large enough to train on a fence, a lattice along the side of a house, or a tall tripod, as at the Bagatelle garden in Paris. It can also be used to make a fragrant arch over a walkway.

'Parade' produces many long canes from the base and also develops numerous long and short continuing laterals off the older canes. When training it, fan out all these canes and laterals on the support to induce the maximum number of blooms. Often the new canes and laterals will bear flowers at their tips, and these will pull the canes down with their weight; if you have enough room, you can create a wonderful effect by letting them cascade into a flower bed.

As with all large-flowered climbers, the canes are heavy and stiff, more difficult to train than the flexible canes of the ramblers. Because of this, it is important to tie the new canes into place while they are developing; later they will become too rigid to manage. The inflexible

growth is difficult to wrap around a pillar, but it is worth the effort; prune the rose severely every winter, removing all the older wood and leaving the young, more pliable canes to attach to the support.

You can grow 'Parade' as a shrub if you are willing to constantly prune it hard with hedge shears. It is easier to control as a hedge. Drive posts into the ground six feet apart, string wires between the posts at two-foot intervals to a height of about six feet, and secure the canes along the wires. Once the hedge is established, it will require little pruning.

Throughout the season, new flowers develop on the ends of the young shoots and all along the laterals that spring from the old canes. Deadhead to induce quick rebloom; otherwise the plant will slow down until autumn. As with 'New Dawn', just pinch off the spent blooms back to the nearest bud. Even without deadheading, 'Parade' will put on an outstanding show in the fall, long after many other roses have stopped flowering.

'Parade', which is hardy in the New York City area, is one of our favorite climbing roses. The dark green foliage is glossy, tough, and very disease resistant. It is a perfect companion for some of the older climbers such as 'Sombreuil', and it can also be combined with many modern roses. Like another Boerner star, 'Aloha', it can be grown as a bedding plant as well as a climber. These two roses combined in a bed create a dazzling effect.

The nodding, fragrant pink flowers of 'Parade', which resemble Bourbon roses, cascade from a high fence.

'WHITE CAP'

Brownell, 1954
Originally introduced as 'Everblooming Pillar No. 3'
An unnamed seedling × 'Climbing Break o'Day'
Plant Patent No. 1273

'WHITE CAP' is a large-flowered climber created by Josephine Brownell of Little Compton, Rhode Island. Originally called 'Everblooming Pillar No. 3', it was one of a number of climbers (many of which were at first provisionally identified as 'Everblooming Pillar') introduced by Mrs. Brownell and her husband, Dr. Walter Brownell. 'White Cap' is no longer in commerce and is very rarely seen today, but it was one of the Brownells' most beautiful contributions to the race of hardy, everblooming, large-flowered climbers.

Stimulated at first by the desire to breed improved yellow climbers, the Brownells crossed wichuraiana hybrids, especially those of Van Fleet, with hybrids of hybrid teas.[113] These second and third generation crosses produced some successful yellow climbers.[114] They also resulted in roses that were exceptionally hardy; these became well known as the Brownells' "sub-zero" roses.

Like all Brownell roses, 'White Cap' has a Van Fleet hybrid in its heritage. Its parent, 'Climbing Break o'Day', is a vigorous climbing hybrid tea that is a sport of another Brownell rose, 'Break o'Day', itself a cross between an unnamed seedling and 'Glenn Dale', a Van Fleet wichuraiana hybrid.

In her patent application for the rose that would eventually be called 'White Cap', Mrs. Brownell clearly defined this type of rose by calling it a variant of the hybrid tea class, "a *Rosa wichuraiana* hybrid tea hybrid," a rose that combines canes like those of a wichuraiana with the hybrid tea ability to bear recurrent blooms on the current seasons's growth. This type of rose was a significant improvement over other wichuraiana hybrids that bear flowers on canes produced the previous season, thus taking two seasons to come into bloom. The Brownell roses act much like hybrid teas during their first season, blooming a lot and remaining bushy. In subsequent seasons they take on a climbing habit.

In addition to its virtues as a climber in the garden, 'White Cap' can be forced into bloom in a pot. Its flowers are also good for bouquets, a point Mrs. Brownell brought out in her patent application, for she was no doubt well aware of the market for cut flowers.

'WHITE CAP', a nonstop bloomer that produces large, double, creamy white flowers from late May right up to the first hard frost, is a wonderful rose that should be brought back into commerce. The ovoid buds, which look like those of hybrid teas, are slightly peach colored, and when the flowers, which have fifty to seventy pointed and reflexed petals, are fully open, they retain a hint of this peach color at their centers. These blooms, as large as four

'White Cap', one of the beautiful everblooming pillar roses created by Josephine Brownell, produces blooms like those of hybrid teas.

inches in diameter, are nearly flat and are quartered at the center, rarely exposing the stamens and pistils. They have an old-fashioned, tea rose fragrance. When left on the bush, the flowers can become messy because of the enormous number of petals. They do not set hips, so nothing is lost by deadheading.

'White Cap', which is never out of bloom, has the hybrid tea characteristic of producing flowers on all its wood—the terminal buds of the new growth and the six-inch laterals that spring from the old wood. Only a few new canes develop at the base of the plant, but continuing laterals as long as eight feet sometimes occur on the upper parts. As the season progresses, other stiff and upright laterals, some up to three feet long, occur on the upper parts of the plant and extend its height. One beautiful way to train this rose is to wrap one or two of its main canes tightly around a tripod; the flower-laden laterals will seem to come cascading out of the support. 'White Cap' can also be trained on an arch. Because it is slow growing, you might want to use this climber as a hedge or even prune it back severely so that it remains a bush.

'White Cap' can grow to a height of about ten feet and requires minimal pruning. During the dormant period, just clean out any old wood that has built up and eliminate any crossing branches. The glossy, dark green leaves are disease free until the end of the season, at which time they may have a little black spot and mildew.

'White Cap' is a beautiful climber that blooms nonstop all season long. Absolutely carefree and hardy, it is a worthy successor to Van Fleet's "dooryard roses."

Other Brownell Climbers

'Coral Creeper'
'Golden Arctic'
'Salmon Arctic'
'Golden Glow'
'Pink Pillar'
'Mrs. Arthur Curtiss James'
'Show Garden'
'Frederick S. Peck'
'Orange Everglow'

'GOLDBUSCH'

Kordes, 1954
'Golden Glow' × *a* R. eglanteria *hybrid*[115]

THE BROWNELLS of Rhode Island were known the world over for their climbing roses, and one of the people who most admired their work was the noted German hybridizer Wilhelm Kordes. Kordes was especially impressed with 'Golden Glow', a yellow climber the Brownells introduced in 1937. This rose, classified in Mrs. Brownell's plant patent application as a "hybrid climbing wichuraiana," was the offspring of two Van Fleet climbers and a hybrid tea.[116] In several issues of *The American Rose Annual* Kordes praised its abundant golden flowers and its hardiness, even going so far as to say, "I think 'Golden Glow' is the Climber we have been expecting for long, long years."[117]

Like the Brownells, Kordes strove for cold-hardy roses. To create 'Goldbusch' he crossed 'Golden Glow' with a hybrid of the hardy species rose, *R. eglanteria*.[118] The result was an eglantine in which the legacies of two distinguished types of roses are combined, the Van Fleet wichuraiana hybrids and the Penzance eglantine hybrids.

Later, another cross between 'Golden Glow' and an *R. eglanteria* hybrid produced for Kordes a shrub rose that can easily be used as a climber, 'Alchymist', which is similar to 'Goldbusch' but has double flowers in shades of yellow and orange. 'Alchymist' was introduced in 1956.

'GOLDBUSCH' puts on an outstanding display of large, semidouble, golden yellow flowers early in the season—at the end of May in the Cranford Rose Garden. The long, pointed buds open quickly to elegant blooms, about three inches in diameter, whose twelve to fifteen petals are arranged in a slight cup shape that beautifully sets off the exposed stamens and pistils. The early season flowers are borne in clusters on three-and-one-half-inch laterals. In the northeastern United States, 'Goldbusch' rarely repeats its bloom in the fall, but when it does, the flowers occur on short, single stems rather than in clusters; their yellow is even more brilliant than in the spring. The flowers of 'Goldbusch' have a sweet but not strong fragrance. Rather, it is the leaves of this rose that contain the perfume. When crushed, they are redolent of the wonderful apple-scented foliage of the eglantine ancestor. This rose sets three-quarter-inch-long hips that retain their sepals and turn vivid orange in the fall.

'Goldbusch' is a vigorous climber. At the Cranford Rose Garden it grew eight feet high and twelve feet wide in three years. The growth is upright yet rampant and bushy enough to be spread out on a lattice, fence, or low wall. This is an ideal rose to train on a pillar or a post. If you wrap two canes around a six-foot pillar, you will have a stunning display of flowers from bottom to top by the second season. During the third season, long canes will develop at the base of the plant, and you can add these to the others on the support; when the canes become too crowded on the pillar, simply cut out the oldest ones. The canes are easy to train the first season, but as they age, they become thick, heavy, stiff, and unwieldy, and they develop strong, hooked prickles. They are attractive spilling out into the garden, however. Once the bush is established it may start to rebloom late in the season.

The light green foliage, leathery and dull, is

susceptible to black spot and, to a lesser degree, mildew. Therefore, plant 'Goldbusch' in a spot with good air circulation and surround it with other, more disease-resistant roses whose leaves will hide its nakedness if it loses foliage during the summer.

Americans have been slow to appreciate 'Goldbusch'. It is still in commerce, however, and it is gaining in popularity, for it is a rose that will gladden any garden with its elegant golden yellow flowers and its deliciously fragrant foliage.

'Goldbusch' has sweetly scented, golden yellow flowers and leaves that, when crushed, have the fragrance of apples.

'DORTMUND'

Kordes, 1955
An unknown seedling × R. kordesii

WILHELM KORDES is noted for introducing a family of roses in which the best characteristics of two hardy species are combined with the desirable qualities of modern hybrids. The genesis of these roses, known as Kordesii hybrids, goes back to 1919 when a rose that was a spontaneous cross between *R. rugosa* and *R. wichuraiana* was discovered in a private garden in Connecticut. This hybrid, called 'Max Graf', had flowers like those of the rugosa; the growth habit of the wichuraiana; and the vigor, hardiness, and disease resistance of both parents. Hybridizers were understandably eager to breed its good qualities into roses of other classes. But in this respect 'Max Graf' was a great disappointment, for it rarely produced seeds, and its pollen was infertile. Kordes, however, planted a specimen of 'Max Graf' in his garden and in 1940, after a fifteen-year wait, it finally produced seed pods, from which he was able to obtain two seedlings. One of the seedlings survived an especially harsh winter in 1941–1942, and, amazingly, proved to be extremely fertile. Because its seeds grew into plants that were just like the parent, it was classified as a new species rose, *R. kordesii*, although it was actually a hybrid of two species roses.[119] By crossing *R. kordesii* with modern hybrids, Kordes developed a whole new race of hardy, disease-resistant, remontant shrub and climbing roses, one of which was 'Dortmund'.

'DORTMUND' bears festive clusters of five to seven large, single, vivid poppy red flowers whose brilliant color is all the more striking because the petals have white bases; this creates a bull's eye at the center of each blossom. The six to eight wavy petals are cupped, and as the flower opens, they reflex lengthwise. There is a light, spicy fragrance. This rose, which blooms from the peak of the hybrid tea season to the first hard frost, sets quantities of medium-sized, glossy, orange hips.

'Dortmund' is a versatile climber that can be used in innumerable ways—as a groundcover, or trained on a fence, lattice, wall, or pillar. We have recently seen a beautiful specimen of 'Dortmund' entwined with a *Pyracantha*. Together the two have made their way to the second story of a Brooklyn brownstone, where the dark, dense foliage and white flowers of the *Pyracantha* make a perfect foil for the intense red of the flowers of 'Dortmund'.

This rose is a slow starter that will climb slowly for the first two years and then suddenly take off, sending out from the base new canes that in one season can shoot up ten or twelve feet. The young canes are easy to work with. If possible, fan them out horizontally so that the flower-producing laterals, which vary in length from six inches to one-and-a-half feet, develop all along their length. Otherwise, all the new growth and repeat blooms may be over your head and out of sight at the top of this vigorous plant.

'Dortmund' is a rose to grow in full sun. In low-light areas it does not bloom profusely, and its glossy, light green foliage becomes diseased

With constant deadheading, 'Dortmund' will produce brilliant red blooms throughout the summer.

and sparse. For the best rebloom, deadhead, even though it means removing the wonderful hips. Without deadheading, rebloom will still occur, but more slowly; the new flowers will appear two or three nodes behind the spent ones.

As one would expect, 'Dortmund' is extremely hardy. It has only recently begun to attract the attention it deserves in the United States, perhaps because Americans have put so much emphasis on climbers with double flowers. Do not overlook this rose, however, for it can provide exceptional color in your garden all season long. It is a favorite in the Cranford Rose Garden, where its red flowers frame an oval window in the white latticework pavilion.

'GOLDEN SHOWERS'

Lammerts; introduced by Germain's, Inc., 1956
'Charlotte Armstrong' × 'Captain Thomas'
Plant Patent No. 1557

SINCE THE INCEPTION of the All-America Rose Selections (AARS) trials in 1938, only three climbers have been chosen as winners, and two of these are yellow varieties created by Dr. Walter E. Lammerts, 'High Noon' and 'Golden Showers'.[120] In 1957 'Golden Showers' also won the Portland Gold Medal, a prestigious award given to roses that perform exceptionally well in the International Test Garden in Portland, Oregon.

This everblooming, large-flowered climber is a cross between a hybrid tea, 'Charlotte Armstrong' (another award-winning rose by Lammerts), and 'Captain Thomas' (one of the parents of 'High Noon'). It resembles 'High Noon' in its growth habit, but it is hardier and its leaves are glossier and more abundant. Through 'Captain Thomas'—which has another Thomas hybrid, 'Bloomfield Perfection', as one of its parents—it traces its heritage back to *R. wichuraiana*.

In spite of its AARS award, 'Golden Showers' did not receive exceptionally high marks in the "Proof of the Pudding" ratings. Correspondents from northern regions noted that it did not grow very tall, an indication that it is not really cold hardy in regions with severe winters, and many people complained that its flowers opened too quickly and faded too fast. Nevertheless, no other yellow climber has the ability to produce such a profuse display of richly colored flowers or such healthy foliage. These qualities, together with its AARS award, brought it instant success, and it is still popular today.

'GOLDEN SHOWERS' starts to bloom early in the season, before the hybrid teas, and continues to produce its spectacular large yellow flowers up until the first frost. These free-form blooms, which open from large, ovoid buds, are usually borne in clusters, and their eighteen to twenty wavy golden petals unfold quickly to expose the dark orange stamens. There is a pleasant tea rose fragrance. After the first impressive flush, many continuing laterals develop, and these often produce clusters of flowers at their tips. In the cooler weather of autumn, there will be a second luxuriant display. Because the flowers open so quickly, reaching their peak within a day, they are not good for cutting.

'Golden Showers' is a beautiful rose to plant in the background of a flower bed, at the corner of a fence, or against the wall of a house. The rich daffodil yellow of its flowers contrasts especially well with dark wood or stone. In the Cranford Rose Garden it grows at a corner of the latticework pavilion, reaching up eight feet to the roof and spreading out to about twelve feet. The canes, which are fairly pliable and not too prickly, are easy to train, which makes this an especially good choice for wrapping around a pillar.

'Golden Showers' is not a vigorous climber. During its first year it will develop four- to five-foot canes that often bear flowers at their tips. Each succeeding year, following the first flush of bloom, the same canes will send out one-foot, flower-bearing laterals. For the first few years after it is planted, the bush stays low and shrubby; then it shoots up to at least eight feet and develops a lovely, arching habit. After two

or three seasons, remove some of the old or crowded wood, leaving behind only the longest canes for training.

Even though 'Golden Showers' has attractive hips, deadhead the spent flowers throughout the season, for the production of hips slows down the repeat bloom. As you cut off the old blossoms, shorten the flower-bearing laterals back by two-thirds. At the end of the summer, stop deadheading so there will be a display of hips in the fall.

The dark, glossy foliage is generally disease resistant, though it is susceptible to black spot.

With its bright yellow flowers and its shiny foliage, 'Golden Showers' is a sleek-looking rose that makes a bold statement in a garden. There is nothing like it for brilliant color.

The brilliant yellow blossoms and glossy foliage of 'Golden Showers' stand out against the lattice pavilion at the Cranford Rose Garden.

'DON JUAN'

Malandrone; introduced by Jackson and Perkins, 1958
A 'New Dawn' seedling × 'New Yorker'
Plant Patent No. 1864

'DON JUAN' is a large-flowered climber developed by Michele Malandrone of Sessant d'Asti, Italy. In his patent application, Malandrone stated that his objective in creating this rose was to combine everblooming, hardy, and climbing habits with a flower size equivalent to that of hybrid teas. Although it is not exceptionally hardy, 'Don Juan' does have extremely large flowers that bloom all summer long.

The most striking characteristic of this climber is the deep red color of its flowers, one of the darkest reds known in roses. This is a modern "black rose," which has in its distant heritage the dark velvety red hybrid tea 'Château de Clos Vougeot', which was introduced in 1908 by the legendary French hybridizer, Joseph Pernet-Ducher. 'Don Juan's connection to 'Château de Clos Vougeot' is through its parent, 'New Yorker', a hybrid tea created by Eugene Boerner for Jackson and Perkins in 1947. Its other parent may have been the same 'New Dawn' seedling that Malandrone used to create his other well-known climber, 'Gladiator'.

'Don Juan' quickly became popular in this country, especially in the South. "Proof of the Pudding" correspondents gave it good marks for its everblooming, fragrant, long-stemmed, velvety red flowers—which are good for cutting—and for its excellent disease resistance. In spite of the fact that it is not particularly vigorous, at the time of its introduction it was thought to be the best red climber on the market because of its large, hybrid tea-like flowers, its excellent color, and its strong fragrance.

'DON JUAN' has pointed, hybrid tea-like buds that are such a dark velvety red they seem almost black. Upon opening, the four- to five-inch double flowers have the classic high-centered shape of a hybrid tea; as they age the flowers become cupped and nearly flat, reflexing a bit to expose slightly the yellow stamens. The thirty to thirty-five wavy, dark red petals sometimes have a hint of orange, and in cold weather their red deepens. The flowers have an outstanding old garden rose fragrance. They set large, brilliant orange urn-shaped hips.

'Don Juan' starts blooming at the end of May and continues its abundant display until winter. It is especially impressive in the fall. At first, most of the flowers are borne on single stems, although a few may be clustered. After the initial bloom period, the flowers are all clustered on short laterals or at the ends of long continuing laterals.

In the heat of the sun the outer petals may take on a scorched look, and the spent flowers, like those of most dark red roses, often look messy. This climber benefits from deadheading; cutting off the spent flowers keeps the bush neat and promotes good rebloom. The flower display is not as copious as on some other climbers, but in this case quality makes up for lack of quantity.

One of the so-called black roses, 'Don Juan' has long-stemmed, fragrant, dark red flowers that are excellent for arrangements.

185

'Don Juan' blooms the first season it is planted. At first it looks very much like a tall hybrid tea, but then it develops four- to five-foot canes; these bear more flowers throughout the season. Most of the repeat blooms occur just a few bud eyes (nodes) behind the previous flowers—a characteristic inherited from 'New Dawn'. You can simply snip off the spent flowers. But you will get larger flowers, more like those of hybrid teas, if after the first flush you cut the laterals back by two-thirds. This process should be continued throughout the season. Other longer canes will develop during the season, and these will also have terminal clusters of flowers.

The two or three main canes are covered with slightly curved prickles, but the laterals are smooth. All the growth is woody and stiff, and if the canes and laterals are not trained, they will grow straight up and eventually produce all the flowers at their tips. You can counter this by spreading them out horizontally. Before the young growth becomes too rigid to bend, fan it out on a fence or a wall, or wrap it around a tripod; this will force the canes to produce flowering laterals all along their length rather than blooming just at the tips.

'Don Juan' flowers more prolifically with each passing year. It is not a vigorous climber in northern regions, where it takes several seasons to reach its maximum size. In a friend's garden in Amagansett, Long Island, Stephen has planted several specimens along a white wall near a pool, attaching the canes with hooks to the wall. The display begins in early spring when the red-green foliage emerges. In late May the dark red flowers appear, and in this warm spot they put on a luxuriant show throughout the summer. Because 'Don Juan' is not a bushy plant, Stephen has filled in the base with an underplanting of 'White Simplicity', an everblooming floribunda.

The only major pruning 'Don Juan' requires is the removal of the oldest growth after the second or third season; this should be done in the winter when the plant is dormant. This rose grows so slowly that you will not have to do much with it for the first two years. In northern regions it has to be treated like a tall hybrid tea, for it dies back to the ground each winter.

'Don Juan' is a good rose for a container, thriving and holding its flowers on even the windiest, hottest rooftop. The foliage is dark, reddish, glossy, and leathery. It is quite resistant to disease, although by the end of the summer it usually has some black spot. It is rarely affected by mildew.

With their long stems, the large blooms are good for bouquets if they are cut early, while they are not fully open. They look lovely combined with the flowers of 'New Dawn', which also should be cut while they are barely open.

Plant 'Don Juan' in a prominent spot where you can easily enjoy its wonderful fragrance, the velvety texture of its flowers, and its lovely red-green foliage.

'ALTISSIMO'

Delbard; introduced by Cuthbert, 1966
'Tenor' × unknown

THE LARGE-FLOWERED climber 'Altissimo' was produced by George Delbard of the firm of Delbard Chabert in Paris and originally distributed by the English firm of R. and G. Cuthbert. Delbard, who is well known as the creator of many of the long-stemmed hybrid teas found in expensive florists' shops, also has a number of successful climbers to his name; some of the best are 'Altissimo', 'Parure d'Or', and 'Messire Delbard'.

The known parent of 'Altissimo' is 'Tenor', another Delbard climber, and one that he has used often in the creation of his new roses. 'Tenor', which is no longer in commerce, has clustered, semidouble, velvety red blooms. 'Altissimo' inherited the red color but not the semidouble flowers; its blooms are single, which made it an unusual introduction at a time when large, full roses with many petals were all the rage. Based on its performance in various trial gardens, 'Altissimo' won a Certificate of Merit from Great Britain's Royal National Rose Society in 1965, but when it was introduced in 1966, it did not become very popular, for climbers with double flowers were more in demand. Today, however, gardeners once again appreciate the simplicity of roses with single flowers, and this beautiful climber is increasingly seen in rose shows, where it often wins ribbons. Visitors to the Cranford Rose Garden are always impressed with it.

'ALTISSIMO' is an old-fashioned-looking rose with magnificent, single, blood red flowers that may be as large as five inches in diameter. The slightly cupped blooms usually have five petals, but sometimes there are seven. The petals, which look as if they had been cut from velvet cloth, surround a massive cluster of yellow pistils and unusual stamens formed of prominent yellow anthers on red filaments. These pistils and stamens remain on the plant even after the petals have fallen. The blossoms, which have a slight clove scent, hold on for a long time and are excellent as cut flowers. There are three-quarter-inch hips.

'Altissimo' is an extremely vigorous rose with a very upright growth habit. It can quickly become ten feet high and twelve feet wide. Left on its own it will produce all of its blooms out of sight at the tips of its long, stiff canes. It should be trained on a support that is broad as well as tall—a fence, wall, or double arch—so that its canes can be spread out in a wide fan shape and induced to produce flowers all along their length. The canes become stiff and inflexible, so train them early. This rose should not be grown on a low support, for that will necessitate the removal of much of its flowering wood to keep it attractive and under control.

During its first year 'Altissimo' produces clusters of flowers at the tips of all of its canes as well as on some shorter flower-bearing laterals. The second season's first flush of bloom, from late May to the end of June, will occur on new laterals from buds all along the first year's canes. Then, after this flush has passed, tall shoots emerge from the base and all along the main canes. All of these new shoots terminate in large clusters of flowers. Deadheading the first flowers as soon as they have faded will encourage new laterals and ensure that the plant will be covered with blooms on all of the old

and new growth throughout the season. This rose responds quickly to an annual hard pruning, which forces it to send out an abundance of new growth from the base.

The rather sparse leaves are large, dark, serrated, and extremely disease resistant. 'Altissimo' is also very hardy.

At the Huntington Botanical Garden in Pasadena, California, a splendid specimen of 'Altissimo' is trained against the white stucco wall of the tea room, the perfect spot to show off its blood red blooms.

George Delbard, the creator of many florists' roses, developed the long-stemmed beauty 'Altissimo' for the garden. The single-petalled blooms have a subtle clove fragrance.

'CADENZA'

Armstrong; introduced by the Armstrong Nursery, 1967
'New Dawn' × *'Climbing Embers'*
Plant Patent No. 2915

'CADENZA', a large-flowered climber created by David L. Armstrong, is a wonderful rose with impressive parents. 'Climbing Embers' is a sport of a scarlet floribunda, 'Embers', which has many important roses in its heritage, including two hardy species roses (*R. roxburghii* and *R. foetida*) and two Kordes roses from the 1930s ('Baby Château' and 'Eva') that were widely used in the development of subsequent fragrant, scarlet red roses. By crossing 'Climbing Embers' with 'New Dawn', Armstrong produced a vigorous and disease-resistant rose that is one of the showiest red climbers ever created.

'Cadenza' received excellent reviews in the "Proof of the Pudding" ratings, where correspondents praised it for the color, quality, and fragrance of its flowers, as well as for its disease resistance. In cold northern climates it lacked vigor and hardiness, but in the rest of the country it was considered a vigorous, nonstop bloomer. It is a great favorite with visitors to the Cranford Rose Garden, where it blooms continuously all summer long. Inexplicably, 'Cadenza', one of the best climbers of the century, went out of commerce. Fortunately, it is now being brought back by a few nurseries.

IN JUNE, when it is in full bloom, 'Cadenza' bears thousands of flowers of the deepest crimson red. The flat-topped buds, in clusters of three to thirty, open to cup-shaped flowers that are sometimes balled in the center. Usually, however, the wavy petals unfurl completely to expose the yellow stamens and pistils. If the weather is not too hot, the blooms remain crisp and fresh looking for two to three weeks, turning a dark (almost black) red as they age. There are sporadic repeat blooms throughout the summer and a respectable display when the weather turns cooler in the fall. The flowers, which have a strong, sweet fragrance, set large orange hips.

'Cadenza' bears flowers on all of its growth the first year it is planted. The June blooms occur mainly on strong laterals about four to six inches long. During the rest of the season, right up until the first hard frost, the flowers are borne at the ends of thick, stiff continuing laterals, some as long as eight feet, that spring from all of the older wood. Shoots that occasionally develop from the base also bear large clusters of flowers.

As with 'New Dawn', for the fastest repeat bloom, simply deadhead back to the first bud behind the faded cluster. From this bud more flowers will emerge.

Most of the new growth occurs from the middle of the plant rather than from the base or the upper parts, and there is rarely a need to thin out basal growth. After a few years, however, it will be necessary to remove some of the older wood from the upper parts of the bush to make room for the new, young canes. Do this only when the growth becomes crowded. The old canes become very woody and hard to manage.

This climber has stiff canes that are easier to

'Cadenza' is the most popular red climber in the Cranford Rose Garden. This specimen has been growing around a window in the pavilion since 1967.

train on a wall or a fence than on an arch. It is so beautiful when the canes are curved that it is worth the trouble to shape them this way. In the Cranford Rose Garden the canes of one specimen are coiled around an oval window in the white latticework pavilion, where they spread out and create a stunning red frame. The same plant also reaches up twelve feet to the roof of the pavilion. It requires very little thinning, for the wide pavilion provides room for all of the canes.

Another specimen of 'Cadenza'' climbs a section of the white lattice fence that surrounds the Cranford Rose Garden. It forms a wonderful backdrop for other roses, although visitors miss its fragrance because it is out of reach. A third bush of 'Cadenza' covers one of the double arches spanning the walkway in the garden. In June this plant produces a fantastic shower of fragrant blooms, but as the season progresses it causes problems, for the long shoots that de-velop impede the passageway unless they are severely pruned. In addition, it is difficult to keep the rampant growth in line with the curve of the arch without removing valuable flower-producing wood. This arch is popular with robins and mockingbirds, for 'Cadenza's dense foliage and numerous deadly prickles make it a safe nesting spot.

'Cadenza' is a slow grower in the summer, but in cool weather it takes off and grows more than fifteen feet high and twelve feet wide. It blooms continuously, slacking off only during periods of heat and drought. The leathery foliage is dark, glossy, and very disease resistant until the fall, when it becomes susceptible to black spot.

This is a truly wonderful climber that will surely become popular again as soon as more nurseries stock it. Until then, if you have an old specimen of 'Cadenza', cherish it, for it is hard to find.

'COUNTRY DANCER'

Buck; introduced by Iowa State University, 1973
'Prairie Princess' × 'Johannes Boettner'

'COUNTRY DANCER' is a shrub developed by Griffith Buck at Iowa State University, where the main objective of his rose-breeding program was the creation of extremely hardy varieties that can withstand the harsh Iowa winters and yet retain all of the desirable qualities of the best garden roses. With 'Country Dancer', Buck achieved this goal.

One of the parents of 'Country Dancer' was 'Prairie Princess', a Buck shrub rose that has in its heritage two very hardy species roses—*R. laxa*, which is native to Siberia, and *R. spinosissima*—as well as 'New Dawn' and 'Inspiration'. The other parent, 'Johannes Boettner', is an early Kordes floribunda.

Buck had high standards for his roses, releasing to the public only those that combined winter hardiness with beauty and fragrance. 'Country Dancer' fulfills this requirement.

Buck considered 'Country Dancer' a floribunda, but it is officially classified as a shrub rose. In some climates it can be treated as a pillar rose.

'COUNTRY DANCER', one of Buck's most informal-looking roses, has high-centered buds, like those of hybrid teas, that open to large, flat, double pink flowers with a strong tea fragrance. These blooms appear to have a yellow center because the anthers and filaments are exposed and the petals are slightly yellow at the base.

This rose blooms in its first year. The initial flowers, which appear at the peak of the hybrid tea season, are borne in clusters on stiff laterals about a foot long. After that, laterals and basal shoots as long as six feet develop; these produce clusters of flowers throughout the season. In the fall, there is a second strong flush of bloom.

Because 'Country Dancer' is often described as a spreading shrub rose, Stephen didn't expect it to be especially vigorous, but after two years in the Cranford Rose Garden, its canes shot up to six feet with no sign of winter kill. After he wrapped the canes around a pillar, they developed long continuing laterals, which extended their length to nearly nine feet. Getting this rose around a pillar was not an easy task, however, for the mature canes are very thick and upright. It is easier to spread them out on a fence; this horizontal training will produce a spectacular display of flowers. No matter what you do with 'Country Dancer', do not train its canes straight up, or they will produce all their flowers at their tips.

This rose requires minimal pruning; after the first flush of flowers has faded, just shorten the laterals that produced the blooms by two-thirds. It is not necessary to deadhead; even though hips develop, the new canes constantly produce more flowers, a trait common in Buck's roses. After several seasons, during the dormant period or immediately after the first bloom period, remove one-third of the canes entirely and cut the rest of them back by at least one-third. This pruning will rejuvenate the plant and encourage it to produce vigorous shoots from the base.

'Country Dancer' has dark, dull leaves that are susceptible to blackspot. Like all Buck roses, it is extremely hardy.

This lovely shrub is one of the many versatile and carefree introductions by a hybridizer who devoted his life to the creation of roses that will survive even in regions with the coldest winters.

COUNTRY DANCER

'JEANNE LAJOIE'

Sima; introduced by Williams, Mini Roses, 1975
('Casa Blanca' × 'Independence') × 'Midget'

'JEANNE LAJOIE' is a climbing miniature raised by Ed Sima of Seattle, Washington. It was introduced by Ernest Williams, who until his recent retirement was the owner of Mini Roses in Denton, Texas. The parents of this rose were 'Casa Blanca', a large-flowered climber; 'Independence', a floribunda; and 'Midget', one of the early miniatures.

Soon after 'Jeanne Lajoie' was introduced, "Proof of the Pudding" correspondents praised it as a vigorous, disease-resistant climber with miniature flowers shaped like those of hybrid teas. At first there were complaints that the blooms were sparse, but this criticism was premature; once 'Jeanne Lajoie' is established, it puts on an incredible display. By 1979 it was rated the best climbing mini in the Midwest.

This miniature is a favorite in rose shows. At one exhibit the judges nearly disqualified it because Jeanne Lajoie was given on the entry card as both the name of the entrant and the name of the rose. As it turned out, the junior exhibitor had not filled out the entry blank incorrectly; she was actually the little girl for whom the rose was named. (Jeanne Lajoie is now twenty-seven years old and an occupational therapist in Texas.)

ALTHOUGH 'Jeanne Lajoie' is such a vigorous climber that it can reach the second story of a house or cover a fence twelve feet long, its small (one-inch) flowers and leaves show that it is a miniature. The deep pink flowers, borne singly or more frequently in clusters, open from long, pointed exhibition-form buds. The twenty to twenty-five pointed petals have a tendency to ball, but otherwise they open wide to disclose the stamens and pistils, and they fade as they age. There is a light tea fragrance. This rose blooms most profusely in cool weather, but it puts on a respectable display throughout the summer. In the fall it sets shiny, orange, quarter-inch hips.

'Jeanne Lajoie' may send up canes as long as twelve feet. Unlike 'Red Cascade', which has a prostrate habit, this climber is upright, with a natural tendency to arch over after it reaches five or six feet. The canes are fairly pliable, good for training on a low fence, a stone wall, or even a short pillar. In the Cranford Rose Garden it grows along a low fence in partial shade.

After the first few seasons, 'Jeanne Lajoie' becomes a prolific bloomer. The first flush consists of a multitude of flowers on short laterals; then many long continuing laterals develop, all producing flowers at their tips. The continuing laterals and the basal growth should all be trained horizontally as soon as they appear to encourage the production of even more flower-bearing laterals. Deadheading after the first flush also promotes rebloom; shorten the laterals by two-thirds. The only other pruning necessary is the thinning out of old or undesirable wood during the dormant season. Jeanne Lajoie's father, Dave, who has four of these roses

'Country Dancer' was introduced in 1973 by Griffith Buck, whose main hybridizing objective was to breed beautiful roses hardy enough to withstand Iowa winters. Unfortunately, most of his fine hybrids are overshadowed by the new, less hardy, shrub roses from Europe.

in his garden in Texas, reports that he often cuts them down to the ground so that they will send out new ten-foot canes for horizontal training.

This is a very hardy climber with small, dark, distinctively glossy leaves that have better-than-average disease resistance.

'Jeanne Lajoie' is an aggressive climber. We have seen a large specimen on a lattice covering the entire side of a house in Boston with thousands of pink blooms. It is one of the best upright climbing miniature roses on the market today.

'Jeanne Lajoie' is a beautiful miniature climber that produces clusters of tiny pink blooms all season long.

'RED FOUNTAIN'

Williams; introduced by Conard-Pyle, 1975
'Don Juan' × 'Blaze'
Plant Patent No. 3615

'RED FOUNTAIN' is a large-flowered climber developed by Ben Williams of J. B. Williams and Associates in Silver Spring, Maryland. Williams, who has been breeding roses for more than twenty years, has produced successful varieties in many classes and has won numerous awards in this country and abroad. His floribunda 'Rose Parade' was an AARS winner in 1975. One of his latest creations is the grandiflora 'Elizabeth Scholtz', named for the director emerita of the Brooklyn Botanic Garden.

Williams considers 'Red Fountain' the perfect cross, for it combines the best qualities of both of its famous parents—clustered flowers, derived from 'Blaze', and a deep, velvety red color inherited from 'Don Juan'. This rose was generally well received by the "Proof of the Pudding" correspondents, who agreed that it was more likely to produce flowers in clusters rather than singly and that its red color held up well. One commentator remarked that left to grow without support, it arched over and actually looked just like a red fountain.

A BUSH OF 'Red Fountain' in full bloom is covered with hundreds of clusters of vibrant, velvety red flowers. These blooms, which average about two inches in diameter, have buds that look like those of hybrid teas, but when open they take on a cupped shape. The fragrance is reminiscent of 'Don Juan.' This rose flowers continuously all season long, right up until a hard frost; hips decorate the bush at the same time as the flowers.

'Red Fountain' is a versatile rose that can be used in a variety of ways. It is often grown as a free-standing shrub or as a hedge. Williams recommends it especially for mass plantings, screens, and barriers. It is also easy to train on pillars, lattices, arches, walls, and fences. At the Hershey Gardens in Pennsylvania, chains draped with this rose surround the central pond.

The care and pruning of 'Red Fountain' is virtually the same as for its parents, 'Don Juan' and 'Blaze'. Deadheading promotes good rebloom, but it is not necessary. 'Red Fountain' is a very hardy rose that has glossy foliage and excellent disease resistance. With its profuse, intensely red flowers, it is a rose that will brighten any setting.

Ben Williams, the hybridizer of 'Red Fountain', considers this high-centered red climber an "improved" 'Don Juan'.

'RED CASCADE'

Moore, Sequoia Nursery, 1976
(R. wichuraiana × *'Floradora'*) × *'Magic Dragon'*

'RED CASCADE' is a climbing miniature by Ralph S. Moore, a pioneer in the development of miniature roses.

The first successfully marketed miniature, 'Peon', was produced in Holland in the 1930s, when Jan de Vink crossed 'Rouletii', a "found" miniature of obscure origins, with 'Gloria Mundi', a polyantha. In 1936 the Conard-Pyle Company introduced 'Peon' into the United States as 'Tom Thumb', the first patented miniature in this country. Moore, who is often called "Mr. Miniature," started working with this type of rose in 1940, crossing 'Tom Thumb' with a rambler, 'Carolyn Dean', to create 'Zee', a climbing mini. Since then he has created hundreds of miniature roses. He also breeds large-flowered shrub roses.

'Red Cascade' opened up new possibilities in miniatures, for it was the first rose of this type that could be used effectively as a decorative climber and a groundcover. Moore saw its potential, and he subsequently brought out many similar varieties, including 'Red Button', 'Pink Cascade', and 'Orange Cascade'. In 1984 he introduced 'Sweet Chariot', a wonderful miniature that is often sold as a climber but is actually more beautiful cascading in a hanging basket or container.

To breed 'Red Cascade', Moore used R. wichuraiana for climbing vigor and disease resistance; 'Floradora', a Tantau floribunda that has in its background 'Baby Chateau' (the Kordes floribunda that has influenced many important red climbing roses); and 'Magic Dragon', another Moore climbing miniature with R. wichuraiana in its heritage.

'RED CASCADE' has ovoid buds that open to flat, brilliant red flowers about one and a quarter inches across. The blooms may have as many as fifty petals, each with a small amount of white at the base. These nearly quartered flowers, which have practically no fragrance, are borne on single stems or in clusters of as many as a dozen at the ends of long, stiff laterals. They hold their form and strong red color for a long time and fall before becoming messy. They do not set hips. Once established in the garden, 'Red Cascade' produces a massive show of blossoms all season long.

In spite of the fact that this rose will grow in a plot of ground as small as six inches square, its canes can reach up to twenty feet in warm climates and from two to ten feet in colder areas. Its growth habit is very much like that of R. wichuraiana, which is why it is such a wonderful groundcover. There is a beautiful planting of this rose at the headquarters of the American Rose Society in Shreveport, Louisiana, where bushes completely cover a bank about three feet high and thirty-five feet long.

A prostrate and vigorous climber, 'Red Cascade' can be trained like any other rambler: wrapped around a pillar, tied to a trellis or lattice, or spread out along a fence. Grafted onto another rose, such as 'Dr. Huey', it makes a

At the headquarters of the American Rose Society in Shreveport, Louisiana, bushes of the climbing miniature 'Red Cascade' cover a thirty-five-foot-long bank.

beautiful weeping standard. Some people plant 'Red Cascade' in containers or hanging baskets, but we consider it too aggressive for this. If you are daunted by its prickles, let it grow on its own, spilling free form over a bank or a wall.

During the first year the first blooms occur on buds at the ends of long canes. The following season a luxuriant first flush is produced on short laterals all along the canes that were established the year before. Throughout each successive growing season, new laterals of varying lengths spring from the base and from the older wood; every bit of this new growth produces clusters of flowers.

Unsupported, a bush of 'Red Cascade' mounds up in the center and becomes a dense mass about three feet high. After a few years the plant becomes crowded, and it is necessary to remove some of the older wood. Other than this, 'Red Cascade' requires little pruning.

In locations with poor air circulation, the long, pointed, dark, glossy leaves of this mini are somewhat susceptible to black spot; occasional thinning keeps this under control.

'Red Cascade' is so beautiful it deserves a prime spot in the garden. It is also a great climber to grow where other roses will not survive—on a site with poor or shallow soil, for example. In the Cranford Rose Garden it is planted over the roots of a dead elm tree, where it thrives in partial shade in soil that is only a few inches deep. It covers the tree stump with a glorious array of bright red flowers from early summer through fall.

'JOHN CABOT'

Svejda; introduced by Agriculture Canada, 1978
R. *kordesii* × *a hardy seedling*

THE CANADIAN DEPARTMENT of Agriculture has been involved for many years in a program to develop roses and other ornamental plants that combine beautiful flowers, disease resistance, and the ability to survive in extremely cold climates. The breeding program is divided between two locations: the Central Experimental Farm at Ottawa (for eastern Canada) and the Morden, Manitoba, Research Station (for western Canada). Many wonderful new shrub roses have been introduced through these programs; among them is 'John Cabot', which is part of a group created at the Ottawa station and called the Explorer series (these roses are named for famous early explorers of Canada).

From 1961 to 1986 the director of the breeding program in Ottawa was Dr. Felicitas Svejda, who produced many hardy shrub roses using R. *kordesii* and R. *rugosa*. 'John Cabot', the first hybrid she released, was a cross between R. *kordesii* and an unspecified hardy seedling. Like some of the other shrubs in the Explorer series, 'John Cabot' is a shrub rose that can be used as a climber. It proved to be the first truly hardy repeat-blooming rose of this type that could survive winters as far north as southern Canada without being taken down from its support and covered.

Dr. Svejda, who is now retired, might be called the "Canadian Dr. Van Fleet," for she has been a pioneer in the creation of roses that are beautiful as well as exceptionally hardy. When Stephen visited her trial fields in Ottawa in 1985, he saw row upon row of glorious shrub roses bred to thrive with little care. Her work is an inspiration for all hybridizers who are attempting to develop hardy, carefree shrub roses. 'John Cabot' won a Certificate of Excellence from the Royal National Rose Society of Great Britain.

'JOHN CABOT' is a shrub that bears large clusters of double, cherry red flowers at the peak of the hybrid tea season. It continues its display for about six weeks and then repeats sporadically in August and September. The individual blooms, two and a half inches in diameter, have thirty to thirty-five wavy, loosely arranged petals that open quickly to a wide, cupped shape, exposing the yellow stamens and pistils. The innermost petals of these virtually scentless flowers have a distinctive white vertical stripe.

This extremely vigorous rose can be left as a shrub or trained on a high fence or wall. A splendid specimen at the headquarters of the American Rose Society in Shreveport, Louisiana, spreads out along a fence. It takes at least four seasons for 'John Cabot' to develop a climbing habit, but after that it easily covers an area twelve feet square. If it is not supported, it needs a lot of room to spread out. In the Cranford Rose Garden 'John Cabot' is so vigorous that one part of the bush has grown to the top of the latticework fence and doubled back down into the bed below, while the rest of the plant has climbed up onto an arch with 'Cadenza'.

'John Cabot' has such an upright growth habit that it will grow very tall even without support. To help it display its lovely, arching habit, during the winter remove much of the older shrubby growth from the center of the bush; this leaves room for the long-growing

canes to develop. As most of the climbing ability results from the very long continuing laterals that develop from the older canes, be careful not to cut out the wood that bears these laterals.

The blooms repeat on laterals that form immediately behind the spent flowers. Late in the season, flowers also appear at the ends of the long canes. Deadheading is not necessary, as the blooms do not become messy before they fall. The plant will put on its best second flush if it has plenty of water and sunlight.

'John Cabot', which has large, dark green, very disease-resistant foliage, seems to flourish in all climates. It is not yet well known in the United States, but it should become popular, for it is a marvelous rose that will thrive anywhere, even in the coldest regions of the country.

Other Canadian Explorer Roses to Use as Climbers
'William Baffin'
'John Davis'
'Henry Kelsey'

'John Cabot' is one of a group of new Canadian Explorer Roses developed for hardiness in extremely cold climates. This very vigorous climber is one of the best for training on a tall support. It can also be encouraged to scramble up into a tree.

'EDEN ROSE '88'

Meilland; introduced in France as 'Pierre de Ronsard', 1987
Introduced into the U.S. as 'Eden Rose '88' by Conard-Pyle, 1988
('Danse des Sylphes' × 'Haender') × 'Climbing Pink Wonder'

'EDEN ROSE '88' is a new climbing rose from the famous house of Meilland et Compagnie in Antibes, France.

The name 'Eden Rose '88' will no doubt cause bewilderment in the rose world for years to come. This rose was introduced in France in 1987 as 'Pierre de Ronsard', but it was brought out in this country by Conard-Pyle in 1988 as 'Eden'. Unfortunately, there were already two other Meilland roses with 'Eden' in the name: 'Eden Rose' (introduced by Conard-Pyle in 1953) and 'Climbing Eden Rose' (1962). When it was discovered that these two roses were still in commerce, the name for the new 'Eden' had to be changed. Since mail-order nurseries had already started a marketing campaign for 'Eden', and the public had become familiar with it, the name was altered just enough to guarantee that there will always be confusion surrounding this rose. Even now, 'Eden Rose '88' is being sold in nurseries and through catalogs simply as 'Eden'. Despite its problematic name, 'Eden Rose '88' is a wonderful rose that is probably the most unusual new climber on the market.

THIS ROSE is a climber that will delight gardeners who love old garden roses, for it resembles a climbing centifolia. The flowers, borne singly or in clusters, are at first globular and white. As they open, the outer petals take on a distinctive greenish cast, and they unfurl to reveal an elaborate shell pink center. Eventually the flowers become flat and quartered, and in the final stage, they are solid shell pink. These huge blooms, some as large as five inches in diameter, have a multitude of petals and a delicious fragrance reminiscent of teas and damasks. They nod even though they are on stiff laterals. 'Eden Rose '88' begins blooming at the same time as the hybrid teas and continues throughout the summer.

At first 'Eden Rose '88' looks like a shrub rose. It blooms in its first year, and after this initial, rather insignificant flush, it begins to take on a climbing form. There are numerous basal shoots, but most of the climbing growth consists of continuing laterals on the upper parts of the plant. This long growth will in about two years cover a fence eight feet high and twelve feet wide. In Atlanta, Georgia, we have seen several dozen of these roses planted together along a four-foot-high fence. They are so vigorous that after one season their excess growth has to be accommodated on arches attached to the fence. They put on a fantastic display of blooms.

The glossy, deep green foliage of 'Eden Rose '88' creates a dense backdrop for the pink blooms, which resemble those of the Meilland's famous hybrid tea 'Peace'. The leaves appear to have above-average disease resistance.

'Eden Rose '88' is a wonderful rose, probably the most unusual climber introduced in the past few years.

The glossy, dark green foliage of 'Eden Rose '88' makes a perfect backdrop for its flowers, which resemble those of old-fashioned cabbage roses.

3

How to Grow Climbing Roses

'Compassion', a wonderful new climber, produces a shower of apricot-pink blossoms. Here it grows with 'Eutin', 'Red Fountain', and 'Spectacular'.

With the exception of training and pruning, the rules for planting and caring for a climbing rose are exactly the same as for any other rose. Follow a few simple guidelines, and you will have a healthy plant with the best possible flowers and foliage.

SITE

This is the first consideration when planting a climber. These roses vary greatly in size and growth habit, so make sure your climber is suitable for the place you have in mind. In a small garden, for example, 'New Dawn' will quickly crowd out all the other plants; 'Aloha' will look pathetic in front of a high lattice it will never be tall enough to scale. Do some homework on the characteristics of various climbers before buying one for your garden.

A climber, like any rose, should be planted in a well-ventilated spot that receives four to six hours of sun a day. Air circulation is especially important for climbers (particularly the early wichuraiana hybrids). In addition, be sure to position the rose where it will not have to compete with trees and other shrubs for nutrients and water.

BUYING YOUR ROSE

Nurseries sell roses in three grades: 1, 1½, and 2. Grade 1 roses, which have at least three canes, are the highest quality. Grades 1½ and 2 have fewer canes and are less expensive. Conventional wisdom says that you should not try to economize by buying a "bargain" rose be-

cause it will probably not develop into a superior plant. Nevertheless, an inexpensive rose from a nursery, or one that has been relegated to the discount bin at a supermarket or chain store, may, with nurturing, grow into a glorious specimen.

You may buy your climber through a mail-order catalog or from a local nursery. Feel free to send away to a mail-order house in a state with a climate different from yours; just be sure to pick a rose suitable for your climate. The rose will be sent in either fall or spring at the right time for planting in your location. It will be a dormant, two-year-old, field-grown plant with its bare roots wrapped in damp material such as sphagnum moss. Open the package immediately to check that you have received the grade you ordered. The root system should be well developed, and the canes should be green and healthy, not shriveled or black.

Plant the climber as soon as you receive it. If you cannot get it into a permanent home right away, heel it into the garden (that is, plant it in a temporary spot) or a compost pile. You can also lay the rose on its side in a trench and cover it with soil. If necessary, it can be kept through the winter this way, provided it is completely covered. You may also store the new rose in a cool place for a few days, leaving it in the damp protective packing material. If you plant the rose in autumn, be sure to get it into the ground at least a month before the soil freezes so it will have time to get established. Many gardeners prefer to plant roses in the fall; this way the roots have a head start on the new leaves and canes that will appear in the spring.

You may want to buy your climber from a

local nursery, in which case it will be in a container. Local nurseries buy bare-root roses wholesale, plant them in pots, and grow them in Quonset huts so they will have leaves and flowers in early spring when they are put on display. Sometimes a visit to a nursery is the best way to choose a rose; the selection may be limited, but you will be able to see what you are getting. The photographs in catalogs put out by large mail-order houses can be misleading. Local nurseries affiliated with the American Rose Society or the Heritage Rose Foundation often have interesting selections of container-grown roses.

PREPARING THE SOIL

Climbers will grow almost anywhere and in just about any type of soil, but they will be healthiest and produce the best flowers in soil that is rich in organic material, well drained, and properly aerated. A good soil mix consists of sixty percent topsoil (a combination of topsoil, compost, and other organic materials), thirty percent sharp sand, and ten percent horticultural peat.

The most difficult site is one near the wall of a house, for this requires digging near a foundation, a place where there will be more cement and other debris than real soil. This is generally not an ideal spot for a rose because, not only will the soil be poor, but the overhanging eaves of the house will also prevent the plant from getting much-needed rainwater. Nevertheless, you can grow a climber successfully next to a house if you remove at least two or two-and-a-

half feet of the compacted earth and replace it with rich, well-drained soil.

If you are planting a hedge of roses in a field, you will also have to do extensive soil preparation, removing the grass sod and earth down to a depth of one-and-a-half to two feet. Break up the sod and throw it into the bottom of the hole before you set the plants in place.

Before planting your rose, test the soil. You can either do this yourself with a soil-testing kit or send a sample to your state agricultural extension service. The soil to be tested should be taken at the depth where most of the roots of the rose will be: six to twelve inches below the surface.

Soil is graded according to its acidity or alkalinity on the pH scale of 0 to 14. Zero is completely acidic, 14 completely alkaline, and 7 neutral. Roses do best in soil that is slightly acidic, with a pH of about 5.6 to 6.6. If your soil is too acidic, add pulverized limestone. If it is too alkaline, add sulfur. (The rates of application will depend on the results of your soil test.) Then enrich it with compost, well-rotted cow or horse manure, leaf mold, or other organic material.

DIGGING THE HOLE

Dig a hole in which the roots can spread out, about two feet deep and a foot and a half wide; shape it to suit the configuration of the roots, which may not be symmetrical. In a field or other previously uncultivated area, you may find clay. If so, dig down another foot, add a loose layer of stones (or similar drainage material) at the bottom of the hole, and cover the stones with sod to bring the hole back up to the proper planting depth.

Once the hole is prepared, throw in a spadeful of rotted manure mixed with a spadeful of composted leaves. You may also put a medium-sized fish head at the bottom of the hole; this will provide nutrients. Cover the fish head with at least an inch of soil so the roots will not come into direct contact with it.

PLANTING THE CLIMBER

Try to plant on a calm day that is misty or overcast so the exposed rose will not be dried out by wind or sun. Before planting, soak the entire plant in a pail of muddy water or diluted manure tea (one part rotted manure to eight parts water) for four to twenty-four hours.

When you are ready to put the rose in the ground, remove it from the water and inspect it carefully for broken or flimsy canes and roots; either remove these altogether or cut them back to healthy, firm tissue. Also cut off any canes that are black (which means they are dead) or thinner than a pencil. Then prune the rest of the canes, cutting each one back by one-third to a healthy, outward-facing bud that is swelling and green. Make the cut at a forty-five-degree angle about one-quarter inch above the bud. This pruning, which will induce vigorous new growth, should be done at planting time in warm climates. In northern regions, if you plant the rose in the fall, postpone this pruning until early spring, just before the plant starts to send out new growth. A container-grown rose, which will already have leaves, should not be pruned at planting time except for the removal of damaged canes.

Combine soil, compost, and rotted manure and use this mixture to make a high mound at the bottom of the hole. Place the rose in the hole, spreading the roots down over the mound. If your rose is grafted on to an understock—as most field-grown roses, except miniatures, are today—the bud union (the bulge at the base of the stem where the rose is grafted to the understock) will determine the planting depth. In a northern climate, position the bud union two or three inches below ground level so it will not be heaved up to the surface when the soil freezes and thaws during the winter. In warmer areas, the bud union can be placed at ground level or a little above, which makes it easy to see suckers that need to be removed. Make sure the roots are not turned up, bent in, or constricted in any way.

Hold the rose firmly in place while you fill in around the roots with a mixture of soil, compost, and rotted manure. Fill the hole half way, then add water. Wait until the soil settles, and then fill the hole to the top again with more of the soil mixture. Mound the soil up around the base of the rose to protect the bud union from the heat of the sun and fluctuations in the weather until the plant is well established. With the remaining soil make a "bowl" around the plant; this will hold the water so that it penetrates the soil rather than flowing away from the plant.

Container-grown roses, which may be in plastic, peat, or cardboard pots, can be planted at any time during spring, summer, or fall so long as the soil is workable. The hole you dig should be the same size as the container. These roses usually have leaves and flowers, so handle them gently. Take the rose out of the pot without disturbing the soil around the roots or letting any of it fall away as you set the plant into the hole. If the container is biodegradable, just score the sides and cut off the bottom; the rest will disintegrate in the ground. Because their roots are usually cramped after weeks or months of confinement, container-grown roses may take longer to establish themselves than bare-root roses.

In the spring, to induce the best possible foliage and flower production, give the new rose regular doses of manure tea (one part rotted manure to five parts water) or fish emulsion (one ounce per gallon of water). Apply chemical fertilizers only after the first flush of bloom has faded, or in midsummer after the rose has put out substantial growth.

When planting a climber that will be trained on a pillar, post, or tripod, set the support in the hole along with the rose so that you will not have to disturb the roots later. Tilt the plant toward the support to direct its growth in that direction.

If several climbers are going to be planted together, the amount of space to leave between them depends on how they are going to be trained. Pillar roses, and roses along fences and walls, should be spaced at least six feet apart. For a dense hedge, three to four feet is sufficient.

Your rose will probably have an identification tag tied around one of its canes. Be sure to remove this when you plant it, otherwise, as the stem grows and expands, the wire holding the tag will cut into the wood. Make another label to stick in the ground next to the rose.

Climbing roses can thrive in planters and other large containers. Each rose should have a container about two feet in diameter and two-and-a-half feet deep. To keep a large tub or barrel as light as possible, use a soilless planting mix. The rules for planting are the same as for roses planted in the ground. When growing a rose in a container, be vigilant about water and fertilizer. The plant must be watered frequently, for wind and sun will dry out the earth, but the constant watering will cause nutrients to leach out of the soil. In addition, check every year to make sure the rose is not root bound. If, after a few years, the plant becomes root bound, move it to a larger container, or prune the roots during the plant's dormant period.

FERTILIZERS

Climbers can benefit from regular applications of fertilizer, but it is important to test the soil before adding nutrients. Also, find out from your local rose society or extension agent whether the soil in your area has any peculiarities you should know about.

Fertilizers are available with differing percentages of nitrogen, phosphorus, and potassium. Once the rose is established in its site, use a 10–6–4 mixture. This provides nitrogen (for healthy, lush foliage), phosphorous (for good root development), and potassium (for the overall health of the plant). Phosphorous is especially important at the beginning of the growing season, when the rose starts sending out new shoots and leaves, and also in the fall to stimulate root development and help the plant "harden off" before it goes into the cold months.

Slow-release fertilizers containing nitrogen, phosphorus, and potassium in even ratios such as 20–20–20 are best for roses grown in containers.

Trace elements—boron, chlorine, copper, iron, manganese, molybdenum, and zinc—are important. Many foliar fertilizers, which are applied in spray form, contain these; test the soil, however, to make sure there is a shortage of these elements before applying them. Too much can be detrimental to the rose.

Epsom salt, which contains magnesium, helps a rose grow strong canes and well-developed roots. Work two tablespoons of the Epsom salt into the soil as soon as the rose shows the first buds in the spring and again after the first flush of bloom.

Banana skins are a natural source of potassium and phosphorous; you can chop up two of these and work them into the ground around a rose every other month. One medium-sized fish per bush will also supply a fairly well-balanced natural fertilizer.

In the Cranford Rose Garden granular fertilizer is applied at the end of winter, before the bushes have budded out; in early July, after the first bloom period; and again in August. In warmer climates where the plants do not go through a dormant period, fertilizing should be done after each flush of flowers. Work a handful of the fertilizer into the soil around the bush, being careful not to get it on the canes or the leaves. Then water well. Many people like to spray the leaves with liquid seaweed, fish emulsion, or liquid fertilizer. This can be applied every two weeks during the growing season, combined with any liquid pesticides you are using.

WATERING

Adequate water is essential to the health of your climbing rose, especially during its first season while the roots are getting established. Do not rely on rainfall alone. Whether you have a sprinkler, a drip system, or a simple garden hose, make sure the rose gets at least one inch of water every week throughout the growing season. The water must penetrate the soil to the bottom of the root system; water that filters down just an inch or two does more harm than good, for the roots will develop only at the surface.

There is an old adage that warns against getting water on the leaves of roses. Actually, wetting the leaves early in the day does no harm as long as they have time to dry off before evening. Wet foliage in the evening, however, will encourage mildew and black spot.

MULCHING

Early in the season, work the soil around the rose lightly with a cultivator, being careful not to injure any shallow roots. This raking will create a top layer of dry soil to aerate the soil and act as a mulch. During the summer, you can apply shredded oak leaves, shredded cedar, licorice root, wood chips, or any bulky mulch that will break down in the soil. Irrigate the earth well before applying any of these mulches.

Avoid using buckwheat hulls as mulch; these are so slow to disintegrate that they tend to compact the soil.

WINTER PROTECTION

In cold regions where roses have a dormant period, a well-cared-for climber that is healthy at the end of the summer has a much better chance of surviving the winter than one that is weak or unhealthy. About a month before the first hard frost, stop deadheading and fertilizing; this will discourage the rose from sending out new growth that will only be killed in the cold weather. Protect a newly planted climber by mounding up around the base six to eight inches of soil mixed with coarse, dry, non-compacting organic material such as shredded oak leaves, wood chips, pine needles, or salt hay. You may want to top this with an additional light covering of evergreen branches; this will protect the base of the plant and give the rose a head start on spring growth.

In the North, the more tender climbers—such as Noisettes, climbing teas, and hybrid sempervirens—need extra protection. They may be wrapped in sheets of Styrofoam or sheltered with large rose cones. Where winter temperatures are likely to fall below ten degrees Fahrenheit, these varieties should be buried in the ground. To protect a climber in this manner, release its canes from the support, tie them together, bury them in a trench, and completely cover them with mulch.

In the spring, remove the rose from its covering after all danger of freezing temperatures is past. The air inside the protective material will be warmer than the air outside, so do not wait too long to remove the cover or the rose will start to put out new growth that will be too weak to withstand spring cold spells.

A weeping standard needs special care in winter. Shorten its canes, cover it completely with salt hay, encase the entire plant in burlap, and tie a rope around the burlap to hold it in place. A weeping standard can also be transferred to a pot and kept in a cool cellar or garage during the cold months. Just remember to water it.

A rose in a planter will overwinter successfully as long as there is plenty of soil between its roots and the edge of the container; this will act as insulation to keep the roots from freezing.

PESTS AND DISEASES

Climbing roses are much less affected by pests and diseases than other roses. Many varieties can thrive with no pest and disease control at all. Nevertheless, your rose will be healthier and produce better flowers if you take some precautions against potential problems and know what to do if they become serious.

The best defense against pests and diseases is to buy a strong, healthy rose; plant it in a spot with good air circulation and adequate sunlight; make sure it has rich, well-drained soil; and keep it well watered. Under these conditions your climber should fight off most diseases and insects on its own, without the use of pesticides. If you do need to use chemicals, seek advice from your local rose society, the local agricultural extension service, or the nearest public rose garden. Remember that insect and disease problems can never be completely eliminated. Don't be overly concerned about them unless they get out of hand.

Insects

Aphids (also called plant lice): These small, soft-bodied, sucking insects may be green, brown, yellow, pink, or black. Usually about an eighth of an inch long, they congregate on tender new shoots, leaves, and flower buds, drawing out the sap and leaving wizened growth behind. They thrive in cool weather. In the Northeast they are usually the first insect of the season to attack. Before resorting to insecticides, try to keep them under control by knocking them off the plant every morning with strong jets of water. Natural predators, such as ladybugs, may help, as well. There are also insecticidal soaps and lightweight horticultural oils (different from dormant oil sprays) that can be applied to the plant to control aphids.

Thrips: These are also tiny sucking insects. Thrips are brownish orange, winged, and even smaller and harder to see than aphids. They cause great damage to developing flower buds. You will know they are there when the buds fail to open or become disfigured with brownish streaks, spots, and bumps. Thrips also feed on leaves, causing them to become whitish and withered. Be sure to remove the parts of the rose that are infested. You may also want to apply foliar insecticide or a systemic poison that the plant will absorb through the soil. Thrips, which seem to be most common in warmer regions of the country and in greenhouses, are

especially evident on roses with yellow or other light-colored flowers.

Spider mites: These are almost infinitesimal red mites that suck the juices from flower buds and the undersides of leaves. They are most prevalent in hot, dry weather. The affected leaves will become yellow, dry, and dusty looking; if you turn them over, you will find the mites moving around in fine webs. You may be able to control this pest with daily jets of cold water. Spray the water early in the morning, covering the entire bush from the bottom up. If a population of mites increases to the point where the webs are obvious, you will probably have to resort to a miticide.

If you have a persistent mite problem or you want to take precautions against these pests, use the following method: Early in the season, just as the leaf buds are breaking, spray the plant with dormant oil to kill the eggs of the mites. Then, at midsummer—usually the time when mites are most troublesome—apply a lightweight horticultural oil.

Japanese beetles: These, the most familiar enemies of the rose, are a serious problem on bush roses, and they will also attack climbers. The Japanese beetle is a shiny, copper green beetle, roughly one-half inch long, that lays its eggs in the ground in midsummer. The grubs (larvae) hatch within twelve days, eat the roots of grass and then go down into the earth to hibernate over the winter. The following June they emerge and begin feasting on all types of plants. They are especially fond of the pollen and nectar of roses and will eat their way through the buds, making holes in all the petals. They also eat the foliage and can completely devour flowers. One way to control Japanese beetles is to treat the soil with a grub-killing insecticide during early spring and late summer. Perhaps the best way to get rid of them is to pick the beetles off the plant by hand and drop them into a pail of water. Many gardeners have had good luck with traps, but others have found that this simply attracts all the Japanese beetles for miles around. A new biological control, milky spore, has recently been developed. This bacterium, once applied, takes several years to build up in the soil; it kills the beetle grubs.

Borers: These larvae of various flying insects do their damage inside canes and twigs. They tunnel down the canes, which eventually turn brown, wilt, and die back. Prune the affected cane back to the area not yet attacked by the borer. Borers enter canes through wounds or pruning cuts, so seal the cut. Destroy the affected canes.

Diseases

One of the most important ways to prevent disease from spreading in the garden is to keep all knives, pruning shears, and other tools scrupulously clean. Dip any tools that have been in contact with infected plants in rubbing alcohol. Avoid crowding plants together, and always water in the morning so the leaves will be dry by nighttime. Throw all diseased cuttings into the trash, never the compost pile.

Black spot: This is probably the most serious rose disease, one every rose grower knows all too well. It is a fungus that infects the leaves of nearly all but the most disease-resistant roses in warm, humid weather. The first visible signs are small black spots on the leaves. Yellow rings form around these spots, and then the leaves turn completely yellow and drop off. Eventually the entire bush can become defoliated. Black spot may not immediately kill your climber, but it can weaken it so much that it may die during the winter. The disease is formed in spores, which are easily carried by water to other plants; this is one reason why rose bushes should not be planted too close together. Take precautions, such as watering early in the day and keeping the beds clean by raking up all dead rose leaves. At the first sign of black spot, remove the infected leaves and throw them into the trash. This is especially important during damp weather. There are fungicides to control black spot, but before you resort to them, try a solution of baking soda and water. To prepare one gallon of this mixture, combine one tablespoon of baking soda with a gallon of water and a few drops of a lightweight horticultural oil. To make twenty-five gallons, use one pound of baking soda, twenty-five gallons of water, and two ounces of oil. Apply this mixture to the foliage once or twice a week, beginning in early spring as soon as new growth appears. This baking soda treatment has worked well in the Cranford Rose Garden. If you must use fungicides, contact your local rose society or your agricultural extension agent for information; these authorities can also tell you about new experimental methods of control with anti-transpirants.

Powdery mildew: This is another all-too-familiar fungus disease, one especially prevalent when days are warm and humid and nights are cool. Plants that are crowded or shaded are most susceptible. Curled and distorted leaves are the first sign; later a layer of grayish white fungus coats leaves, leafstalks, flowers, stems, and buds, especially on new growth at the top of the plant. The disease will probably not kill the rose, but it will stunt the young canes and interfere with the development of the flowers. It spreads when conditions are cool and humid. Damp air, not water, is the culprit. Hosing down the plant early in the morning helps control this fungus by washing away the spores.

Modern climbers with glossy foliage, such as 'New Dawn' and its offspring, are less suscep-tible to powdery mildew than many other varieties.

GENERAL RULES FOR PRUNING

The following are general principles that apply to all climbers. Directions for pruning specific types of climbing roses will be found in the portraits of individual plants.

Regular pruning keeps a rose healthy and attractive. You may not realize it, but every time you deadhead or cut flowers for bouquets, you are pruning the bush. On repeat-blooming roses, this also helps promote new blooms. When deadheading, cutting flowers, or doing any other pruning on canes smaller than about a half inch in diameter, use sharp secateurs (scissor-action pruning shears with blades that cross). Avoid anvil-type pruners because they can crush the canes. For larger canes use long-

After the flowers of 'Chevy Chase' fade, all the canes that bore flowering laterals should be removed. The new, pliable canes originating from the base of the plant are then trained in a fan shape along a low fence, where they will produce a fantastic display of red blooms the following year. This simple training procedure applies to all ramblers.

When training any type of climber, tie the canes securely to the support with jute or some other soft, durable material. Good air circulation is essential, so avoid crowding the canes.

In late winter and early spring, the canes of climbers are carefully wrapped around the arches spanning the walkways of the Cranford Rose Garden. This training induces flowering laterals along the entire length of the canes.

handled pruners (loppers). Old climbers with very heavy wood may even require a saw. Keep all your tools sharp; dull pruners can tear the wood and open up the canes to insects and disease. Remember to wear long, heavy gloves and protective clothing.

Start pruning in late winter or early spring, just before the growing season starts. At this time of year, concentrate on removing dead and diseased canes; cut these out at the base of the plant. A healthy cane will have green bark and white pith; unhealthy wood will be brown or black. If there are canes that have died back during the winter or that have borers in them, cut them back to healthy tissue. Then thin out the center of the plant to promote good air cir-culation, cutting away canes that are weak, crowded, or crossing each other. Leave as many of the sound canes as possible, especially if you are training the climber to cover a wall or other large surface.

When and where to prune throughout the rest of the season will depend on the type of climber. The basic rule for making the cut is that it should be about one quarter inch above a healthy leaf bud. This bud should be one that is facing away from the center of the plant, in order to direct the new growth outward. Make the cut at a forty-five-degree angle, with the upper edge of the cut just above the bud. You may want to seal the cut with glue, wax, tree-wound compound, or even lipstick.

4

WAYS TO USE
CLIMBING ROSES

'Excelsa', which has clusters of cherry red flowers from mid-June to mid-July, decorates an arch in a park in Bourges, France.

There are an unlimited number of ways to use climbers in the garden and the landscape. However, the growth habits of these plants vary greatly. When buying a climbing rose, be sure to select one that will adapt to the type of training you have in mind.

There are a few basic points to remember about training climbers. First, use only the sturdiest, most durable materials. Wooden supports such as posts, pillars, and lattices should be made of hard wood; cedar, cypress, chestnut, locust, redwood, or hickory are best. Soft wood in contact with the ground is sure to rot after a few years, bringing down both the support and your carefully trained rose. Metal is even stronger than wood, and can be just as attractive. If you do use a wooden support, you can protect the parts below ground by inserting them into hollow metal pipes driven into the earth. No matter what kind of support you use, set it deeply and securely into the ground, or anchor the base in concrete.

Wire for fences, chains, and mesh should be extra heavy and galvanized so it will not rust. Stretch it tightly, or it will sag under the weight of the roses.

Do not weave canes in and out of narrow spaces; you will find them nearly impossible to remove when you have to take them down for the winter, prune them, or cut them out because they have died or become invasive. Tie the canes to the surface of the support instead.

Use soft, durable, long-lasting material such as raffia, cotton jute (soft twine), strips of leather, or even nylon stockings to tie the canes into place. Cross the tie behind the cane so that it, not the cane, is next to the support; this prevents chafing. In the rose garden at the Château de Bagatelle in Paris, thin, fresh-cut willow shoots about one foot long are used to fasten

Climbing roses can be trained on many types of supports. In a garden in Amagansett, New York, cedar posts create a rustic pergola and a series of pillars. In two years the structure will be completely covered with roses.

Ramblers can cover great expanses. Here 'Wedding Day' climbs up and over the roof of the library of the Royal National Rose Society at Chiswell Green, England.

climbers to their supports. While the laterals are still green, they can be tied just like heavy string, and as they dry they become permanent and blend in with the canes.

CLIMBERS AS SHRUBS

If some climbers are left on their own, they will become attractive shrubs or large bushes. They may take up a lot of space, but they require very little care; just prune out dead wood, cut away invasive canes, and shape them if necessary. Varieties with stiff stems will need no support; others can be helped to assume an attractive form if their canes are tied to a strong stake. Use a short post about three feet long that will be masked by the rose. Attach the canes to it at different levels; this will give the rose height. For an even more interesting effect, leave some of the canes free to follow their own natural habit.

Climbers in shrub form are useful for camouflaging tree stumps and wellheads, decorating the supports of mailboxes, or encompassing the bases of birdbaths and feeders to deter cats and wild animals. You can make an especially bold statement with these shrubs by grouping several of them together. In the Cranford Rose Garden 'Excelsa', 'Max Graf', and the Brownell large-flowered climber, 'Coral Creeper', grow on embankments and slopes; their very stiff, arching canes cover large areas. You can combine different varieties that have similar growth habits, but do not mix too many colors. Space the bushes about four feet apart.

Repeat-blooming climbers are wonderful for planting on the tops of walls. A decorative effect is most easily achieved with ramblers, which will send flowers spilling over the sides on their long, pliable canes. Climbers with stiff canes may need a little training in order to cascade.

CLIMBERS AS HEDGES

All types of climbers can be used as hedges. Such hedges can serve as screens, boundary barriers, enclosures for gardens, or substitutes for stone walls. Besides enlivening the landscape with their flowers, rose hedges provide cover for birds and wild animals.

The best climbers for hedging are those that have arching habits. If you use varieties that are not invasive, you can keep them at the desired height with minimal pruning. When planting a hedge around a small garden, use climbers that are not too tall or too expansive, and leave plenty of space between the hedge and the other plants in the garden.

To create a rose hedge, plant the bushes in a row, about four feet apart, closer if the varieties you are using are not vigorous. The strongest roses for hedge plantings are R. multiflora—whose canes will knit together to form an impenetrable barrier strong enough to contain livestock—and R. setigera. Unless you have a ranch or other large property that needs this kind of utilitarian hedge, concentrate on a display of modern everblooming large-flowered climbers. Many of these have such stiff canes that they will form upright hedges with no support at all. Other climbers—wichuraiana hybrids with pliable canes, for example—will need some type of framework, such as a series of iron or wooden posts connected by wires. Use posts that are only about five feet high so that they will be hidden. Space them about ten feet apart and drive them roughly two feet into the ground. Extend a wire, or a series of wires eighteen inches apart, between them. As the bushes grow tall, stretch the canes out and attach them to the wires with soft twine. For the most pleasing effect, use bushes of one variety or different varieties with similar growth habits.

Hedges of *R. multiflora* or *R. setigera* will eventually become overgrown and tangled; you can ruthlessly shear them back at midsummer, after they have bloomed. Other shrub types require only minimal pruning; remove the dead wood, cut back invasive canes, and open up the centers of the bushes.

A series of everblooming Brownell roses makes a beautiful natural fence. Other types that are especially good for hedges are 'Westerland', 'Autumn Sunset', 'Frau Karl Druschki', and 'Mme. Hardy'.

CLIMBERS AS GROUNDCOVERS

R. wichuraiana and its early hybrids, which are often called "trailers," can easily be used as groundcovers because they have numerous canes that grow out from the base and creep along the ground. They root repeatedly, forming a dense carpet that will smother weeds and hold the soil. Earlier in the century, 'Dorothy Perkins' and 'Excelsa' were often used as groundcovers along railway embankments. Other hybrids that have retained the procumbent wichuraiana growth habit are 'Lady Godiva' and 'Minnehaha'.

Climbers that need no care, pruning, or training are the best candidates for groundcovers; *R. setigera, R. wichuraiana*, 'Max Graf', 'Rote Max Graf', 'Weisse Max Graf', 'Excelsa', 'Coral Creeper', and 'Red Cascade' are all excellent choices. These require no work; they form such dense and thorny mats that you could not prune them even if you wanted to.

Miniature climbers can be used for edging garden paths. Try 'Red Cascade', 'Pink Cascade', or 'Sweet Chariot'.

PEGGED CLIMBERS

Climbers can be trained along the ground by pegging—attaching some of the canes to short stakes that hold them in a horizontal position a few inches above the earth. Almost any variety can be trained this way. The effect is spectacular because horizontal positioning causes all the bud eyes on the canes to bloom. The pegged canes may be shaped to radiate out from the center of a circle, trained as edging around a bed or along a path, or formed in a series of low hoops or arches. Almost any climber or rambler can be pegged, but the hybrid perpetuals and Bourbons, which often produce long canes, are especially good for this.

Any rose with long canes can be pegged. Secure the tips of the canes to the ground with wooden or metal pegs driven firmly into the earth. A pegged rose needs a large space, but it will reward you with a carpet of blooms.

Pegging should be done as soon as the canes are long enough to be trained in this fashion. After the rose has bloomed, new canes can be used to replace those that were previously pegged. This training can also be done during the winter when the rose is dormant and the canes are more manageable because they have no leaves.

The canes can be either pegged right into the soil or tied to stakes. If you choose the latter method, drive foot-long stakes of strong wood or metal into the ground, arranging them in the desired pattern. Make sure the stakes are well anchored, for the canes will exert a strong pull on them. Tie the canes to the stakes with twine; notches in wooden stakes will help hold the ties. If the canes resist bending and feel as though they might break under pressure, pull them down gradually, a little bit every day until you get them into place. If the canes refuse to bend all the way down, pull them down as far as possible and attach them to the stakes with long pieces of twine.

A pegged rose takes up a lot of space, but it is not necessary to peg all the canes. If some are left to grow free-form above the others, they will create a luxuriant effect. At the beginning of each season, if there are young canes to work with, cut away the old pegged canes and replace them with the new ones.

Many tender roses will survive winters in cold climates with their canes pegged close to the ground. Pegging is also a way of propagating many of the wichuraiana and multiflora ramblers, for wherever the canes come into contact with the earth, they send out roots.

Any climber that makes a good groundcover is suitable for pegging. A few suggestions are 'Mme. Ernst Calvat', 'Splendens', 'Alister Stella Gray', 'Félicité Perpétue', 'Fisher Holmes', 'Frau Karl Druschki', and 'Eugène Fürst'.

CLIMBERS TRAINED UP INTO TREES

Many climbers can be induced to scramble up into trees, where they will form an airy column of flowers. The blooms are beautiful combined with any type of foliage. This is also an effective way to decorate a dead tree.

A climber growing near a tree will often make its way into the branches on its own, but many varieties can be planted expressly for this purpose. Plant the climber near the drip line of the branches, tilting it toward the tree. A long bamboo pole stretching from the ground to the nearest low-hanging branch will help the rose grow into the tree. Tie the pole to the branch, and guide the canes of the rose along it. Once the rose has grown up into the tree and attached itself securely to the branches, remove the pole.

Climbing roses in trees require no care. Just be sure to use varieties whose canes will survive the winters in your area, for disentangling dead thorn-covered canes from the branches of a tree is a tedious and sometimes hazardous task. If this does become necessary, be careful not to yank a long cane out of the tree, for it may whip back into your face.

Some of the roses that do well in trees are 'Seagull', 'Albéric Barbier', 'Climbing Cécile Brünner', 'Bloomfield Courage', 'Complicata', 'Veilchenblau', and 'Chevy Chase'. Small-flowered climbers are commonly found growing up into trees, but many of those with larger flowers can also be used. Stephen has had good luck with 'Silver Moon', 'Dr. W. Van Fleet', and 'Christine Wright'.

CLIMBERS ON FENCES OR WALLS

A rose on a white picket fence is as American as apple pie. An exuberant climber will quickly engulf a fence, so make sure the structure is strong and firmly anchored in the ground, or it may be pulled down by the weight of the bush.

Ramblers, climbers with pliable canes, are easy to train on fences about four feet high. Prune the rose immediately after it has flowered, cutting out all the old, dead, or crowded wood; then pull the young canes over the fence in a series of wide curves and tie them in place with soft twine.

You can help a climber scale a high wall by covering the wall with netting, to which the canes can attach themselves. Use brackets to position a wire "lattice" about a foot out from the wall; this will leave room for air to circulate behind the canes. Stone walls become very warm in the sun. The reflected heat may enable tender climbers to survive winters in regions where they are not ordinarily hardy. On the other hand, cold-hardy climbers may suffer from the extra heat during the summer.

For the best bloom, the canes of all climbers trained on walls and fences should be fanned out horizontally as much as possible. To create the most sumptuous effect, use every cane and cover every inch of the surface.

For training on fences and walls, try repeat-blooming climbers—especially those with large, fragrant flowers that will create a massive display all summer long. Climbers that flower once can also be very impressive in these situations. The nonrepeating multiflora rambler 'Ghislaine de Féligonde' puts on a glorious show against a wall in the rose garden at Castle Howard in England. Some of the best climbers to grow on walls and fences are 'Zéphirine Drouhin', 'Sombreuil', 'Conrad Ferdinand Meyer', and 'Lawinia'.

CLIMBERS ON THE WALLS OF HOUSES

The appearance of a house can be transformed by a climbing rose. Many people attach the canes directly to the wall, but this is not good for either the house or the rose: nails or hooks will damage the siding, the canes will have to be taken down every time the house is painted, and the rose will suffer from reflected heat and lack of proper air circulation. It is much better to train a rose on a lattice that is set about a foot out from the wall of a house and held in place by brackets or blocks of wood. Lattices may be attached to walls, porches, or verandas; affixed beside doors and windows; or fastened to roofs.

Climbers of all types can be used to decorate houses. Fragrant varieties are the best choices for framing doors and windows; their perfume will be a constant delight inside the house and out. Large-flowered climbers such as 'New Dawn' are lovely around windows, doorways, and porches. Climbing miniatures are attractive trained to lattice frames against the walls of small buildings such as cabins and garden sheds. For the best bloom, always spread the canes out horizontally as much as possible when training a climber against the wall of a house.

CLIMBERS ON LATTICES AND TRELLISES

Fan-shaped trellises are often placed against the sides of houses, in front of stone walls, or at the backs of gardens. Properly used, a rose-covered trellis can be the main decorative element in a small space. A trellis or a lattice will look unstable and out of place in the middle of a lawn, however.

Lattices and trellises act as ladders, enabling climbing roses to reach great heights. There are any number of ways to train roses on these structures. One way to expand the rose display in a garden is to plant climbers on both sides of a lattice. You may combine types with different growth habits and varying degrees of vigor, pruning the most rampant ones to keep them from taking up all of the space.

When training a rose on a lattice, do not be tempted to weave the canes in and out of the interstices; it may seem logical to do this when the canes are young and flexible and their thorns are not fully developed, but you will regret it later on. Attach the canes to the surface of the support, fanning them out as much as possible.

Lattices and trellises are traditionally made of wood, but metal is just as good, and more durable. One way to make a metal lattice is to drive galvanized iron posts into the ground and string stout wires, spaced about a foot apart, between them. Wooden lattices are often white, but green, black, and the natural color of unpainted wood also look good with roses. Painted lattices will eventually have to be repainted; this job is best done at a time when you are pruning and thinning out the climber.

A white latticework fence covered with climbers encircles the Cranford Rose Garden. In addition to this, the central architectural element of the garden is an ethereal pavilion composed entirely of latticework and covered with many varieties of climbers.

When the canes of a rose are spread horizontally on a fence or wall, laterals emerge from all the nodes. Throughout the season, these laterals will produce clusters of flowers all along the canes.

CLIMBERS ON ARCHES AND PERGOLAS

Every garden should have at least one rose-covered arch, preferably serving as a fragrant, inviting entranceway. Arches enveloped with the flowers of climbing roses lift color and texture into the air and enliven the garden all season long; they are especially exciting in the spring when the green mantle of leaves suddenly explodes into bloom. A rose-covered arch can frame a doorway, top a gate, span a walkway, or lead enticingly from one space to another. A series of such arches can create a fragrant arbor, tunnel, canopy, or bower. An arch is by nature functional and should look as though it serves some purpose. Avoid placing a rose arch all by itself out in the middle of a lawn.

Many mail-order houses offer ready-made arches, but you can construct a simple one yourself. Drive two posts into the ground, top them with a horizontal board, and nail two narrow boards in an inverted V-shape to this 'lintel." To make a round arch, shape a strip of iron into a curve and insert the ends into hollow pipes set firmly into the ground. Rebars, the heavy, ribbed steel bars used by construction workers when they pour concrete, can also be made into arches. They are heavy, but they become invisible when covered with roses. A stunning display of 'Eden Rose '88' is trained on this type of arch in a private garden in Atlanta, Georgia. In the Cranford Rose Garden, double metal arches span the walkways; these are about one foot wide and are formed of bent one-inch metal pipes and iron mesh. Double arches look sturdier than single ones.

Rose arches can be created using just the canes of tall climbers with very stiff, upright growth habits; the Penzance hybrids and species roses such as *R. eglanteria* and *R. canina* are especially suitable for this. Plant two bushes six feet apart and use temporary supports to guide their canes toward each other; the canes will eventually meet and interlock, creating a marvelous free-standing canopy; this kind of arch will be especially delightful if you use *R. eglanteria* or any of its hybrids that have the apple-scented eglantine foliage.

When making a rose arch, leave at least six feet between the posts so the canes of the roses will not block the opening. Do not make the arch too tall; otherwise, the flowers will bloom out of sight over your head.

Different types of climbers with similar growth habits can be combined on an arch, but limit the number of colors or the effect will be garish. Ramblers or climbers with pliable canes are the best choices for arches. Try to keep the canes horizontal. A rose arch should be neat; remove dead canes and invasive growth and keep the laterals well pruned.

A series of arches can be used to create a spectacular tunnel of climbing roses. French rose gardens are famous for their magical rose tunnels—fragrant, shady vaults that offer relief from the sun. 'American Pillar' and other wichuraiana hybrids are frequently used for creating tunnels. For a tunnel of repeat-blooming climbers, try 'Pink Perpétué', 'Pink Cloud', 'Rhonda', and 'Sombreuil'.

Pergolas are even more elaborate structures on which to train climbing roses. These covered walkways are constructed of double rows of pillars or posts, and their roofs are often formed of trelliswork. There is an especially impressive rose-covered pergola in the gardens of the Royal National Rose Society at Chiswell Green, near St. Albans, England.

'Climbing Orange Triumph', 'American Pillar', and 'Paul's Scarlet Climber' surround Cupid in the Temple of Love at La Roseraie de l'Haÿ-les-Roses.

CLIMBERS ON PILLARS AND POSTS

In the past, climbers of moderate height were called "pillar roses" because they were often wound around pillars or posts. This form of training used to be more popular than it is today, but do not overlook it. It is a wonderful way to create a vertical accent in the garden, especially when space is limited. Rose pillars are important ornamental features in the rose gardens at Bagatelle and La Roseraie de l'Haÿ-les-Roses.

Roses with long, vigorous canes can also be trained on pillars, but they will have to be severely pruned. Do not use extremely rampant climbers because to keep them under control you will have to cut away many of the valuable canes and flower-bearing laterals.

Rose pillars, which should be six to eight feet high, can be constructed of many kinds of materials. Dead tree trunks or limbs make good pillars. Leave the stumps of the branches for the roses to climb on; the pillar can also be covered with wire mesh for this purpose. Cedar is especially attractive and rustic-looking. Wrap

Three plants of a promising new climbing floribunda, 'Climbing Rimosa', cover a ten-foot-high tripod with their pure yellow blooms.

them in spiral fashion around chains, wires, or ropes.

CLIMBERS ON TRIPODS

If you have enough space, you can place three pillars together and create a pyramid of climbing roses. To make a tripod, space three metal or wooden posts about three feet apart and drive them into the ground on a slant so that the tops meet over a central point where they can be tied together. For a colorful display, plant a different variety of climber at the base of each post. Cedar or larch will give the tripod a rustic effect. More sophisticated-looking structures can be made of metal. (Spectacular metal tripods lift climbers fifteen feet into the air at the Bagatelle rose gardens and at La Roseraie de l'Haÿ-les-Roses.)

CLIMBERS AS WEEPING STANDARDS

Climbers trained as weeping standards are rarely seen today in the United States, but they are common in England and on the Continent. There are several ways to train a rose in this fashion. The most common method is to use a rose such as 'Excelsa', 'Dorothy Perkins', or 'Red Cascade' that is budded onto R. rugosa or 'Dr. Huey' stock. The canes of some climbers, such as those of 'Dorothy Perkins', will fall naturally into a weeping position. Sometimes umbrellalike mesh frames are constructed for the canes to spread out over.

the canes around the support, placing them horizontally as much as possible. If you let the canes grow higher than the pillar, they will cascade back down and enhance the effect. Each season, remove all the old and dead canes, and replace them on the pillar with new, young canes. Keep all the laterals short.

A series of pillars or posts planted twelve feet apart can be connected with festoons of climbing roses. When the canes have surmounted the uprights, continue their training by wrapping

Another, more difficult, method of creating a weeping standard is to use a rose that is growing on its own roots. Cut away all the canes but one and tie this single cane to a straight support. Remove all the side buds from the growing rose, leaving only the top branches, which can be pulled down with fishing weights to create the weeping effect.

CLIMBERS TRAINED IN POTS

Earlier in the century florists did a big business in container-grown roses that were forced into bloom for holidays. Often these were ramblers, whose long, flexible canes made possible a variety of intricate shapes, including windmills, ships, umbrellas, and other fantasies. The firm of Ellwanger and Barry, which introduced 'Crimson Rambler' to this country in 1895, supplied its customers with instructions for growing a rambler in a pot and forcing it into bloom: Dig up a two-year-old plant in the fall, plant it in a seven-inch pot with regular potting soil, and prune it severely. By February it will be eighteen to twenty-four inches high and eighteen inches wide and will have produced many new, healthy canes covered with large clusters of flowers. These arching canes can be trained on hoops and arches.

Ramblers and other types of climbers are still trained this way today. For example, every December 25 Stephen brings into the house a mini-climber, 'Sweet Chariot'. He plants it in good potting soil, cuts away all but four of its canes, and shortens these remaining canes back to four inches. If there are any leaves left, he removes them as well. The plant receives plenty of water and light, and by late January it has developed eight to ten new canes that are covered with flowers. The rose remains in full bloom until late spring, at which time Stephen replants it in the garden.

GLOSSARY

AARS. All-America Rose Selections, Inc. An association of commercial rose growers who test and select new roses.

ARS. The American Rose Society.

Balling. When the outer petals of a flower adhere together and fail to open, they are said to have balled. This condition is usually due to cool and damp weather.

Bedding plant. Rose varieties such as polyanthas, floribundas, grandifloras, hybrid teas, and miniatures that are suitable for planting together in beds.

Bristle. A hairlike prickle.

Bud. A swelling that will develop into a shoot or a flower.

Budded rose. A rose that is bud-grafted onto an understock to give it increased vitality.

Bud eye. The site on a bud from which growth occurs.

Button eye. The effect created when the central petals of a very double rose curve inward and form a small, round, "buttonlike" center. Usually seen in certain old garden roses.

Cane. The stem of a rose. Rose canes have hard outer coverings and pithy centers.

Climber. A vigorous shrub rose that has long canes and can be trained on a wall, trellis, or other support.

Continuing lateral. A very long rose cane that grows from a main cane. Continuing laterals, which occur at random points along main canes, bloom either from terminal buds or on short laterals.

Deadheading. The practice of removing spent blooms to encourage rebloom.

Double. A rose flower with at least sixteen petals arranged in many rows.

Entire. A leaf whose edges have no serrations or indentations is said to be entire.

Everblooming. Flowering continuously from the beginning of the season until the dormant period.

Exhibition quality. A rose blossom whose innermost petals hold a high center while the outer petals unfurl symmetrically.

Extended. Long and tapered. Sepals that are extended are longer than the closed flower bud.

Feathered. Having a distinctly cut edge. *See* Lacinate.

Foliage. The leaves.

Fringe. An edge of fine indentations.

Gland. A minute organ emitting a sticky, resinous substance.

Glandular. Having glands. Glandular parts of a plant are sticky to the touch.

Grafting. Uniting a desired variety of rose with

a stronger, more vigorous rootstock. The form of grafting most commonly used for roses is bud-grafting, or budding.

Heel in. To store temporarily a dormant, bare-root plant in a trench where it is covered with soil and kept moist until it can be planted in its permanent site.

Hip. The fleshy seed capsule of a rose.

Hybrid. A cross between two different species or varieties of plants.

Hybridizing. Crossbreeding between different species or varieties. This can occur in the wild through natural pollination of one plant by another, or through the hybridizer's deliberate transference of the pollen from one variety to the stigmas of another.

Imbricate. A flower that has short, reflexed petals arranged in an open, rosette shape.

Inflorescence. A bloom cluster.

Lacinate. Having a deeply cut edge with feathery, fingerlike projections.

Large-flowered climber. A vigorous shrub rose that produces long canes with large flowers that are at least two or three inches in diameter.

Lateral. Any rose cane that grows from a main cane.

Layering. Vegetative propagation through contact of a cane with a rooting medium.

Leaflet. One unit of a compound leaf.

Leaf set. Having a group of leaflets joined by a common stalk or petiole.

Margin. The edge.

Matte. A dull surface.

Node. The joint on a stem that marks the place where a leaf or a bud emerges.

Ovate. Egg-shaped.

Own-root. A rose that has not been budded to an understock.

Panicle. An inflorescence in which the flowers are in a more or less pyramidal arrangement.

Pedicel. An individual flower stem, directly connected to the receptacle.

Pegging. The practice of training the canes of a rose along the ground by securing the ends to short stakes. This horizontal training causes all the bud eyes on the canes to bloom.

Perpetually blooming. See Everblooming.

Petal. One of the units of the showy part of a flower that surrounds the stamens and pistils.

Petiole. Leaf stalk.

Pillar rose. A rose whose canes are just the right length for training on a pillar or a post.

Pistil. The female part of a flower, consisting of the stigma, the style, and the ovary.

Polyantha. A rose variety that has clusters of many small flowers. The original polyantha is thought to have been a cross between a China rose and a multiflora. Polyanthas were the forerunners of the floribundas.

Pollen parent. In hybridizing, the male parent.

Prickle. The correct term for a rose "thorn." A true thorn is a modified branch. A prickle is a superficial growth on a stem, and it can easily be detached.

Procumbent. Trailing or spreading along the ground. Procumbent roses have lax canes that are easily trained.

Proof of the Pudding. A section of *The American Rose Annual* (the publication of the American Rose Society) in which gardeners from around the United States evaluate newly introduced roses. Each rose is evaluated for five years.

Pubescence. A slight fuzzy, soft coating.

Quartered. Flowers whose central petals are divided into four sections. Sometimes there are three or five segments rather than four. Quartering is common in old garden roses.

Rambler. A type of climbing rose with long, lax, easily trainable canes, the majority of which emerge from the base of the plant. Ramblers usually bloom once a season.

Receptacle. The part of a flower stalk that is immediately above the pedicel and bears the floral organs.

Reflexed. A petal that has curled back upon itself. Reflexed petals often create star shapes and other interesting patterns.

Remontant. A rose that repeats its bloom after the main bloom but does not flower continuously (as opposed to everblooming).

Rootstock (understock). A strong, vigorous rose onto which another rose is grafted.

Rose rustlers. Collectors of old garden roses who search out neglected and forgotten varieties.

Rugose. Having a rough texture.

Seed parent. In hybridizing, the female parent.

Seedling. A new rose variety grown from a seed, the result of crossing two different species or varieties (hybridizing).

Semidouble. A rose flower with two rows of petals, or from seven to twenty-four petals. Semidouble roses often have exposed stamens.

Sepal. One of the group of leaflike structures that enclose the flower bud.

Single. A rose blossom with one row of five petals or two rows of five petals each.

Smooth. Without hairs, bristles, glands, or prickles.

Species rose. A rose that occurs naturally in the wild and remains true to type when grown from seed.

Sport. A mutation that results when one of the branches on a plant is different from the rest of the plant. A plant grown from this genetically altered branch is also called a sport.

Stamen. The male, pollen-producing part of a flower consisting of a filament and an anther.

Standard rose (tree rose). A tall, treelike rose that is created by grafting one rose to the main cane of another, sturdy rose at a point several feet above the ground. The cane to which the rose is grafted may itself be budded to another rootstock.

Stigma. The sticky apex of the pistil. During pollination, the stigma receives the pollen.

Stipule. One of a pair of leaflike appendages at the base of a leaf or a leafstalk.

Stud roses. Roses that were grown in the West during the nineteenth century expressly for purposes of hybridization.

Suckering. Suckering occurs when new canes arise from the roots of a rose and form another plant. In grafted roses the suckers come from the rootstock and sap the strength of the desired rose, which will eventually die. In roses that grow on their own roots, the suckers are not harmful because they are the same as the main plant; if there are so many suckers that they become invasive, they can be removed and planted elsewhere.

Thorns. Modified branches composed of the same material as the stem of the plant. Roses have prickles, which are often incorrectly referred to as thorns.

Tomentose. Hairy; covered with soft bristles.

Understock. See Rootstock.

Very double. A rose blossom with a great many petals. Very double roses are often quartered, and they frequently have button eyes.

BOTANICAL HIGHLIGHTS

Listed below are significant botanical characteristics of each of the sixty-five roses profiled in the text. These can be used for purposes of comparison, and they may also provide clues to the identities of "mystery" roses. Included for each rose are descriptions of its pedicels (flower stems), receptacles (extensions of the flower stalks that are immediately above the pedicels and that bear the floral organs), sepals (leaflike structures enclosing the flower buds), stipules (leafy appendages at the points where the leaf stalks join the stems), prickles ("thorns"), and foliage (the leaves). All the botanical terms are defined in the glossary.

Rosa moschata
Pedicels: tomentose; glandular bristles
Receptacles: tomentose; glandular bristles
Sepals: tomentose; glandular bristles
Stipules: information not available
Prickles: hooked; numerous
Foliage: long; pointed

Rosa eglanteria
Pedicels: green bristles
Receptacles: smooth
Sepals: glandular; extended
Stipules: entire; wide; glandular
Prickles: hooked; numerous; dense
Foliage: matte; 5 leaflets; apple fragrance when crushed

Rosa canina
Pedicels: smooth
Receptacles: smooth
Sepals: smooth; extended
Stipules: entire; glands on margins; wide
Prickles: hooked; usually located at each node; sparse
Foliage: glossy; 5 leaflets

Rosa setigera
Pedicels: glandular bristles
Receptacles: glandular
Sepals: glandular
Stipules: entire; wide; distinct red center stripe
Prickles: curved; red when new; large
Foliage: matte; tomentose; rugose; 3 or 5 leaflets

Rosa multiflora
Pedicels: glandular
Receptacles: smooth
Sepals: glandular
Stipules: extremely lacinate; very glandular
Prickles: curved
Foliage: matte; tomentose; long; 7 leaflets

'Félicité Perpétue'
Pedicels: become red as they age; small red bristles
Receptacles: smooth
Sepals: bristles
Stipules: fringed; tipped with red glands; rose-red center stripe
Prickles: thin; curved; dense; originate immediately below inflorescence
Foliage: glossy; large; pointed; 3 or 5 leaflets; petioles covered with red bristles; small hooked prickles on undersides

'Malton'
Pedicels: glandular; tomentose
Receptacles: smooth
Sepals: glandular; extended

Stipules: entire; wide; glands on margins; red center stripe
Prickles: curved; thin; red when young; numerous, but eventually disappear on older wood
Foliage: matte; rugose; large; 3 or 5 leaflets; petioles glandular

'Mme. Hardy'
Pedicels: dense, soft, glandular bristles, some red, some colorless; strong resin fragrance
Receptacles: bristles
Sepals: long and feathered; glands along margins
Stipules: wide; rose-red center stripe; no fringe
Prickles: originate immediately below inflorescence; very dense; nearly straight; arranged on a slant; nearly absent on wood more than two years old
Foliage: dark green; rugose; tomentose on underside; 3 or 5 leaflets; petioles covered with tiny glands

'Fellenberg'
Pedicels: tomentose
Receptacles: smooth
Sepals: tomentose when young, smooth when mature
Stipules: no fringe; red glands along margins; indistinct rose-red center stripe
Prickles: large and hooked; originate near the lower two-thirds of lateral; evenly dispersed
Foliage: glossy; long; pointed; 5 or 7 leaflets; new leaves have a red margin

'Russell's Cottage Rose'
Pedicels: dense, sticky, glandular bristles

Receptacles: dense, sticky, glandular bristles
Sepals: dense, sticky, glandular bristles; extended
Stipules: extremely lacinate; wide; distinct rose-red center stripe
Prickles: nearly straight; dense; originate immediately below first leaf
Foliage: large; rugose; 5 or 7 leaflets; red margins

'Great Western'
Pedicels: red bristles; small and glandular; sparse
Receptacles: smooth
Sepals: glandular; extended
Stipules: entire; wide
Prickles: small and straight; very dense on new growth; originate immediately below the first leaf; nearly nonexistent on older wood
Foliage: light green; rounded; 3, 5, or 7 leaflets

'Coupe d'Hébé'
Pedicels: become red as they age; glandular bristles
Receptacles: smooth
Sepals: glandular
Stipules: wide; glands on the margins; hint of rose-red in center
Prickles: nearly straight; many sizes; dense and red on laterals; originate below first leaf on lateral; gray on older canes
Foliage: coarse; 3 or 5 leaflets; petioles very glandular

'Splendens'
Pedicels: glandular; tomentose
Receptacles: smooth

Sepals: glandular; tomentose
Stipules: slightly lacinate; distinct red center stripe
Prickles: curved; dense; originate immediately below inflorescence
Foliage: dull, dark green; 3 or 5 leaflets; petioles with hooked prickles on undersides

'Blairii No. 2'
Pedicels: tomentose; tiny red glands
Receptacles: smooth
Sepals: glandular
Stipules: slight rose-red center stripe
Prickles: curved; long; greenish-red
Foliage: glossy; 3 or 5 leaflets; petioles tomentose and glandular

'Baltimore Belle'
Pedicels: tiny, glandular bristles
Receptacles: smooth
Sepals: bristles
Stipules: entire; red glands on the margins; a red center stripe develops as the stipule ages
Prickles: curved; thin; originate immediately below inflorescence; dense on older wood
Foliage: 3 or 5 leaflets; petioles with prominent prickles on undersides; petioles glandular

'Paul Ricaut'
Pedicels: dense bristles
Receptacles: smooth
Sepals: dense bristles; long
Stipules: entire; red glands on edges; rose-red when new
Prickles: sparse on laterals;

slightly curved, large, and
dense on main canes
Foliage: matte; large; dark green;
5 leaflets; petioles and leaf
margins red on new growth

'Sombreuil'
Pedicels: smooth
Receptacles: smooth
Sepals: red glands along margins
Stipules: entire; red glands along
margins
Prickles: hooked; red when new;
usually originate below the
second or third set of leaves;
dense
Foliage: glossy; large; 3 or 5
leaflets; petioles glandular;
new foliage red

Rosa wichuraiana
Pedicels: smooth
Receptacles: smooth
Sepals: smooth
Stipules: lacinate; glands along
margins
Prickles: hooked; small; numer-
ous; a pair at each node
Foliage: glossy; small; 9 or 11
leaflets

'Zéphirine Drouhin'
Pedicels: glandular bristles
Receptacles: smooth
Sepals: glandular bristles
Stipules: entire; red glands along
margins; red center stripe
Prickles: none
Foliage: 3 or 5 leaflets; dark
green; new growth dark red

'Crimson Rambler'
Pedicels: extremely glandular;
glands are red and sticky
Receptacles: glandular
Sepals: glandular; extended

Stipules: extremely lacinate;
glandular
Prickles: curved; sparse
Foliage: long; dull green; 7
leaflets

'Alister Stella Gray'
Pedicels: tomentose; red
Receptacles: tomentose
Sepals: tomentose; extended
Stipules: slightly lacinate; red
glands along margins
Prickles: curved; very sparse
Foliage: matte; dark green; 3 or
5 leaflets; petioles red, cov-
ered with glands; red,
hooked prickles on under-
sides of petioles

'Aglaia'
Pedicels: tomentose
Receptacles: smooth
Sepals: densely glandular
Stipules: narrow; lacinate; red
glands along margins
Prickles: hooked; red on new
growth; develop on oldest
parts of laterals; dense on
oldest wood
Foliage: glossy; long; 3, 5, or 7
leaflets; dense glands on petioles; hooked prickles on undersides of petioles

'Conrad Ferdinand Meyer'
Pedicels: red glands
Receptacles: some glands
Sepals: glandular; extended
Stipules: entire; wide; glandular;
new stipules red
Prickles: nearly straight; dense;
originate immediately below
first set of leaves
Foliage: ovate; slightly rugose;
margins of new foliage red;
5 or 7 leaflets; petioles glandular and tomentose

'Albéric Barbier'
Pedicels: smooth
Receptacles: smooth
Sepals: tomentose
Stipules: entire; wide; red in center when young; red glands
along margins
Prickles: curved; originate below
second or third leaf set;
sparse
Foliage: glossy; long; petioles
covered with bristles; 3, 5,
or 7 leaflets

'Dorothy Perkins'
Pedicels: tiny red glands, not
dense
Receptacles: smooth
Sepals: red glands along margins
Stipules: lacinate; wide; red
glands along margins
Prickles: curved; yellow-red on
new growth; originate imme-
diately below inflorescence;
sparse
Foliage: glossy; long; 7 leaflets

'Frau Karl Druschki'
Pedicels: slightly glandular
Receptacles: smooth
Sepals: red glands along margins
Stipules: entire; wide; red glands
along margins
Prickles: bristlelike; small; concentrated near bases of laterals; curved and dense on
older wood
Foliage: ovate; slightly rugose;
petioles tomentose and covered with bristles

'American Pillar'
Pedicels: glandular
Receptacles: glandular
Sepals: glandular
Stipules: lacinate; wide
Prickles: thin; hooked; often

found within the inflorescence

Foliage: glossy; dark green; long; 3, 5, or 7 leaflets; petioles covered with tiny bristles

'Silver Moon'
Pedicels: glandular
Receptacles: smooth
Sepals: smooth
Stipules: entire; wide; glands along margins; slight rose-red center stripe on older growth
Prickles: hooked; large; dense; sometimes found on pedicels
Foliage: glossy; 3 or 5 leaflets; petioles are covered with bristles

'Dr. W. Van Fleet'
Pedicels: tiny bristles
Receptacles: smooth
Sepals: glands along margins
Stipules: entire; glands along margins
Prickles: hooked; large; usually originate immediately below the inflorescence; pink when new, gray as they age; dense
Foliage: glossy; ovate; 3 or 5 leaflets; petioles covered with bristles

'Trier'
Pedicels: tomentose
Receptacles: smooth
Sepals: tomentose
Stipules: lacinate; narrow; glands along margins
Prickles: hooked; large; sparse; do not occur on laterals
Foliage: glossy; long; 5 or 7 leaflets; petioles turn plum-red as they age

'Hiawatha'
Pedicels: dense bristles; glandular

Receptacles: smooth
Sepals: smooth
Stipules: very lacinate; wide
Prickles: hooked; yellow-brown; originate immediately below inflorescence; dense
Foliage: glossy; long; narrow; 5 or 7 leaflets; petioles covered with bristles

'Evangeline'
Pedicels: dense bristles; glandular
Receptacles: smooth
Sepals: glands along margins
Stipules: lacinate; glands along margins
Prickles: hooked; amber-colored; a pair at every node; originate immediately below inflorescence
Foliage: glossy; long; 3, 5, or 7 leaflets; petioles glandular

'Tausendschön'
Pedicels: glandular
Receptacles: glandular
Sepals: glandular
Stipules: lacinate; narrow; glands along margins
Prickles: none
Foliage: glossy; long; 5 or 7 leaflets; petioles glandular

'Excelsa'
Pedicels: slightly glandular; red
Receptacles: smooth
Sepals: glands along margins
Stipules: lacinate; wide
Prickles: curved; large; sometimes in the inflorescence; a pair at each node; sparse
Foliage: glossy; long; 5 or 7 leaflets; petioles not glandular

'Christine Wright'
Pedicels: glandular bristles
Receptacles: smooth
Sepals: glands along margins
Stipules: slightly lacinate; wide; glands along margins
Prickles: hooked; amber when new; dense; originate immediately below inflorescence
Foliage: glossy; ovate; 3 or 5 leaflets; petioles covered with bristles; prickles on undersides hooked and very prominent

'Clytemnestra'
Pedicels: tomentose; plum-red
Receptacles: tomentose
Sepals: tomentose
Stipules: slightly lacinate; glands along margins; plum-red center stripe
Prickles: none on laterals; a few hooked prickles on older canes
Foliage: glossy; long; 3, 5, or 7 leaflets; petioles plum-red

'Mary Lovett'
Pedicels: tiny bristles
Receptacles: smooth
Sepals: smooth
Stipules: entire; wide; glands along margins
Prickles: hooked; large; brown; dense; originate immediately below inflorescence
Foliage: glossy; 3 or 5 leaflets; petioles covered with bristles

'Thisbe'
Pedicels: tomentose
Receptacles: tomentose
Sepals: tomentose
Stipules: slightly lacinate; narrow; glands along margins
Prickles: curved; large; rust-col-

ored; dense; originate immediately below inflorescence

Foliage: matte; long; undersides tomentose; 5 or 7 leaflets; petioles tomentose and glandular

'Penelope'

Pedicels: tomentose; slightly glandular

Receptacles: smooth

Sepals: tomentose; glandular; extended

Stipules: slightly lacinate; wide; glands along margins; hint of rose-red center stripe

Prickles: curved; thin; small; sparse on laterals and older wood

Foliage: matte; dark green; ovoid; 5 or 7 leaflets; petioles tomentose and glandular

'Bloomfield Courage'

Pedicels: glandular

Receptacles: smooth

Sepals: smooth

Stipules: slightly lacinate; rose-red center stripe; glands along margins

Prickles: curved; amber; found only at base of new growth; prickles disappear as canes age

Foliage: glossy; light green; long; 5 or 7 leaflets; petioles covered with glands; new foliage has a red margin

'New Dawn'

Pedicels: tiny bristles

Receptacles: smooth

Sepals: glands along margins

Stipules: entire; glands along margins

Prickles: hooked; large; usually originate immediately below

inflorescence; pink when new, gray as they age

Foliage: glossy; ovate; 3 or 5 leaflets; petioles covered with bristles

'Blaze'

Pedicels: dense glandular bristles

Receptacles: smooth

Sepals: glandular

Stipules: entire; glands along margins

Prickles: curved; small; brown; sparse on laterals; dense on new growth

Foliage: glossy; 3 or 5 leaflets; petioles glandular; no prickles on undersides of petioles

'Climbing Summer Snow'

Pedicels: glandular; majority of glands colorless

Receptacles: glandular

Sepals: glandular

Stipules: lacinate

Prickles: none on canes or laterals

Foliage: glossy; long; 5 or 7 leaflets; petioles glandular; undersides of petioles have small hooked prickles

'Chevy Chase'

Pedicels: tomentose

Receptacles: tomentose

Sepals: tomentose

Stipules: entire; narrow; glands along margins

Prickles: curved; amber when new; large; originate immediately below inflorescence; dense

Foliage: matte; gray-green; ovate; 5 or 7 leaflets

'Thor'

Pedicels: smooth

Receptacles: smooth

Sepals: smooth

Stipules: entire; wide; glands along margins

Prickles: hooked; yellow when new; large; originate immediately below inflorescence; dense

Foliage: glossy; dark green; ovate; 5 leaflets, petioles glandular

'Dream Girl'

Pedicels: scattered bristles

Receptacles: smooth

Sepals: smooth

Stipules: slightly lacinate; wide; glands along margins

Prickles: nearly straight; yellow-red when new; large; originate immediately below inflorescence; dense

Foliage: glossy; long; 3, 5, or 7 leaflets; petioles smooth

'City of York'

Pedicels: scattered bristles

Receptacles: smooth

Sepals: smooth

Stipules: entire; glands along margins

Prickles: curved; large; originate immediately below inflorescence; dense

Foliage: glossy; 3 or 5 leaflets

'Inspiration'

Pedicels: smooth

Receptacles: smooth

Sepals: smooth

Stipules: entire; wide; glands on margins

Prickles: curved; amber when new; originate immediately below inflorescence; large; dense

Foliage: glossy; ovate; large; 3,

5, or 7 leaflets; scattered bristles on petioles; no prickles underneath

'High Noon'
Pedicels: glandular
Receptacles: smooth
Sepals: glandular; extended
Stipules: entire; narrow; glands along margins
Prickles: curved; amber when new; large; found at base of laterals and on older wood; sparse
Foliage: glossy; long; large; 3 or 5 leaflets; petioles tomentose

'Aloha'
Pedicels: glandular
Receptacles: smooth
Sepals: smooth; glands along margins
Stipules: slightly lacinate; glands along margins; rose-red on new growth
Prickles: curved; large; originate immediately below inflorescence; dense
Foliage: glossy; ovate; 3 or 5 leaflets; petioles glandular

'Temptation'
Pedicels: scattered bristles
Receptacles: smooth
Sepals: smooth
Stipules: entire; glands along margins
Prickles: curved; plum-red when new; large; originate immediately below inflorescence; dense
Foliage: glossy; ovate; 3 or 5 leaflets; petioles glandular

'Parade'
Pedicels: bristles
Receptacles: smooth

Sepals: smooth
Stipules: entire; glands along margins
Prickles: hooked; originate immediately below inflorescence; dense
Foliage: glossy; large; 5 or 7 leaflets; new growth red

'White Cap'
Pedicels: smooth
Receptacles: smooth
Sepals: tomentose
Stipules: slightly lacinate; a few glands on the margins
Prickles: nearly straight; amber when new; large; scattered along bases of laterals; dense on older canes
Foliage: glossy; long; 3 or 5 leaflets; petioles smooth except for prominent hooked prickles on undersides

'Goldbusch'
Pedicels: bristles
Receptacles: smooth
Sepals: smooth
Stipules: entire; narrow; glands along margins
Prickles: hooked; develop inside inflorescence
Foliage: matte; 3 or 5 leaflets

'Dortmund'
Pedicels: bristles
Receptacles: smooth
Sepals: bristles; extended
Stipules: entire; narrow; glands along margins
Prickles: hooked; thin; none on laterals; dense on older wood
Foliage: glossy; long; 3 or 5 leaflets; scattered bristles on petioles; prominent hooked prickles on undersides

'Golden Showers'
Pedicels: tomentose
Receptacles: tomentose
Sepals: tomentose; extended
Stipules: slightly lacinate; glands along margins
Prickles: curved; large; found on bases of laterals and scattered throughout the older canes
Foliage: glossy; large; 3 or 5 leaflets

'Don Juan'
Pedicels: smooth
Receptacles: smooth
Sepals: glands along margins
Stipules: slightly lacinate; glands along margins; rose-red center stripe
Prickles: curved; large; occur only at bases of laterals; dense on older wood
Foliage: glossy; dark green; 3, 5, or 7 leaflets; new foliage plum-red

'Altissimo'
Pedicels: scattered bristles
Receptacles: smooth
Sepals: smooth; extended
Stipules: entire; glands along margins
Prickles: curved; red; large; originate immediately below inflorescence; dense
Foliage: glossy; large; dark green; 5 leaflets

'Cadenza'
Pedicels: glandular
Receptacles: smooth
Sepals: glandular
Stipules: slightly lacinate; wide
Prickles: curved; large; yellow when new; originate immedi-

ately below inflorescence; dense

Foliage: glossy; large; dark green; 5 leaflets

'Country Dancer'

Pedicels: smooth; rose-red

Receptacles: smooth

Sepals: tomentose; extended

Stipules: entire; wide; glands along margins

Prickles: curved; thin; amber when new; usually originate below second set of leaves on lateral; dense

Foliage: matte; ovate; large; 3 or 5 leaflets; petioles tomentose and glandular; no prickles on undersides

'Jeanne Lajoie'

Pedicels: tiny red glands

Receptacles: smooth

Sepals: tiny red glands

Stipules: slightly lacinate; wide; glands along margins

Prickles: straight; large; originate immediately below inflorescence; dense

Foliage: glossy; 3 or 5 leaflets

'Red Fountain'

Pedicels: scattered bristles

Receptacles: smooth

Sepals: smooth

Stipules: entire; glands along margins

Prickles: curved; large; originate immediately below first leaf; scattered

Foliage: glossy; 3 or 5 leaflets

'Red Cascade'

Pedicels: scattered bristles

Receptacles: smooth

Sepals: smooth

Stipules: slightly lacinate; wide

Prickles: curved; thin; sparse on laterals; usually originate immediately below inflorescence; dense on older wood

Foliage: glossy; long; 5 or 7 leaflets; petioles covered

with bristles; prominent hooked prickles on undersides

'John Cabot'

Pedicels: smooth

Receptacles: smooth

Sepals: smooth

Stipules: slightly lacinate; wide

Prickles: curved; thin; found at base of laterals; dense on older wood

Foliage: glossy; long; dark green; 5 or 7 leaflets; petioles tomentose and bristly; prominent long prickles on undersides

'Eden Rose '88'

Pedicels: smooth

Receptacles: smooth

Sepals: smooth

Stipules: entire; glands along margins

Prickles: curved; large; sparse on laterals and older wood

Foliage: glossy; 5 leaflets

LOCATION OF CLIMBING ROSES IN THE CRANFORD ROSE GARDEN

ON THE LATTICE PAVILION

'Silver Moon'
'Aloha'
'Bess Lovett'★
'Climbing Yesterday'★
'Alida Lovett'★
'Red Fountain'
'Champneys' Pink Cluster'
'Handel'
'Russell's Cottage Rose'
'Snowfall'
'Mermaid'

'Cadenza'
'Swan Lake'
'Penelope'
'Blaze'
'Pink Perpétué'
'Golden Showers'
'Piñata'
'Christine Wright'
'Breeze Hill'★
'High Noon'

'Gold Star'
'Blossomtime'
'Paul's Scarlet Climber'
'Climbing Dainty Bess'
'Climbing Queen Elizabeth'
'Dortmund'
'Grand Hotel'
'Dr. W. Van Fleet'
'Climbing Cécile Brünner'
'White Dorothy'

IN THE ROSE ARC POOL AREA

'White Dorothy'
'Ivy Alice'
'Excelsa'
'Thelma'
'Dorothy Perkins'
'Dr. Huey'
'Bloomfield Courage'

'Antique 89'
'Chevy Chase'
'Albertine'
'Jeanne Lajoie'
'Rocky'
'Altissimo'
'Climbing White Cécile Brünner'

'Red Fountain'
'Clytemnestra'
'Violette'
'Awakening'
'Climbing Snowbird'
'E. Veyrat Hermanos'

LOCATION OF CLIMBING ROSES IN THE CRANFORD ROSE GARDEN

ON THE LATTICE FENCE ENCLOSING THE MAIN AREA

'Dr. W. Van Fleet'
'May Queen'
'Excelsa'
'Blaze'
'Paul's Scarlet'
'Lawinia'
'Messire Delbard'
'Ghislaine de Féligonde'
'High Noon'
'Fellenberg'
'Great Western'
'Christine Wright'
'Cupid'
'Cadenza'
'Mme. Grégoire Staechelin'
'Sombreuil'
'Climbing Pinkie'
'Chaplin's Pink Climber'
'Evangeline'
'Dorothy Perkins'
'Casa Blanca'
'Dr. Huey'
'Bloomfield Courage'
'Zeus'

'America'
'Climbing Spartan'
'Thor'
'Red Fountain'
'Mary Lovett'
'Tempo'
'Silver Moon'
'Climbing First Prize'
'June Morn'
'The Climbing Doctor'*
'Mystery White Rambler'*
'Félicité Perpétue'
'Jeanne Lajoie'
'Thelma'
'Dream Girl'
'Don Juan'
'Inspiration'
'Chevy Chase'
'Non Plus Ultra'
'Frederick S. Peck'
'Golden Arctic'
'Temptation'
'Gladiator'

'Elegance'
'Compassion'
'Royal Sunset'
'Mrs. Arthur Curtiss James'
'Dortmund'
'Climbing Mme. Pierre S. du Pont'
'Etain'
'Climbing Cécile Brünner'
'Trier'
'White Dawn'
'Zéphirine Drouhin'
'Variegata Di Bologna'
'Handel'
'Wichmoss'
'Papa Rouillard'
'Dublin Bay'
'Climbing Charlotte Armstrong'
'New Dawn'
'John Cabot'
'Casino'
'Meg'
'Joseph's Coat'

ON WOODEN PILLARS IN THE SIDE BEDS

'Nova Zembla'
'Maigold'
Rosa multiflora
'Moonlight'
'Malton'
'Blairii No. 2'
'Earl of Dufferin'
'Eden '88'
'Lavender Lassie'
'Mme. Hardy'
Rosa canina
'Ballerina'

'Thisbe'
'Country Dancer'
'John Davis'
'Hamburger Phoenix'
'Schoolgirl'
'Conrad Ferdinand Meyer'
'Paul Ricaut'
Rosa setigera
'Baltimore Belle'
'Duc de Fitzjames'
'Seven Sisters'*
Rosa multiflora platyphylla

'Adelaide Hoodless'
'Jacotte'
'Thor'
'Viking Queen'
'Dr. J. H. Nicolas'
'Dublin Bay'
'Goldbusch'
'Variegata di Bologna Rouge'
'Frau Karl Druschki'
'Constance Spry'
'Clair Matin'

CLIMBING ROSES

ON CEMENT PILLARS AND CONNECTED BY CHAINS, CREATING FESTOONS IN THE MAIN BEDS

'Evangeline'
'Dorothy Perkins'
'Excelsa'
'Tausendschön'
'Climbing Sutter's Gold'
'Climbing Charlotte Armstrong'
'Hiawatha'
'Bloomfield Courage'

'Lady Godiva'★
'Lady Gay'★
'Coronation'
'Gruss an Freundorf'
'Climbing Summer Snow'
'Ghislaine de Féligonde'
'Ivy Alice'
'Apple Blossom'

'Bobbie James'
Rosa multiflora
'New Dawn'
'Ruga'
'Baltimore Belle'
'Phyllis Bide'
'Venusta Pendula'

ON ARCHES OVER THE PATHS

'Royal Gold'
'Climbing Summer Snow'
'François Juranville'
'Excelsa'
'White Dorothy'
'City of York'
'Cadenza'
'Etain'
'New Dawn'
'Antique 89'

'Piñata'
'Gladiator'
'Dr. Huey'
'Chevy Chase'
'Coral Dawn'
'Freifrau von Marschall'
'Complicata'
'Veilchenblau'
'Dorothy Perkins'
'Hiawatha'

'Bloomfield Courage'
'Shalom'
'Aglaia'
'Paul's Lemon Pillar'
'Alexandre Girault'
'Zeus'
'Malton'
'White Cap'
'Le Rêve'

ON PILLARS AND LATTICE FENCING ON THE HILLSIDE AND THE OVERLOOK

'White Cap'
'Fred Loads'
'Frau Karl Druschki'
Rosa setigera
'Pink Pillar'
'Rhonda'
'Pelé'
'Seagull'

'Kiftsgate'
'Jeanne Lajoie'
'Red Cascade'
'Ghislaine de Féligonde'
'Spectacular'
'Mendocino Delight'
'Excelsa'
Rosa wichuraiana

'Splendens'
'Adélaide d'Orléans'
'Paul Noël'
'Thérèse Bugnet'
'Henry Kelsey'
'Morgengruss'
'Alister Stella Gray'
'Scarlet Meidiland'

★ *We are not certain about the identification of this rose.*

PROVENANCE OF THE CLIMBING ROSES PROFILED IN THE TEXT

All sixty-five roses profiled grow in the Cranford Rose Garden. The following list gives the original source of each and the date it was introduced in the Cranford Rose Garden. An asterisk (*) after the date indicates that the source is no longer in existence.

ROSE NAME	ORIGINAL SOURCE
Rosa moschata	The specimens discussed in the text are located in Hollywood Cemetery, Richmond, VA, and on the grounds of the Burwell school in Hillsborough, NC.
Rosa eglanteria	Arnold Arboretum, 1925
Rosa canina	Arnold Arboretum, 1925
Rosa setigera	Arnold Arboretum 1925
Rosa multiflora	The Conard-Pyle Company, 1936
'Félicité Perpétue'	Old Rose Nursery, Lusby, MD, 1933*
'Malton'	Lowe's Own Root Roses, 1987
	Heritage Rose Gardens, 1988
'Mme. Hardy'	Bobbink & Atkins, Rutherford, NJ, 1958*
'Fellenberg'	Pickering Nurseries, Inc., 1987
'Russell's Cottage Rose'	Antique Rose Emporium, 1988
'Great Western'	Lowe's Own Root Roses, 1987
'Coupe d'Hébé'	Lowe's Own Root Roses, 1987
	Pickering Nurseries, Inc., 1990
'Splendens'	Heritage Rose Gardens, 1990
'Blairii No. 2'	Lowe's Own Root Roses, 1987
'Baltimore Belle'	No Record
'Paul Ricaut'	Pickering Nurseries, Inc., 1987
'Sombreuil'	Pickering Nurseries, Inc., 1987
Rosa wichuraiana	Bobbink & Atkins, 1928*
'Zéphirine Drouhin'	Bobbink & Atkins, 1928*
'Crimson Rambler'	Bobbink & Atkins, 1928*
	No longer in Cranford Rose Garden. The specimen studied is located on the campus of Lebanon Valley College in Annville, PA. It dates to pre-1900.

'Alister Stella Gray'   Pickering Nurseries, Inc., 1990

'Aglaia'   Pickering Nurseries, Inc., 1987

'Conrad Ferdinand Meyer'   Bobbink & Atkins, 1927*

'Albéric Barbier'   Pickering Nurseries, Inc., 1987

'Dorothy Perkins'   Bobbink & Atkins, 1928*

'Frau Karl Druschki'   Bobbink & Atkins, 1934*

'American Pillar'   The Conard-Pyle Company, 1929

'Silver Moon'   Bobbink & Atkins, 1928*

'Dr. W. Van Fleet'   Bobbink & Atkins, 1930*

'Trier'   Pickering Nurseries, Inc., 1987

'Hiawatha'   Bobbink & Atkins, 1928*

'Evangeline'   Bobbink & Atkins, 1930*

'Tausendschön'   Bobbink & Atkins, 1928*

'Excelsa'   Bobbink & Atkins, 1928*

'Christine Wright'   No Record

'Clytemnestra'   Bobbink & Atkins, 1937*

'Mary Lovett'   Heritage Rose Gardens, 1989

'Thisbe'   Pickering Nurseries, Inc., 1987

'Penelope'   Pickering Nurseries, Inc., 1987

'Bloomfield Courage'   Bobbink & Atkins, 1930

'New Dawn'   The Conard-Pyle Company, 1932

'Blaze'   Bobbink & Atkins, 1933

'Climbing Summer Snow'   Jackson & Perkins Company, 1933

'Chevy Chase'   Bobbink & Atkins, 1943*

'Thor'   Wayside Gardens Company, 1941

'Dream Girl'   Bobbink & Atkins, 1943*

'City of York'   Kern Rose Nursery, Mentor, OH, 1962*

'Inspiration'   Bobbink & Atkins, 1949*

'High Noon'   Armstrong Nurseries, Inc., 1950

'Aloha'   Jackson & Perkins Company, 1951

'Temptation'   No Record

'Parade'   Jackson & Perkins Company, 1953

'White Cap'   Brownell Rose Research Gardens, Little Compton, RI, 1952*

'Goldbusch'   Pickering Nurseries, Inc., 1987

'Dortmund'   Roses of Yesterday and Today, 1986

'Golden Showers'   Germain's, Inc., Los Angeles, CA, 1956*

'Don Juan'   Jackson & Perkins Company, 1962

'Altissimo'   Roses by Fred Edmunds, 1983

'Cadenza'   No Record

'Country Dancer'   Roses of Yesterday and Today, 1986

'Jeanne Lajoie'   Nor'East Miniature Roses, Inc., 1986

'Red Fountain'   The Conard-Pyle Company, 1986

'Red Cascade'   Nor'East Miniature Roses, Inc., 1986

'John Cabot'   Pickering Nurseries, Inc., 1988

'Eden Rose '88'   The Conard-Pyle Company, 1991

The addresses of the above nurseries that are still in existence

The Antique Rose Emporium
Route 5, Box 143
Brenham, Texas 77833

PROVENANCE OF THE CLIMBING ROSES PROFILED IN THE TEXT

Armstrong Nurseries—Wholesale Only
Bear Creek Gardens, Inc.
P.O. Box 9100
Medford, Oregon 97501–9899

The Conard-Pyle Company—Wholesale Only
372 Rose Hill Road
West Grove, Pennsylvania 19390–0904

Edmunds' Roses (formerly Roses by Fred Edmunds)
6235 S.W. Kahle Road
Wilsonville, Oregon 97070

Heritage Rose Gardens
16831 Mitchell Creek Drive
Fort Bragg, California 95437

Hortico, Inc.
723 Robson Road
R.R. 1
Waterdown, Ontario LOR 2H1 Canada

Jackson & Perkins Company
One Rose Lane
Medford, Oregon 97501–0702

Lowe's Own Root Roses
6 Sheffield Road
Nashua, New Hampshire 03062

Nor'East Miniature Roses, Inc.
P.O. Box 307
Rowley, Massachusetts 01969

Pickering Nurseries, Inc.
670 Kingston Road
Hwy. 2
Pickering, Ontario L1V 1A6 Canada

Roses of Yesterday & Today
802 Brown's Valley Road
Watsonville, California 95076

Wayside Gardens (formerly in Mentor, Ohio)
1 Garden Lane
Hodges, South Carolina 29695–0001

Other Sources of Climbing Roses

Butner's Old Mill Nursery
806 South Belt Highway
St. Joseph, MO 64507

Gloria Dei Nursery
36 East Road
High Falls Park
High Falls, NY 12440

High Country Rosarium
1717 Downing Street
Denver, CO 80218

Historical Roses
1657 West Jackson Street
Painesville, Ohio 44077

Howertown Rose Nursery
1656 Weaversville Road
Northampton, PA 18067

Kimbrew—Walter Roses
Route 2
Box 172
Grand Saline, TX 75140

V. Krause Nurseries Ltd.
P.O. Box 180
Carlisle, Ontario LOR 1HO Canada

Magic Moment Miniatures
P.O. Box 499
Rockville Centre, NY 11571

Sequoia Nursery
Moore Miniature Roses
2519 East Noble Ave.
Visalia, CA 93277

Roses Unlimited
Route 1
Box 587
Laurens, SC 29360

Vintage Gardens
3003 Pleasant Hill Road
Sebastopol, California 95472

Weeks Wholesale Rose Grower, Inc. (wholesale only)
430 E. 19th Street
Upland, CA 91786

NOTES

1. As stated in the American Rose Society's *Annual Proceedings and Bulletin 1908* (New York: The American Rose Society, 1909), 90, the life of the society is counted from March 13, 1899.
2. Although N[arcisse Henri François] Desportes, in *Rosetum Gallicum* (Paris, 1828), 111–12, claimed that John Gerard introduced the musk rose into England in 1596, it probably arrived there much earlier in the sixteenth century. See Roy E. Shepherd, *History of the Rose* (1954; facs. rpt., New York: Coleman, 1978), 25; Graham Stuart Thomas, *Climbing Roses Old and New* (New York: St. Martin's Press, 1966), 36; and John Fisher, *The Companion to Roses* (Topsfield, Mass.: Salem House, 1987), 136.
3. John Gerarde, *The Herball or General Historie of Plantes* (London, 1597), 1084. (The spelling of Gerard's name on the title page of this edition is Gerarde.)
4. Ibid., 1086.
5. John Parkinson, *Paradisi in Sole Paradisus Terrestris* (London, 1629), 418.
6. Ibid., 417.
7. Thomas, "The Mystery of the Musk Rose," in *Climbing Roses Old and New*, 48–57.
8. Gerarde, *The Herball or General Historie of Plantes* (1597), 1087–88.
9. Robert Buist, *The Rose Manual* (1844; facs. rpt., New York: Coleman, 1978), 26.
10. Ibid., 27.
11. Many nineteenth-century sources refer to the variety *R. multiflora carnea* as simply *R. multiflora*; but the species itself, *Rosa multiflora* Thunb., was included in David Hosack's *Hortus Elginensis: or a Catalogue of Plants, Indigenous and Exotic, Cultivated in the Elgin Botanic Garden, in the Vicinity of the City of New-York*, 2d ed. (New York, 1811), 48. The Elgin Botanic Garden was the first public botanic garden in this country.
12. See W[illiam] J[ackson] Bean, *Trees and Shrubs Hardy in the British Isles*, vol. 4, 8th ed. revised, 1980 (rpt. with corrections, 1981; rpt. London: John Murray, 1989), 119.
13. These qualities had been touted as early as 1820 by William Prince, who, in *A Treatise on Fruit and Ornamental Trees and Plants, Cultivated at the Linnaean Botanic Garden* (New York, 1820), 27, advertised *R. multiflora* as "a vine flowering in wreaths, of very quick growth, a single plant now covers the side of a house 40 feet long and 20 feet high, and has produced at least ten thousand flowers in one season, 50 cents."
14. J[ean] H[enri] Nicolas, "The Three Musketeers," *The American Rose Annual* (1937), 134–36.
15. T. W. Girdlestone, "Rosa Polyantha," *The Gardeners' Chronicle* (November 26, 1887), 659.
16. According to P.-Ph. Petit-Coq, "Rosa Sempervirens (Linné): Variété Félicité Perpétue," *Journal des Roses*, 8ᵉ Année (1884), 56–57, Jacques used *R. sempervirens major*. A list of recently introduced Noisettes in *Revue Horticole*, 1 (1829), 114, includes several by Jacques. This provides evidence suggesting that Jacques used Noisettes in a number of his hybrids. Further proof that one of the parents of 'Félicité Perpétue' was a Noisette is found in William Robert Prince, *Prince's Manual of Roses* (1846;

facs. rpt., New York: Coleman, 1979), 94, for he says that it was sold under a variety of names, including 'Noisette floribunda' and 'Noisette compacta'.

17. [Antoine] Jacques and [François] Herincq, *Manuel général des plantes, arbres et arbustes*, vol. 1 (Paris, 1845), 575.

18. There has been a good deal of confusion about the name. It has been said that Guérin dedicated it to his niece, but he actually named another of his roses for her: 'Joséphine Malton', a yellow rose classed either as a tea or a Bengal, which is no longer in commerce. See P. du P., "Rose Malton (Hybride de Bengale)," *Journal des Roses*, 20e Année (1896), 121–22.

19. Stephen bought plants of this rose from two nurseries. One nursery called it 'Malton'; the other, 'Fulgens'. They were identical.

20. The excellent color print that accompanies the article on 'Malton' cited above in n. 18 helped in the identification.

21. Louis Chaix, "Histoire du rosier île Bourbon," *Flore des Serres et des Jardins de l'Europe*, 7 (1851–1852), 80.

22. Thomas Rivers, *The Rose Amateur's Guide*, 4th ed. (1846; facs. rpt., New York: Coleman, 1979), 47–48.

23. William Paul, *The Rose Garden* (1848; facs. rpt., New York: Coleman, 1978), Division I, 15–16.

24. P.-Ph. Petit-Coq, "Rose Madame Hardy: Hybride de Damas remontant," *Journal des Roses*, 4e Année (1880), 126.

25. *Le bon Jardinier, almanach pour l'année 1836* (Paris, 1836), 879, where it is spelled 'Fellemberg'. 'Fellenberg' is not listed in the 1826–1830 catalogues of the French nurseryman Jean Pierre Vibert or in Desportes, *Rosetum Gallicum*, 1828. It appears in the list of Noisettes in the nursery catalogue of George Thorburn in New York City in 1838, where it is spelled 'Felemberg'.

26. 'Belle Marseillaise' was listed separately in *Le bon Jardinier* (1836), 878 (see note 25), as well as in other early literature. Robert Buist, *The Rose Manual*, discussed these as two separate roses, as did Jacques and Herincq in *Manuel général des plantes*, vol. 1 (1845), 572. 'Belle Marseillaise' seems to be one of the many nineteenth-century roses that has completely disappeared.

27. *Travaux du comice horticole de Maine et Loire* (Angers, 1852), 231. On a trip to France in 1992, Stephen learned that the name Fellenberg was spelled with an *m* ('Fellemberg') in early French garden catalogues because the convention at that time was to avoid the combination of the letters *nb*.

28. A note in *The Gardeners' Chronicle* (October 16, 1841), 689, is interesting in this regard, for the writer says that "Noisette roses have been so much hybridized that they are now difficult to define. They may, however, be generally known by the small size of their flowers, their clustering tendency, and the large number in one corymb."

29. Prince, *Prince's Manual of Roses*, 91.

30. Thomas, *Climbing Roses Old and New*, 62.

31. Ibid., 71.

32. Buist, *The Rose Manual*, 22.

33. Paul, *The Rose Garden*, Division I, 13–14.

34. On the history of the Bourbon rose, see "Extrait d'une lettre de M. Jacques, directeur du jardin du roi, datée de Villiers, le 17 février 1841," *Travaux du comice horticole de Maine et Loire*, 3 (1848), 224–26; and Louis Chaix, "Histoire du rosier île Bourbon," 77–80. The article by Chaix was partially translated by Dennison H. Morey in "The Bourbon Rose," *American Rose Annual* (1953), 163–67.

35. Rivers, *The Rose Amateur's Guide*, 60–61.

36. *The Gardeners' Chronicle* (May 27, 1843), 356.

37. It seems that with 'Coupe d'Hébé', Laffay was coming close to his goal of a hardy, remontant rose, for not long after this, his famous hybrid perpetual 'La Reine' appeared. 'La Reine' was praised by British nurserymen as early as 1841. Laffay's first hybrid perpetuals, 'Princesse Hélène' and 'Reine Victoria', first bloomed in 1837 (see T. Rivers Jr., "Effects of the Winter on Roses," *The Gardeners' Chronicle* [May 15, 1841], 308–309).

38. Rivers, *The Rose Amateur's Guide*, 59.

39. The British botanist John Lindley attempted to sort out their history in his *Rosarum Mono-*

graphia (London, 1820), 118. In 1822 Joseph Sabine, secretary of the Horticultural Society of London (now the Royal Horticultural Society), presented an intricate account of the Ayrshire roses to the society (see his "On the Ayrshire Rose," *Transactions of the Horticultural Society of London*, 4 [1822], 456–67).

40. Many Ayrshire roses are listed in nineteenth-century garden catalogs. In 1823, Prince's nursery on Long Island sold a 'White Ayrshire Creeper'. The 1843–1844 catalog listed six Ayrshires, one of which was called " 'Ayrshire Creeper', or 'Rosa arvensis'," further evidence of the suspected relationship to *R. Arvensis*.

41. *The Rose Garden* (1848), Division II, 97.

42. *The Garden* (July 16, 1892), 44.

43. The date usually given for 'Blairii No. 2' is 1845; but as it was listed by Thomas Rivers in the 1843 edition of *The Rose Amateur's Guide*, 3d ed. (London, 1843), 200, it must be dated no later than that. 'Blairii No. 1' is cited in *The Gardeners' Chronicle* (July 3, 1841), 441.

44. Joseph Breck, "Miscellaneous Intelligence: Art. I: Massachusetts Horticultural Society," *The Magazine of Horticulture, Botany, and all Useful Discoveries and Improvements in Rural Affairs*, 12 (1846), 155.

45. Buist, *The Rose Manual*, 27.

46. H[enry] B[rooks] Ellwanger, *The Rose* (New York: Dodd, Mead & Co., 1882), 14–15.

47. For example, it is listed as a hybrid Bourbon by Shirley Hibberd, *The Rose Book* (London, 1864), 23. Robert Buist, who did not distinguish between hybrid Bourbons and hybrid Chinas, included it in his catalog of 1859 as one of a select group of hybrid Chinas.

48. Ellwanger, *The Rose* (1882), 134.

49. H[enry] B[rooks] Ellwanger, *The Rose*, rev. ed. (New York: Dodd, Mead & Co., 1923), 205. Portemer introduced many roses: 'Paul Ricaut', 1845; 'De Candolle', 1847 or 1857; 'Herman Kegel', 1848; 'Comtesse Doria', 1854; 'Alfred de Dalmas', 1855; 'Duchesse de Verneuil', 1856; 'Pierre Notting', 1863; 'Arthur Young', 1863.

50. Virginia Hopper, " 'Sombreuil' v. 'Colonial White'," *The Rose Letter* [quarterly newsletter of the Heritage Roses Group], 12 (1987), 13–14.

51. J. Cherpin, "Rosier Thé Sombreuil," *Journal des Roses et des Vergers: Revue des Jardins*, 4ᵉ Année (1857), plate XVIII; H. Nestel, *Nestel's Rosengarten*, 3 (Stuttgart, 1867), plate 9, which is captioned "Rosa Thea, Mme. de Sombreuil"; Paul Hariot, *Le Livre d'or des roses* (Paris, 1903), plate 12. Hariot's plate, captioned "Sombreuil, The; Robert, 1850," is an excellent likeness of this rose.

52. M. Millet, "Description des fleurs et des fruits nés dans le département de Maine et Loire," *Travaux du comice horticole de Maine et Loire* (Angers, 1851), 161.

53. *The Rose Book*, 204. The fact that Nestel discussed it in *Nestel's Rosengarten* in 1867 indicates that it was hardy enough to grow in Germany.

54. Rivers, *The Gardeners' Chronicle* (October 2, 1841), 647; Jacques and Herincq, *Manuel général des plantes*, vol. 1 (1845), 564; Buist, *The Rose Manual*, 113. This rose, which seems to have disappeared, is not the hybrid perpetual of the same name.

55. Ellwanger, *The Rose* (1882), 282.

56. 'Rose Sombreuil' is dated 1820 in J. P. Vibert, *Observations sur la nomenclature et le classement des roses* (Paris, 1827), 40.

57. "Rosiers Nouveaux," *Flore des Serres et des Jardins de l'Europe*, 7 (1851–1852), 112.

58. C[harles] S[prague] S[argent], "New or Little-Known Plants: Rosa Wichuraiana," *Garden and Forest: A Journal of Horticulture, Landscape Art and Forestry*, 4 (1891), 570.

59. M[ichael] [Henry] Horvath, "The First Wichuraiana Hybrids," *The American Rose Annual* (1930), 203.

60. The credit for Horvath's early wichuraiana hybrids was taken by W. A. Manda. Many years later, J. Horace McFarland discovered that Horvath had been the true originator of these roses. See especially McFarland's introductory note to the article cited in note 59 and two other articles by McFarland: "Really Hardy Roses," *The Flower Grower*, 19 (1932), 49–50; and "M. H. Horvath's Place in Rose History," *The American Rose Annual* (1945), 168–70.

61. See H. Dauthenay, "L'Origine et les synonymes de la rose Zéphyrine Drouhin," *Revue Horticole*, 71e Année (1899), 398.

62. In France, the name was written in several ways: 'Zéphyrine Drouhin' 'Zéphyrine Drout', 'Zéphyrine Drouot', and 'Zéphyrine Drouhot'. In Germany, it was spelled 'Zéphyrine Drouhin'.

63. S[éraphin Joseph] Mottet, "Les Mérites du rosier Zéphirine Drouhin," *Revue Horticole*, 73e Année (1901), 356–57. Mottet called this rose a hybrid Bourbon.

64. J. Horace McFarland, "The Look Ahead for Roses," *The Flower Grower*, 19 (1932), 394.

65. *The American Florist*, 13 (1897), 2.

66. See W. Watson's entry Rose Crimson Rambler in "Foreign Correspondence," *Garden and Forest*, 5 (1892), 330.

67. One firm that specialized in pot-grown 'Crimson Ramblers' was the Louis Schmutz Nursery in Brooklyn, New York, which in 1897 had three hundred 'Crimson Rambler' bushes trained on two-foot arches in six-inch containers. Sold wholesale at $18 a dozen, these were available just before Easter and Memorial Day, their buds fully formed and ready to burst into bloom (*Garden and Forest*, 10 [1897], 139).

68. It appears on a list of leading new roses published by J[oseph] H[ardwick] Pemberton in "New Roses," *Journal of the Royal Horticultural Society*, 20 (1897), 242. 'Alister Stella Gray' was also highly praised by George Paul in his "More Varied Use of Roses in Gardens," *Journal of the Royal Horticultural Society*, 25 (1900–1901), 87–89.

69. *Journal of the Royal Horticultural Society*, 16 (1894), p. lxxvii.

70. Otto Ballif, "Les Roses: Mademoiselle Jeanne Philippe (Thé) et Alister-Stella Gray (Noisette Sarmenteux)," *Journal des Roses*, 27e Année (1903), 119. Here 'Alister Stella Gray' is said to be a rose of American origin that was obtained by A. H. Gray and put into commerce in Europe by G. Paul in 1895. The writer may have confused Alexander Hill Gray with Andrew Gray of Charleston, South Carolina, who had some years earlier raised a golden yellow Noisette, 'Isabella Gray', from a seedling of another yellow Noisette called 'Chromatella' or 'Cloth of Gold'. 'Isabella Gray', which he named for his oldest daughter, was sent to England by Robert Buist in 1854 (see T[homas] Rivers, "The Isabella Gray Rose," *The Gardener's Chronicle* [July 4, 1857], 470). Andrew Gray was at one time first foreman in Robert Buist's nursery in Philadelphia. As Buist was a Scotsman by birth, it is possible that Andrew Gray was also from Scotland and that there may have been some family connection with Alexander Hill Gray, who was originally from Scotland. One might even speculate that it was Andrew Gray's success with 'Chromatella' that inspired Alexander Hill Gray to use that rose in his own work.

71. See Arthur William Paul, "On the Derivation of Some Recent Varieties of Roses," reprinted from the *Report of the [Third International] Conference on Genetics* (London: Royal Horticultural Society, 1907), 7.

72. In the 1899 catalog of the Farquhar Nursery in Boston, it was described as " 'Aglaia' also known as 'Yellow Rambler'. A climbing rose of the style of 'Crimson Rambler' but with double flowers of clear decided yellow." This firm was honest enough to include a note cautioning that it required protection.

73. Two of these were 'Eugénie Lamesch' ('Aglaia' × 'William Allen Richardson'), a yellow polyantha; and 'Léonie Lamesch' ('Aglaia' × 'Kleiner Alfred'), an orange-blend polyantha. Both of these were introduced by Peter Lambert in 1899.

74. Arthur William Paul, "On the Derivation of Some Recent Varieties of Roses," 6.

75. M[ichael] H[enry] Horvath, "The First Wichuraiana Hybrids," *The American Rose Annual* (1930), 203–204. When Horvath first came to this country from Hungary around 1890, he was employed at the Newport Nursery Company in Newport, Rhode Island, and it was there that he began his hybridizing experiments with *R. wichuraiana*. Later he moved to Ohio.

76. See "Roses Abroad: Correspondence with the Editor," *The American Rose Annual* (1926), 174–75.

77. J[ean] H[enri] Nicolas, "Roses as Plants the Year Round," *The Garden Magazine*, 45 (1927), 36.

78. H[ayward] R[adcliffe] Darlington, "Some American Roses in an English Garden," *The American Rose Annual* (1938), 44.

79. See the comments of David Fairchild in "Dr. Walter Van Fleet, American Rosarian and Plant Hybridist: An Appreciation by Some of his Friends and Associates," *The American Rose Annual* (1922), 16.

80. Letter to L[eonard] B[arron] in "American Pillar Rose," *The Garden Magazine*, 28 (1918), 90. See also W[alter] Van Fleet, "Possibilities in the Production of American Garden Roses," *The American Rose Annual* (1916), 34.

81. The Conard and Jones Company was established in 1897 as a mail-order firm selling seeds, roses, and other plants. In 1908, the year 'American Pillar' was introduced, the company began to specialize in roses.

82. Van Fleet, "Possibilities in the Production of American Garden Roses," 31. See also "Dr. Walter Van Fleet, American Rosarian and Plant Hybridist," 16–17.

83. Van Fleet, "Possibilities in the Production of American Garden Roses," 33.

84. "Roses for All America," *The Garden Magazine*, 39 (1924), 24–25.

85. Van Fleet, "Possibilities in the Production of American Garden Roses," 31.

86. G[lendon] A. Stevens, *Climbing Roses* (New York: Macmillan, 1933), 173.

87. "The Favored Roses of America," *The American Rose Annual*, (1927), 196–99.

88. See the comments of David Fairchild in "Dr. Walter Van Fleet, American Rosarian and Plant Hybridist," 16–17.

89. G[eorge] L[aing] Paul in "Rambling Roses," *Journal of the Royal Horticultural Society*, 36 (1911), 532, reported that Lambert said 'Trier' was a seedling from 'Rêve d'Or'.

90. Ann P. Wylie, "The History of Garden Roses," Masters Memorial Lecture, 1954, *Journal of the Royal Horticultural Society*, 80 (1955), 19–21.

91. Ibid., 21.

92. R. Marion Hatton, "The Walsh Ramblers," *The American Rose Annual* (1943), 22–24.

93. G[eorges] T.-Grignan, "La Rose Hiawatha," *Revue Horticole*, 79ᵉ Année (1907), 31.

94. H. G. Reading, "Tausendschön, a Climbing Rose of Merit and Distinction," *The Flower Grower* 5 (1918), 9.

95. Rudolf Bier, "Tausendschön," *Rosen-Zeitung*, 28. Jg. (1913), 61.

96. Reading, "Tausendschön, a Climbing Rose of Merit and Distinction," 9.

97. [J. Horace McFarland], "The Rose Pioneers of America," *The American Rose Annual* (1916), 46.

98. *The Gardeners' Chronicle* (September 15, 1923), 159.

99. This estate no longer exists; part of the Morris Arboretum is now on the site.

100. J. Horace McFarland, "Roses Remade for America, "*The Garden Magazine*, 31 (1920), 94.

101. Pp. 231–32.

102. The patent application, number 416, reads: "The new variety originated as a sport of the climbing rose plant disclosed in the co-pending application of Alphonse Couteau, Serial No. 314,550, filed January 18, 1940, now Plant Patent 400." The application goes on to give the rose a botanic classification of "large flowered polyantha" and a commercial classification of "floribunda." Eugene Boerner, research director at Jackson and Perkins, called it a floribunda in an article, "Roses on Parade in 1940," *The American Rose Annual* (1940), 156. At a time when the public wanted roses with large flowers, any new bush with clustered flowers larger than miniatures was called a floribunda, no matter what its true heritage.

103. "New Roses of the World," *The American Rose Annual* (1936), 230.

104. J. Horace McFarland, "Newer Roses at Breeze Hill," *Breeze Hill News*, 4 (October 1941), 12.

105. Ibid. McFarland refered to 'Eblouissant' as a Bengal polyantha. It is suspected to be the result of a cross between an unknown China and 'Cramoisi Supérieur', also a China.

106. Romaine B. Ware, "Dooryard Roses: The story of a man who creates new and better roses," *Nature Magazine*, 33 (1940), 141.

107. M[ichael] H[enry] Horvath, "Progress in

Breeding Hardy Climbers," *The American Rose Annual* (1935), 118.

108. The Conard and Jones Company became The Conard-Pyle Company in 1923. This firm, which introduced 'American Pillar' in 1908, has brought out many other superb roses, including one of the most famous of all time, 'Peace', a hybrid tea that was introduced in 1945, the same year as 'City of York'.

109. The proclamation in which this rose was declared the official flower of the city was printed in the Conard-Pyle catalog: "On this 2nd day of June in the year 1945, it is the unanimous decision of the governing council of the city of York that a certain white rose be named "City of York"; that this fragrant white blossom is found worthy of being the official flower of this historic city, once the capitol of the United States in other perilous times and that the acts of the official council become effective as of the moment this white rose is duly christened.

"It is further decreed and proclaimed: That on the First day of June of each year two white blossoms of the 'City of York' rose be taken from the Memorial Garden and presented to the Mayor of York; one flower as a symbol of perpetual thought and tribute to those men and women who served their country and the second flower presented as a token of love, peace, honor, and goodwill to all mankind from the hearts of all the citizens of York, the White Rose City."

110. At the end of World War II, his son, Mathias Tantau, Jr., also a world-renowned rose hybridizer, took over the direction of the firm. Mathias Tantau, Sr., was named honorary president of the *Verein des deutscher Rosenfreunde* [Association of German Friends of Roses] in 1953.

111. Boerner was a prolific creator of new roses. Because the remarkable success of floribundas in America was largely due to his efforts, he was called "Papa Floribunda."

112. *The American Rose Annual* (1954), 134.

113. On the work of the Brownells, see "The Brownell Roses," *The American Rose Magazine*, 3 (July 1939), 67–68; and Stephen F. Hamblin, "Hybrid Tea-Hybrids," *The American Rose Annual* (1956), 144–45.

114. A notable example is the Brownell rose 'Mrs. Arthur Curtiss James' (introduced by Jackson and Perkins in 1933), a climber that combines wichuraiana growth with large, yellow hybrid tea flowers. One of its parents was a Van Fleet climber, 'Mary Wallace', which was a cross between *R. wichuraiana* and a pink hybrid tea.

115. Gerd Krüssmann, *The Complete Book of Roses*, trans. and rev. by Krüssmann and Raban (Portland, Oregon: Timber Press, 1981), 346.

116. 'Glenn Dale' × ('Mary Wallace' × a hybrid tea).

117. [Wilhelm Kordes], "As Germany Sees the New Roses," *The American Rose Annual* (1940), 169. See also "Anyhow, from Nazi Germany!" *The American Rose Annual* (1941), 129.

118. He did not identify the eglantine hybrid, but it may have been 'Magnifica', a rose he used extensively in his work. 'Magnifica' (formerly called *R. rubiginosa magnifica*), is a seedling of one of the Penzance hybrid eglantines.

119. *R. kordesii* had twenty-eight chromosomes, double the number of chromosomes of either of its parents, and this resulted in the fertility that allowed it to be crossed with modern garden roses. On the genetics of this rose, see H. D. Wulff, "*Rosa Kordesii*, eine neue amphidiploide Rose," *Der Züchter*, 21 (1951), 123–32, where it is first referred to as *R. kordesii*. Kordes also traced its history in his article "The Problem of Winter Hardiness," *The Rose Annual* [publication of the National Rose Society of Great Britain] (1952), 32–34.

120. The third climber to win the AARS trials was 'America', a large-flowered climber with coral-colored flowers that was developed by Bill Warriner and introduced by Jackson and Perkins in 1976.

BIBLIOGRAPHY

The American Rose Society. *The American Rose Annual*, 1916–.

André [René-Edouard]. "Rosiers sarmenteux pour la décoration pittoresque des parcs et des jardins." *Revue Horticole*, 72ᵉ Année (1900), 384–87.

Ballif, Otto. "Les Roses: Mademoiselle Jeanne Philippe (Thé) et Alister-Stella Gray (Noisette Sarmenteux)." *Journal des Roses*, 27ᵉ Année (1903), 119.

Beales, Peter. *Classic Roses*. New York: Holt, Rinehart and Winston, 1985.

Bean, W[illiam] J[ackson]. *Trees and Shrubs Hardy in the British Isles*. Volume 4. Eighth edition revised, 1980. Reprinted with corrections, 1981. Reprint. London: John Murray, 1989.

Bier, Rudolf. "Tausendschön." *Rosen-Zeitung*, 28. Jg. (1913), 61.

Boitard, Pierre. *Manuel complet de l'amateur de roses*. Paris, 1836.

Le bon Jardinier, almanach pour l'année 1836. Paris, 1836.

"The Brownell Roses." *The American Rose Magazine*, 3 (1939), 67–68.

Buck, Griffith J. "Cold Hardiness of Rose Varieties." *The American Rose Annual* (1959), 133–38.

———. "*Rosa Laxa*, Source of Hardiness in Rose Breeding." *The American Rose Annual* (1962), 90–95.

Buist, Robert. *The Rose Manual*. Philadelphia, 1844. Facsimile Reprint. New York: Coleman, 1978.

Butler, Edward K. "Multiflora Ramblers." *The American Rose Annual* (1918), 82–85.

Carlisle, J. P. "Rose Pax." *The Gardeners' Chronicle* (September 15, 1923), 159.

Chaix, Louis. "Histoire du rosier île Bourbon." *Flore des Serres et des Jardins de l'Europe*, 7 (1851–1852), 77–80.

Cherpin, J. "Rosier Thé Sombreuil." *Journal des Roses et des Vergers: Revue des Jardins*, 4ᵉ Année (1857), 4, plate XVIII.

Combined Rose List 1992. Compiled and edited by Beverly R. Dobson and Peter Schneider. Rocky River, Ohio: Peter Schneider, 1992.

Corbett, L. C. "Continuing Dr. Van Fleet's Work." *The American Rose Annual* (1924), 27–28.

Crépin, François. "Histoire du *Rosa Multiflora* Thunbg." *Révue de l'Horticulture Belge et Etrangère*, 2 (1876), 199–201.

Darlington, H[ayward] R[adcliffe]. "Some American Roses in an English Garden." *The American Rose Annual* (1938), 43–49.

Dauthenay, H. "L'Origine et les synonymes de la rose Zéphyrine Drouhin." *Revue Horticole*, 71ᵉ Année (1899), 398.

———. "Rosiers hybrides du *Rosa Wichuraiana*." *Revue Horticole*, 70ᵉ Année (1898), 479–80.

Desportes, N[arcisse Henri François]. *Rosetum Gallicum*. Paris, 1828.

Dobson, Beverly R. *Bev Dobson's Rose Letter*. Irvington, N.Y.: Beverly R. Dobson, 1983–.

"Dr. Walter Van Fleet, American Rosarian and Plant Hybridist: An Appreciation by Some of his Friends and Associates." *The American Rose Annual* (1922), 13–22.

Drennan, Georgia T. *Everblooming Roses for the Outdoor Garden of the Amateur*. New York: Duffield, 1912.

Ellwanger, H[enry] B[rooks]. *The Rose*. New York: Dodd, Mead & Co., 1882.

———. *The Rose*. Revised edition. New York: Dodd, Mead & Co., 1923.

Farrington, E[dward] I[rving]. "Newer Climbing Roses of Merit." *The Garden Magazine*, 27 (1918), 72–73.

"The Favored Roses of All America." *The American Rose Annual* (1923), 38–42.

"The Favored Roses of America." *The American Rose Annual* (1925), 145–50.

"The Favored Roses of America." *The American Rose Annual* (1927), 196–99.

Fisher, John. *The Companion to Roses*. Topsfield, Massachusetts: Salem House, 1987.

Gamble, J[ames] A[lexander]. "Our Useful Wild Roses." *The American Rose Annual* (1941), 54–56.

———. "Better Roses for All Regions of North America." *The American Rose Annual* (1942), 50–60.

Garden and Forest: A Journal of Horticulture, Landscape Art and Forestry. 10 volumes. New York, 1888–1897.

The Gardeners' Chronicle. London, 1841–1976.

Gerarde, John. *The Herball or General Historie of Plantes*. London, 1597.

Girdlestone, T. W. "Rosa Polyantha." *The Gardeners' Chronicle* (November 26, 1887), 659.

[Gravereaux, Jules.] *Roseraie de l'Haÿ (Seine): Catalogue 1900*. [Paris: 1900.]

T.-Grignan, G[eorges]. "La Rose Hiawatha." *Revue Horticole*, 79ᵉ Année (1907), 31.

Hamblin, Stephen F. "Hardy Yellow Climbing Roses." *Horticulture*, 8 (1930), 131–32.

———. "Hybrid Tea-Hybrids." *The American Rose Annual* (1956), 141–46.

Hariot, Paul. *Le Livre d'or des roses*. Paris, 1903.

Harkness, Jack. *Roses*. London: Dent, 1978.

———. "Tantau." *The Makers of Heavenly Roses*. London: Souvenir Press, 1985.

Hatton, R. Marion. "In Praise of Ramblers." *The American Rose Annual* (1935), 109–13.

———. "The Walsh Ramblers." *The American Rose Annual* (1943), 22–24.

Hibberd, Shirley. *The Rose Book*. London, 1864.

———. *The Amateur's Rose Book*. Revised edition. London, 1874.

———. *Les Roses du XIXᵐᵉ siècle: Catalogue annoté des roses horticoles*. Liège, 1882.

Hopper, Virginia. " 'Sombreuil' v. 'Colonial White'." *The Rose Letter* [Quarterly newsletter of the Heritage Roses Group], 12 (1987), 13–14.

Horvath, M[ichael] H[enry]. "The First Wichuraiana Hybrids." *The American Rose Annual* (1930), 203–204.

———. "Progress in Breeding Hardy Climbers." *The American Rose Annual* (1935), 117–20.

Hosack, David. *Hortus Elginensis: or a Catalogue of Plants, Indigenous and Exotic, Cultivated in the Elgin Botanic Garden, in the Vicinity of the City of New-York*. 2d ed. New York, 1811.

Van Hulle, H. J. "Les Rosiers sarmenteux," *Revue de l'Horticulture Belge et Etrangère*, 2 (1876), 201–203.

Jacques, [Antoine], and [François] Herincq. *Manuel général des plantes, arbres et arbustes*. 4 vols. Paris, 1845–1857.

Joret, Charles. *La Rose dans l'antiquité et au moyen age: Histoire, légendes et symbolisme*. Paris, 1892.

Journal des Roses (Rosa inter Flores). Melun and Paris, 1877–1914.

[Kordes, Wilhelm.] "As Germany Sees the New Roses." *The American Rose Annual* (1940), 167–69.

[———.] "Anyhow, from Nazi Germany!" *The American Rose Annual* (1941), 127–29.

———. "The Problem of Winter Hardiness." *The Rose Annual* [Publication of the National Rose Society of Great Britain] (1952), 26–36.

Krüssmann, Gerd. *The Complete Book of Roses*. Translated and Revised by Gerd Krüssmann and Nigel Raban. Portland, Oregon: Timber Press, 1981.

Le Rougetel, Hazel. *A Heritage of Roses*. Owings Mills, Maryland: Stemmer House, 1988.

Lindley, John. *Rosarum Monographia*. London, 1820.

Lindsay, Robert. "The Garden at Easter Duddingston." *The Gardeners' Chronicle* (September 1, 1894), 248–49.

[McFarland, J. Horace.] "The Rose Pioneers of America." *The American Rose Annual* (1916), 44–47.

———. "New Uses of Climbing Roses." *The American Rose Annual* (1918), 86–89.

———. "Climbing Roses" (Abridgment from *The Mother's Magazine*). *The Flower Grower*, 5 (1918), 51, 57.

———. "Roses Remade for America." *The Garden Magazine*, 31 (1920), 93–98.

[———.] "What New Roses Does America Need?" *The American Rose Annual* (1922), 23–27.

———. "Really Hardy Roses." *The Flower Grower*, 19 (1932), 49–50.

———. "The Later Climbing Roses." *Horticulture* (July 1–15, 1932), 281.

———. "The Look Ahead for Roses." *The Flower Grower*, 19 (1932), 394.

———. "Climbing Roses." *The National Horticultural Magazine*, 12 (1933), 86–92.

———. "M. H. Horvath's Place in Rose History," *The American Rose Annual* (1945), 168–70.

Michaux, Andreas. *Flora Boreali-American*. Vol. 1. Paris and Strasbourg, 1803.

Modern Roses 6: A Check-list of Rose Names Prepared in Cooperation with the International Registration Authority for Roses. Harrisburg, Pa.: McFarland, 1965.

Modern Roses 7: The International Check-list of Roses. Harrisburg, Pa.: McFarland, 1969.

Modern Roses 8: The International Check-list of Roses. Edited by Catherine E. Meikle. Harrisburg, Pa.: McFarland, 1980.

Modern Roses 9: The International Checklist of Roses. Edited by P. A. Haring. Shreveport, La.: The American Rose Society, 1986.

Morey, Dennison H. "The Bourbon Rose." *The American Rose Annual* (1953), 163–67.

Morrison, B[enjamin] Y[oe]. "'Carrying on Dr. Van Fleet's Work." *The American Rose Annual* (1926), 41–46.

Mottet, S[éraphin Joseph]. "Rosa Wichuraiana." *Revue Horticole*, 70ᵉ Année (1898), 104–106.

———. "Les Mérites du rosier Zéphirine Drouhin." *Revue Horticole*, 73ᵉ Année (1901), 356–57.

National Rose Society. *A Descriptive Catalogue of Exhibition and Garden Roses*. 4th rev. ed. London, 1899.

Neil, Mr. "Account of the Ayrshire Rose." *The Edinburgh Philosophical Journal*, 2 (1820), 102–107.

Nestel, H. *Nestel's Rosengarten*. 8 volumes. Stuttgart, 1866–1869.

Nicolas, J[ean] H[enri]. "Roses as Plants the Year Round." *The Garden Magazine*, 45 (1927), 36, 84.

———. "The Three Musketeers." *The American Rose Annual* (1937), 134–36.

Nietner, Th[eodor]. *Die Rose*. Berlin, 1880.

Ogilvie, Ian S., and Neville P. Arnold. "Roses from the North." *Horticulture* (February, 1992), 26–32.

P. du P. "Rose Malton (Hybride de Bengale)." *Journal des Roses*, 20ᵉ Année (1896), 121–22.

Parkinson, John. *Paradisi in Sole Paradisus Terrestris*. London, 1629.

Paul, Arthur William. "On the Derivation of Some Recent Varieties of Roses." Reprinted from the *Report of the [Third International] Conference on Genetics*. London: Royal Horticultural Society, 1907.

Paul, George. "More Varied Use of Roses in Gardens." *Journal of the Royal Horticultural Society*, 25 (1900–1901), 85–90.

Paul, G[eorge] L[aing]. "Rambling Roses." *Journal of the Royal Horticultural Society*, 36 (1911), 529–33.

Paul, William. *The Rose Garden*. London, 1848. Facsimile Reprint. New York: Coleman, 1978.

Pemberton, J[oseph] H[ardwick]. "New Roses." *Journal of the Royal Horticultural Society*, 20 (1897), 237–48.

Peters, Ruth Marie. "The Man Who Dreamed Up Dream Girl." *The Flower Grower*, 34 (1947), 623, 655–56.

Petit-Coq, P.-Ph. "Rose Madame Hardy: Hybride de Damas remontant." *Journal des Roses*, 4ᵉ Année (1880), 126.

———. "Rosa Sempervirens (Linné): Variété Félicité Perpétue." *Journal des Roses*, 8ᵉ Année (1884), 56–57.

Phillips, Roger, and Martyn Rix. *Roses*. New York: Random House, 1988.

Prince, William. *A Treatise on Fruit and Ornamental Trees and Plants, Cultivated at the Linnaean Botanic Garden*. New York, 1820.

Prince, William Robert. *Prince's Manual of Roses*. New York, 1846. Facsimile Reprint. New York: Coleman, 1979.

"Rambler Roses." *The American Florist*, 55 (1920), 1296–97.

"Rambler Roses for Easter." *The American Florist*, 52 (1919), 48.

"Rambling Observations of a Roving Gardener." *Horticulture* (March 15, 1930), 128-29.

Reading, H. G. "Tausendschön, a Climbing Rose of

Merit and Distinction." *The Flower Grower*, 5 (1918), 9.

Revue Horticole. Paris, 1829–1974.

Rivers, Thomas. *The Rose Amateur's Guide*. 3d ed. London, 1843.

——. *The Rose Amateur's Guide*. 4th ed. London, 1846. Facsimile Reprint. New York: Coleman, 1979.

——. "The Isabella Gray Rose. *The Gardeners' Chronicle* (July 4, 1857), 470.

Rivers Jr., T. "Effects of the Winter on Roses." *The Gardeners' Chronicle* (May 15, 1841), 308–309.

"Rosa Setigera." *Meehans' Monthly*, 8 (1898), 65–66.

"Rose Veilchenblau." *The Gardeners' Chronicle* (January 2, 1932), 14.

"Roses for all America." *The Garden Magazine*, 39 (1924), 24–25.

Sabine, Joseph. "On the Ayrshire Rose." *Transactions of the Horticultural Society of London*, 4 (1822), 456–67.

S[argent], C[harles] S[prague]. "New or Little-Known Plants: Rosa Wichuraiana." *Garden and Forest: A Journal of Horticulture, Landscape Art and Forestry*, 4 (1891), 570.

Scanniello, Stephen, and Tania Bayard. *Roses of America: The Brooklyn Botanic Garden's Guide to Our National Flower*. New York: Henry Holt, 1990.

Schery, Robert. "The Curious Double Life of Rosa Multiflora: Innocent Garden Rose or Ecological Villain?" *The American Rose Annual* (1977), 70–76.

Shepherd, Roy E. *History of the Rose*. New York, 1954. Facsimile Reprint. New York: Coleman, 1978.

Simon, Léon, and Pierre Cochet. *Nomenclature de tous les noms de roses connus, avec indication de leur race, obtenteur, année de production, couleur et synonymes*. Metz, 1899.

Snyder, Margaret R. "Two Early American Rose Hybridizers." *The American Rose Annual* (1953), 129–32.

Stevens, G[lendon] A. *Climbing Roses*. New York: Macmillan, 1933.

Stock, K. L. *Rose Books: A Bibliography of Books and Important Articles in Journals on the Genus Rosa, in English, French, German and Latin, 1550–1975*. Milton Keynes, England: K. L. Stock, 1984.

T. "Rambler Roses in Pots." *The Gardeners' Chronicle* (July 9, 1921), 17.

Thomas, Jr., George C. "The Hardy Everblooming Climber." *The American Rose Annual* (1920), 33–39.

——. *The Practical Book of Outdoor Rose Growing*. Philadelphia and London: Lippincott, 1914.

——. *Roses for All American Climates*. New York: Macmillan, 1924.

Thomas, Graham Stuart. *Climbing Roses Old and New*. New York: St. Martin's Press, 1966.

Van Fleet, W[alter]. "Possibilities in the Production of American Garden Roses." *The American Rose Annual* (1916), 27–36.

——. "New Pillar Rose." *Journal of Heredity*, 10 (1919), 136–38.

——. "Rose-Breeding in 1920 at Bell Experiment Plot." *The American Rose Annual* (1921), 25–31.

Verein des deutscher Rosenfreunde. *Rosen-Zeitung*. Frankfurt am Main, 1886–1933.

Vibert, J. P. *Observations sur la nomenclature et le classement des roses*. Paris, 1827.

Ware, Romaine B. "Dooryard Roses: The story of a man who creates new and better roses." *Nature Magazine*, 33 (1940), 141–43.

Wells, Robert W. *Papa Floribunda: A Biography of Eugene S. Boerner*. Milwaukee: BBG Publishing Company, 1989.

White Rose. "Rose Hedges." *The Gardeners' Chronicle* (September 20, 1919), 149.

——. "Climbing Roses in August." *The Gardeners' Chronicle* (August 28, 1920), 108.

Wilson, E[rnest] H[enry]. "Some New Roses Introduced by the Arnold Arboretum During the Past Decade." *The American Rose Annual* (1916), 37–41.

——. "What Roses Does America Need?" *The American Rose Annual* (1924), 23–25.

Wilson, Helen Van Pelt. *Climbing Roses*. New York: M. Barrows, 1955.

Wulff, H. D. "*Rosa Kordesii*, eine neue amphidiploide Rose." *Der Züchter*, 21 (1951), 123–32.

Wylie, Ann P. "The History of Garden Roses." Masters Memorial Lecture, 1954. *Journal of the Royal Horticultural Society*, 79 (1954), 555–71; 80 (1955), 8–24, 77–87.

Index

Page numbers in **bold** refer to main entries; those in *italic* to illustrations.